"ZEKE" BRATKOWSKI · JOHN CARSON · ART DeCARLO

RAN TARKENTON · JIMMY VICKERS · BOBBY WALDEN

PAT HODGSON · JOHN KASAY · TOMMY LAWHORN

E PATTON · BILLY PAYNE · PRESTON RIDLEHUBER · B

ORGE COLLINS · RAY GOFF · GLYNN HARRISON · RAN

MAC McWHORTER · TOM NASH · MATT ROBINSON

MIKE WILSON · CHIP WISDOM · PETER ANDERSON

TERRY HOAGE · JOHN LASTINGER · REX ROBINSON

HEL WALKER · EDDIE WEAVER · CHAMP BAILEY · M

EIER · BOSS BAILEY · DAVID GREENE · FRED GIBSON

O · DAN MAGILL · LARRY MUNSON · ERK RUSSEL

I-VI · VINCE DOOLEY · MARK RICHT · BILL HARTMA

JOE TERESHINSKI SR. · CHARLEY TRIPPI · EDMU

ARLO · PAT DYE · CLAUDE HIPPS · JIMMY ORR · THER

EN · MIKE CAVAN · BOBBY ETTER · STEVE GREER · L

E · KENT LAWRENCE · TOMMY LYONS · KIRBY MOO

· BILL STANFILL · BOB TAYLOR · JIM WILSON · DI

ON · RANDY JOHNSON · HORACE KING · BILL KRU

NSON · MIXON ROBINSON · BUZY ROSENBERG · ROY

RSON · KEVIN BUTLER · KNOX CULPEPPER · FRED

10"n

WHAT IT MEANS TO BE A BULLDOG

VINCE DOOLEY, MARK RICHT,
AND GEORGIA'S GREATEST PLAYERS

TONY BARNHART

TRIUMPH
B O O K S
CHICAGO

Library of Congress Cataloging-in-Publication Data
What it means to be a Bulldog : Vince Dooley, Mark Richt, and Georgia's greatest
    players / edited by Tony Barnhart.
        p. cm.
    ISBN 1-57243-645-X
        1. University of Georgia—Football—History. 2. Georgia Bulldogs (Football
    team)—History. I. Barnhart, Tony.

GV958.G44W53 2004
796.332'63'09758—dc22

                                                                    2004047852

This book is available in quantity at special discounts for your group or organization. For further information, contact:

Triumph Books
601 South LaSalle Street
Suite 500
Chicago, Illinois 60605
(312) 939-3330
Fax (312) 663-3557

Printed in U.S.A.
ISBN 1-57243-645-X
Design by Nick Panos; page design by Wagner/Donovan Design.
All photos courtesy of the University of Georgia except where indicated otherwise.

CONTENTS

FOREWORD
What It Means to Be a Bulldog

W HEN I LOOK BACK ON MY LIFE, it's hard to remember a time when I didn't know about the Georgia Bulldogs.

I can still remember, as a little boy, putting together a scrapbook of great college football players. Among the figures I cut out for my book were great Georgia players like Frank Sinkwich, Herb St. John, and Charley Trippi. They were some of my early heroes.

On January 1, 1947, I left my home in Mobile, Alabama, and found a way to New Orleans because I wanted to see Georgia and the great Charley Trippi play North Carolina and their star running back, Charlie "Choo Choo" Justice, in the Sugar Bowl. I was hoping to buy a ticket for a dollar, but I never got in.

As a player at Auburn there always seemed to be something unusual happening whenever we would play Georgia. I remember in 1952 we were playing down at that old stadium in Columbus. We found out that if you sat on the toilet and flushed, steaming hot water would come back out and scald your bottom. Our coaches were running around telling us not to do that.

Johnny Carson, Georgia's great end, was not so lucky. He really scalded himself badly, and before the game we were told that he was not going to be able to play. But he somehow got on the field and caught a touchdown pass to beat us [13–7].

In 1953 we played Georgia and their great passer, Zeke Bratkowski. I was the Auburn quarterback, but I wasn't a very good passer. Well, that day we won the game [39–18], but Zeke didn't play well. I think I completed something like six of nine passes. The headline in the paper the next day said,

After winning 201 games as Georgia's head coach (1964–1988), Vince Dooley went on to become one of the most successful administrators in the history of college athletics.

"Dooley Outpasses Bratkowski!" That was a headline I enjoyed, but I knew I would probably never see it again.

In 1959, when I was a coach at Auburn, I was in the press box at Sanford Stadium on the day that Georgia beat Auburn [14–13] to win the Southeastern Conference championship. I remember Bryant Harvard running wide, the ball coming loose, and somebody falling on it for Georgia. That somebody was Pat Dye. Fran Tarkenton used that turnover to drive Georgia down the field for the victory. It felt bad that day because I worked for Auburn, but later on, when I became head coach at Georgia, that incredible game would be a source of pride.

When I was at Auburn there always seemed to be some kind of connection with Georgia.

I remember riding in the car on recruiting trips with Gene Lorendo, a fellow assistant coach. He played at Georgia, and more than anything in the world, he wanted to beat coach [Wally] Butts. But the more he would talk

Coach Dooley (right) with Oklahoma legend Bud Wilkinson. Dooley was offered the head coaching job at Oklahoma in 1965, but stayed at Georgia.

about coach Butts, the more emotional he would get about what the little round man had done for him.

Coach [Shug] Jordan, my head coach at Auburn, spent the 1950 season at Georgia before he came back to Auburn in 1951.

Coach Dooley rides on the shoulders of his players after a win over Georgia Tech in 1980 capped an undefeated regular season.

And of course coach Joel Eaves left as Auburn's basketball coach in 1963 to be the athletic director for Georgia. It was coach Eaves who brought me to Georgia as head football coach at the tender age of 31. Little did I know that 41 years later I would still be at Georgia. That's because once you become a Bulldog, it's hard to see yourself as anything else.

When I became head coach at Georgia, I immediately wanted to learn everything I could about the university and about the state. I decided to start with the bulldog.

I learned that bulldogs are among the most tenacious animals on earth. They are bred in some places to control bull herds, and if they have to bite a bull to

Dooley's first huge upset win at Georgia came in 1965, when the Bulldogs beat Alabama, the defending national champions, 18–17 in Athens.

get him to stop, they will, and they never let go. They never say die, so the bulldog was symbolic of the kind of team we wanted to be at Georgia.

You can learn all about Georgia's symbols and its traditions by doing a lot of reading. And I did that. But you don't truly learn about Georgia until you know its people, and that takes time. I can't say that right away I understood the depths to which the Georgia people love their university. It's very much like a marriage. The longer you are together, the more you learn and the deeper you come to love that person.

In 41 years I can say that I considered only two offers to leave Georgia. The first was after our second year here (1965) when Oklahoma called. That wasn't the right move since I had just gotten to Georgia.

The other was in 1980 when Auburn called and made a very attractive offer for me to return to my alma mater as head coach and athletic director. Had that come earlier in my career, I would have been very tempted to take it. But by then I had been at Georgia for 17 years. My family had grown up in Athens and knew nothing about Auburn. By then my roots were too deep and my love for Georgia was too great. When I said no to Auburn, I knew my transformation into a Georgia Bulldog was complete. I'm sure it happened earlier, but at that point there could be no doubt—I was a Bulldog for life.

Georgia is a place that grows on you, and your feeling for it takes on a bigger part of your life with every year that passes.

A lot of my former players, whom you will find in this book, have come to realize that. As they get older and have children of their own, their time at Georgia becomes increasingly more important to them. They realize the lessons they learned here have been very important to them in their lives. In times both good and bad, they draw on the experiences they had here at Georgia and apply them.

It's the same way when you are the coach. As the years go on, the victories mean less and less, but the phone calls and letters you get from the players mean more and more. That is one of the special rewards of coaching.

As they share their memories with you in this book, I hope one thing comes through: their pride in being Bulldogs—yesterday, today, and always.

At Georgia we always worked very hard to build a reputation that our players could embrace and that opponents would have to acknowledge. And that reputation was this:

- When you play Georgia, you better buckle up your chin strap, because you're going to be in a battle.

- When you play Georgia, we are going to hit you for 60 minutes and the game is going to go down to the wire.

- We may not win, but if you play for Georgia, then you better be laying it on the line every play in every game. If you do that, then we'll win our fair share.

When I think about what it means to be a Bulldog, I always go back to tenacity and loyalty. Georgia people are committed to their state, their university, and their football team. Once you become a part of the Georgia family, you have a support structure that is second to none.

Many times, when a former player of ours is in trouble, his teammates quickly rally around to help. It doesn't matter if they spoke to the teammate last week or 10 years ago. The bond that is formed by their shared sacrifice is unbreakable—and it lasts forever.

In this book, you will read the stories of how players from all walks of life came to Georgia and created a lifelong bond with their teammates and their university. That bond is what being a Georgia Bulldog is all about.

—Vince Dooley

Vince Dooley was the head football coach at Georgia from 1964 to 1988. In 25 years Dooley won 201 games, six SEC championships, and one national championship (1980). He was named Georgia's athletic director in 1979 and remained in that capacity until his retirement in June of 2004. In 1994 Vince Dooley was inducted into the College Football Hall of Fame.

FOREWORD

How I Became a Bulldog

Not long after I was named head coach at Georgia, I remember going back to Florida State to finish up some business. We had a young lady working in the football offices who had come from Athens. As soon as she saw me that day she came up and said, "Please smell the air for me."

It was clear to me that she loved Georgia and had embraced everything about it. It was also clear that she really missed being in Athens, because it is such a special place. Once I got to Georgia, it didn't take me long to understand exactly how she felt.

As a player at Miami [1978–1982] I was certainly aware of Georgia, because you always know where the really good teams are. And Georgia was certainly in one of its most successful periods at that time. If you asked me about Georgia back then, I would probably mention Vince Dooley, Herschel Walker, and Between the Hedges. [Editor's note: Georgia's playing field is surrounded by beautiful hedges, which were part of the stadium when it was built in 1929. They were replaced after the 1996 Olympics. Georgia fans are always happy to get an opponent Between the Hedges.] That much I knew. I also knew that Georgia was very, very good.

One of the great joys in my first three years as head coach has been the opportunity to learn more and more about our great traditions. About the Silver Britches and ringing the bell after victories. [Editor's note: Georgia traditionally wore silver pants as part of their uniform until Vince Dooley became head coach in 1964, when they went to white pants. In 1980, Dooley brought the Silver Britches back. Georgia won the national championship that year, and the Bulldogs have been wearing them ever since.] About the fact that not a lot of people around here like Georgia Tech.

Mark Richt (right) is introduced as Georgia's new head football coach by athletic director Vince Dooley on December 26, 2000.

When I first started thumbing through the media guide, there were so many great past players that I didn't know were Bulldogs—guys like Jake Scott, who I saw play for the Dolphins. From the outside, you know that Georgia has had a lot of great players, but when you really look at it, you realize that the list goes on and on. It is a very impressive thing and something that should make us all proud.

But the thing that has struck me the most in my time here is the passion of the Georgia people. Looking at the program from the outside, I always thought that Georgia fans were some of the best in the country. But to see it on a daily basis makes me appreciate how special the Georgia people really are. The love fans have for Georgia is felt very deeply, and it is passed on from generation to generation. That love for this program and this university is why Georgia is such a great place.

Some people think you can't live in the past when dealing with today's student-athletes, but at Georgia our past is very important to us. We've tried to reach back and embrace those things that have always meant a lot to Georgia's program.

Coach Richt and his new friend, UGA VI.

I remember the "Junkyard Dawgs" of coach Erk Russell. We've tried to incorporate a number of coach Russell's sayings. We believe in "G.A.T.A." [Editor's note: In 1965, during a game with Georgia Tech, Russell created the term "G.A.T.A.," which stands for "Get After Their Ass."]

We believe in the "Big Team, Little Me" concept often seen on T-shirts that coach Russell used here.

What can you say about the opportunity to work for a Hall of Fame coach like Vince Dooley? In his 25 years as head coach, he set a standard of excellence—both on the field and off—that we are challenged to meet every single day. To have him here as a resource has meant more than I can possibly say.

Today our motto is "Finish the Drill." It means something to our players, and I hope in years to come that our people will consider it part of the same great tradition as those other sayings.

We think it is very important for our current players to understand the great players who came before them and built Georgia's tradition. We have pictures of former players in our meeting rooms to highlight the accomplishments of the past. In the Butts–Mehre building we list every bowl we've ever gone to and every major award won by our players.

We do this because it is important to show recruits what we have accomplished and what we expect to accomplish. It is also important for former players to be able to come back and show their families what they accomplished while they were here. One of the things Georgia has always tried to do is tie its past, present, and future together.

When we first got to Georgia, it was really hard for me to believe that we hadn't won an SEC championship since 1982. So to be a part of a championship team in 2002 was very, very special. Winning that first championship was a great feeling, and it is something that I really want to feel again. At Florida State, conference championships were getting to be old hat. Here at Georgia we had people in our building who were here the last time we won a championship, and to see them smile and celebrate is something that I will always remember.

Since I was a Miami Hurricane player and a Florida State Seminoles assistant coach, people often ask when I started to feel like a Bulldog.

The emotional connection began when we started our first off-season conditioning program and I had my first chance to bond with the players. That's when the Red and Black really started meaning something to me. I had to make an emotional transition from where I had been for such a long

Coach Richt takes part in the "Dawg Walk" before a Georgia home game.

time, and the players helped me do that. That's when you start getting emotionally invested in being a Bulldog.

I'd have to say that the transition was complete when I participated in my first Dawg Walk. That's when it really hit home. To see the passion of the Georgia people and how much they care really made an impact on me. I came to the realization that we're really here and we're really about to do this thing. It was an emotional time for me and one that will stick with me for the rest of my life.

Georgia is such a special place, and Athens is a true college town. I understand why so many of our players are drawn back to the place that, for many of them, represents the best time in their lives.

And now I completely understand why that young lady at Florida State wanted me to "smell the air" for her when I got to Athens. Being a part of Georgia is something I get to do every day—and I am very grateful for it.

—Mark Richt

Mark Richt was named head football coach at Georgia on December 26, 2000. His 2002 team won Georgia's first SEC championship since 1982.

EDITOR'S ACKNOWLEDGMENTS

No one puts together a book like this without a lot of help along the way. I was fortunate to receive the assistance of some very talented and dedicated people at the University of Georgia.

First of all, this book could not have been written without the support of athletic director Vince Dooley, head coach Mark Richt, and sports information director Claude Felton. They enthusiastically embraced the project when I presented it to them and then backed it up with some very important assistance when it was needed most.

By the time this book is published, coach Dooley will have completed his 41st and final year at Georgia as either head football coach or athletic director. Given what has transpired in those 41 years, he is the single most influential figure in the history of athletics at the University of Georgia. There is no way to adequately thank him for the help he has given me in my career, but I thank him nonetheless. My hope is that the gratitude that flows to him from the former players in these pages will be considered partial payment for everything he has done for me.

Every great administrator has a great administrative assistant. For coach Dooley it is Becky Stevens. I thank her for putting up with all my phone calls.

Claude Felton is the best sports information director in the United States, period. Lucky for me, he happens to work at Georgia. Claude did it all, from addresses to phone numbers to background information to photographs. I'm also lucky because he has been my friend for over 30 years. Many thanks to Karen Huff, Claude's talented office manager, who was of great help as I tracked down the right photographs.

I got to know Mark Richt when he was a successful assistant coach at Florida State. All of us who covered Mark knew that someday he would make one lucky school a very good head coach. Little did I know that it would be the University of Georgia, my alma mater. In just three short years coach Richt has put the Bulldogs back among the elite in college football. And he has done it with an extraordinary level of class and dignity. His Foreword, describing how he has become a Bulldog, tells it all. Sharon Hudgins, coach Richt's administrative assistant, has always been patient and helpful, and I thank her for that.

Two other men I would like to thank are Ray Goff, who was Georgia's head coach from 1989 to 1995, and Jim Donnan, who was the head coach from 1996 to 2000. While their careers at Georgia did not end on a positive note, their contributions to the football program were significant. They were always very helpful to me, and I'm proud to say that I still consider them both friends.

Anyone who presumes to write a book on football at the University of Georgia realizes early on that he or she must lean heavily on the expertise of Loran Smith. For when it comes to recording Georgia football and its history, Loran set the standard long ago. The rest of us are just trying to catch up.

His long list of books, which includes *Glory, Glory; Between the Hedges;* and *Dooley's Dawgs,* are incredibly well written and researched. Those books, and 30 years' worth of Claude's football media guides, were my primary reference tools through this almost-70-year journey through Georgia football history. Loran was supportive of this project from the beginning. I thank him for that and for his friendship over the years.

Like Loran, I was one of the lucky ones who had the chance, as a student at Georgia, to learn from the great Dan Magill. I could learn more about Georgia in a 30-minute conversation with coach Magill than I could in 10 hours of reading dusty books. Even though he did not play football at Georgia, coach Magill knows more about what it means to be a Bulldog than any man alive. He is why the Honorable Mention section of this book was created. You can't write a book with a title like *What It Means to Be a Bulldog* and not have Dan Magill in it.

Last, but certainly not least, I would like to thank the scores of UGA lettermen who were so generous with their time in the preparation of this book. My only regret is that for every one who made the book, there were dozens more I wish I could have included, but time and space did not allow it. By no means is this the definitive list of the greatest players in the history of Georgia football, but it is a representative sample of each decade covered.

It was obvious in our conversations that these former players enjoyed taking a detailed trip down memory lane. But believe me, fellas, when I tell you that the pleasure was all mine. I thank you for that and hope you enjoy the finished product.

INTRODUCTION

When I decided to take on this project, I did so with a high level of confidence—maybe even a little arrogance. When it came to the history of Georgia football and understanding what it means to be a Bulldog, I thought I had a pretty good grasp on the subject. I felt I had lived it.

Growing up in Union Point, Georgia, about 30 miles from Athens, I became a Georgia football fan on September 18, 1965. I was 12 years old. On my television that day I saw Georgia beat Alabama, the defending national champions, 18–17, on the famous flea flicker play. That was the day that "Moore to Hodgson to Taylor" became a permanent part of the Georgia vocabulary. The following week, I attended my first Georgia game at Sanford Stadium against Vanderbilt. After that I was hooked.

From that point on I witnessed, either in person or on television, Georgia football history as it was being made. These memories are just as vivid as if they had happened yesterday:

- I watched in horror in 1968 when Tennessee came back to tie Georgia 17–17 on that damned rug in Knoxville.

- On Thanksgiving Day, 1971, I sat at home and watched one of the greatest games in history between Nebraska and Oklahoma. Then I got a call from Jackie Perkins, saying he had an extra ticket to the Georgia–Georgia Tech game for that night in Atlanta. So I was there when Andy Johnson led Georgia down the field in the final two minutes and Jimmy Poulos went over the top for the victory.

- Also in 1971, I was in Sanford Stadium when Buzy Rosenberg ran back two punts for touchdowns against Oregon State. I was outside the stadium peering over the fence when Auburn's Pat Sullivan won the Heisman Trophy by beating undefeated Georgia 35–20.

- As a student at Georgia in 1974, I had the great misfortune to sit through the most miserable weather day and perhaps the worst game in Sanford Stadium history, a 34–14 loss to Georgia Tech.

- In 1975 I was with several hundred other students at the Fifth Quarter when Richard Appleby hit Gene Washington on the end-around pass that beat Florida 10–7. We almost tore the place down. In that same season I was at Vanderbilt when the shoestring play worked and at the Cotton Bowl when it didn't.

- In 1976 I was working at my first newspaper job in Union, South Carolina. I talked my boss into letting me go to Athens for the Georgia–Alabama game. The players in this book back up my claim: the celebration in Athens that followed the 21–0 victory remains unmatched in the history of Georgia football.

xxii

- In 1978 I was working in Greensboro, North Carolina, and wanted to watch the Georgia–Georgia Tech game, which was on regional television. The ABC affiliate in Greensboro picked up another game, so I had to drive to Bob Bevan's house in Burlington, about 30 minutes away, because he could get the stations in Raleigh, which were carrying the Georgia game. I'm glad I did. Georgia won 29–28 in what would today be called an instant classic.

- In 1980, I was in Tallahassee, Florida, on assignment when Georgia played Florida in Jacksonville. I thought about driving to Jacksonville for the game but realized I couldn't get back in time for my assignment that night. So I watched from my hotel room as Buck Belue hit Lindsay Scott, who ran his way into Georgia history. I jumped so high that I broke a lamp and had to apologize to the folks at the Econo Lodge. They were Florida State fans, and since I was cheering the University of Florida's loss, they didn't make me pay for the lamp.

- I couldn't talk my bosses at the *Greensboro Daily News* into sending me to the Sugar Bowl to watch Georgia play Notre Dame for the national championship. So Bob Kinney, a buddy of mine and an Ohio State man, and I threw the first "Buckeyes and Bulldogs" party ever in Greensboro, North Carolina.

I sat there and watched every nail-biting minute of that Sugar Bowl surrounded by people who had no idea what all the fuss was about. They didn't understand that not only was Georgia playing for the national championship, they had to beat Notre Dame, that hated bastion of Northern superiority, to do it.

I learned a very important lesson that day after Georgia had won [17–10] to complete the miracle 12–0 season. If you drink champagne out of a beer mug you will get very happy, very fast.

This list could go on and on. I came to *The Atlanta Journal-Constitution* in 1984, where I had a chance to be the Georgia beat writer and to cover the Bulldogs on a regular basis. Every major story that has come out of the Georgia football program over the past 20 years I either witnessed firsthand or had a part in covering.

So when I had a chance to write a book titled *What It Means to Be a Bulldog,* I figured I pretty much knew it all.

As it turned out, I knew absolutely nothing.

In the process of interviewing these players, many of whom had been my boyhood heroes, I learned that the true measure of what it means to be a Bulldog cannot be found in the recorded history of so many Saturday afternoons. Instead, it is found in the incredible bond that still exists among the men who played the game together and in the unshakable love they have for the great university that changed their lives forever.

George Collins, an All-American guard in 1977, said it best when I asked him what it means to be a Bulldog.

"That's easy," said Collins, now a high school football coach. "It means that if I'm in trouble, I can pick up the phone at 3:00 in the morning and call John Kasay. If I needed him to be here, he wouldn't ask what, and he wouldn't ask why. He would get here and give me the shirt off his back if I needed it."

John Kasay was an offensive guard on Georgia's early teams under coach Vince Dooley. He later became Georgia's strength and conditioning coach and lived for many years in McWhorter Hall, the school's athletic dormitory. The number of lives he touched and molded in that capacity cannot be counted. But it is significant to note that at least six former Georgia players have named one of their children after him.

One of those children is Kaysie Smith, the daughter of the late Royce Smith, an All-American guard at Georgia in 1971. Royce Smith was scheduled to be interviewed for this book when he died suddenly last January at the age of 54. It had been over 32 years since he played his last game at Georgia. Still, more than 45 of his teammates attended the funeral in Statesboro, Georgia.

That is what it means to be a Bulldog.

Kaysie and her brother, Royce Jr., were kind enough to give us some remembrances of their father so that Royce Smith could be included in this book.

The true meaning of being a Bulldog is also found in the handwritten letters that former defensive coordinator Erk Russell would send to the parents of senior players. Russell would even send letters to the parents of players on the offense, whom he didn't personally coach. Mac McWhorter tells us in his chapter that the letter his parents received from Russell in 1973 still hangs on the wall of their home.

The true meaning of being a Bulldog is also found in the stories of those players who overcame adversity—sometimes of their own creation—to have successful careers at Georgia and after. Some of the stories you will read include:

- The great Charley Trippi, who admits that he had two choices in life: to play football at Georgia or to go back to the coal mines of Pennsylvania. He chose the former and never looked back. He still lives in Athens today.

- Theron Sapp, who had to overcome three broken vertebrae in his neck and the doubts of doctors and even coach Wally Butts that he would ever play again. He went on to glory by scoring the winning touchdown to break Georgia Tech's eight-game winning streak in 1957. He is one of only four Georgia players to have his jersey retired.

- Horace King, the first African-American man to sign a scholarship to play football at Georgia. Horace didn't want to be a pioneer when he came to Georgia. He just wanted to be a Bulldog. He became both. He played with pride and dignity and was proud to be a Bulldog when he left Athens. Today he lives in Detroit and is still proud to be a Bulldog.

- Dr. Tommy Lawhorne, who came from Sylvester, Georgia, with the strong belief that he could compete—athletically and academically—with anybody. He made himself into an outstanding football player and became the valedictorian of Georgia's 1968 senior class. He was a finalist for the Rhodes Scholarship and went to medical school at Johns Hopkins.

- Billy Payne, who took the leadership skills he learned from his father, also a player at Georgia, and from coach Vince Dooley and applied them to his own life. He was an All-SEC player who went on to law school and would later bring the 1996 Summer Olympic Games to Atlanta.

- Mike Wilson, who tried to quit the Georgia team five times as a freshman because he was confused and thought he didn't love the game anymore. He credits coach Dooley with teaching him to love the game again. Wilson became an All-American and played 12 seasons in the NFL.

- Frank Ros, who came to this country from Spain as a young boy who spoke no English. He would become the captain of Georgia's 1980 national championship team.

xxv

- Terry Hoage, who almost gave up football in 1982 because he wasn't sure it was compatible with his academic goals—which were considerable. After getting assurances from coach Dooley and others, Hoage stayed and became a two-time All-American defensive back. In December of 2000 he was inducted into the College Football Hall of Fame.

These stories and many others like them are the true essence of what being a Bulldog is all about.

And as these former players take a pleasant stroll down memory lane in this book, I hope the Georgia people recognize and embrace some of the same special moments from their lives as fans and students:

- Going to Hodgson's Pharmacy for an ice-cream cone or to the Varsity for a hot dog.

- A cheeseburger wrapped in waxed paper from Allen's.

- Listening to the chapel bell ring into the night after a victory and walking under the Arch.

- Singing "Glory, Glory" and shouting "How 'Bout Them Dawgs!"

- Sitting on the tracks at the east end of Sanford Stadium, which, sadly, Georgia people can no longer do. You could get an education in one long weekend on those tracks.

- Tailgating with friends on those brilliant fall Saturdays that make Athens one of the most special places on earth.

- Listening to the Redcoat Band as it remains in the stadium to play after the game. I still get chills every time they play "Tara's Theme" from *Gone with the Wind.*

- The Dawg Walk. If you're not ready to play after you walk through the Georgia people and the Redcoat Band, then, brother, you're never going to be ready.

When you read the words of these former players, I hope you will come away with a universal truth: the University of Georgia is not a location on a map, but is instead a place in the heart. It is a living, breathing entity much like one's mother or father. Because, like the time we spend with our parents, our years at Georgia ultimately turned us from children into adults.

To a man, every former player interviewed for this book said the same things about Georgia:

- That the time they spent as football players and students served as the foundation upon which they built the rest of their lives.

- That the lessons learned at Georgia, both on the field and off, were applied over and over again as they made their way through life after football.

- That any success they have had as adults must be credited to the fundamentals that were drilled into them as football players and students at Georgia.

- And that, ultimately, there is no way that they can ever repay Georgia for those important lessons other than by passing them on to the next generation of Bulldogs.

Their memories are our memories, too. I hope you enjoy them.

The
THIRTIES
AND FORTIES

BILL HARTMAN

Fullback
1935–1937

IN MANY WAYS IT ALWAYS seemed like I was destined to go to Georgia.

When I was growing up we lived in Columbus, Georgia, for a while, and back then Georgia was playing Auburn in Columbus every year. My father took me to see my first Georgia game against Auburn in 1925. I had never seen anything quite like it.

I was still very young, but I remember Georgia going to play Yale in New Haven, Connecticut, in 1927 and Georgia winning the game 14–10. Yale was a power back then, so it was a tremendous accomplishment for Georgia to go up there and beat them. But that was also the same year that we lost to Georgia Tech 12–0, and it cost us a trip to the Rose Bowl and the national championship.

There are not many of us still around, but I was in Athens on that day in 1929 when Sanford Stadium was dedicated. Yale came down to help Georgia dedicate the stadium, and we beat them 15–0. That was such a glorious day.

I was a lucky fellow growing up. I was the captain of the 1931 team at Madison [Georgia] High School, and then I went on to Georgia Military College [GMC] for prep school. I spent a couple of years there and was the captain of the 1933 team. Wallace Butts, who would become the head coach at Georgia in 1939, was my coach at GMC.

When it came time to pick a college, I had a lot of options. Little did I know that when I picked Georgia, it would start an association that would still be going on when I was 88 years old.

I began to be heavily recruited in my first year at GMC in 1932. Ralph "Shug" Jordan was the freshman coach at Auburn, and he would referee some of our games. I remember during one of those games I got knocked down, and he ran over to pick me up because he wanted to recruit me for Auburn.

I was only 17 years old, so coach Butts talked me into coming back to GMC for another season in 1933. That was the year that Bobby Dodd left Tennessee and went to Georgia Tech as an assistant—and he started recruiting me, too.

I thought seriously about going to Tech. They were going to get me a job in the off-season, and the idea of working in Atlanta appealed to me.

General Robert Neyland, the legendary coach at Tennessee, offered me a job with the Tennessee Valley Authority in the summers that would pay $50 a week. That was really good money for a boy who used to work for a dollar a day at the grocery store. Neyland also said he would put me up in the Andrew Johnson hotel in Knoxville so I wouldn't have to live in the dorm. All that kind of stuff was legitimate back then.

Then I met Mr. Harold Hirsch Jr., an executive with Coca-Cola and a big Georgia supporter, who offered me and three of my GMC teammates summer jobs with his company. We would make $75 a week, plus expenses, traveling as investigators for Coca-Cola. I liked Mr. Hirsch and I liked Georgia, so I decided to become a Bulldog. It was the best decision I ever made in my life.

The campus at Georgia was so different then. There were only three thousand students—1,500 girls and 1,500 boys—and it seemed like everybody knew everybody else. Football players were not isolated as they are now but were part of the social scene. We all belonged to the various fraternities and honor societies that were so much a part of campus life. It is the most enjoyable time that I can remember.

On the field there were a lot of memories, too. I remember that in 1934 we lost the freshman game to Georgia Tech before forty thousand people. The score was 20–14, and we lost the game on a mistaken decision by the referee.

In 1935, when I was a sophomore, I played in most of the games. I clearly remember one game against Alabama. Paul "Bear" Bryant was a senior on that Alabama team and was supposedly playing on a broken leg. We ran the ball up and down the field, but they beat us 17–7.

In 1936 we went up to New York and played a Fordham team that was supposed to be heading to the Rose Bowl. They called their offensive line "The

3

Bill Hartman has been associated with the University of Georgia since he enrolled as a freshman in 1934.

Seven Blocks of Granite," and one of those blocks was Vince Lombardi. Their offensive line coach was Frank Leahy, who would go on to be the head coach at Notre Dame.

We were just a bunch of little Georgia boys, and they had a marching band with about 100 people in it. I remember they kept playing the song "California Here We Come" because the Rose Bowl was supposed to invite them after the game.

We led 7–0 for most of the game, but they came back and tied us 7–7. We knocked them out of the Rose Bowl, though. We took the train back to Athens and got there about 5:30 Monday morning. There were over ten thousand people there to meet us.

One of my favorite memories of 1937, my senior year, was when we played Holy Cross at Fenway Park in Boston. Holy Cross had a great All-American fullback named Bill Osmanski, who played the same position as I did. The Boston papers were calling the game "Wild Bill H. versus Wild Bill O." I played about 58 minutes in that game, but they beat us 7–6.

I will always remember my last game in Athens. Tulane was a power and about a three-touchdown favorite over us. They ran up and down the field on us, but we beat them 7–6.

In my last game against Georgia Tech, I remember that the score was tied 0–0 at the half. Coach Harry Mehre was late getting out of the locker room and was still in the end zone when Tech kicked off to us to start the second half. While coach Mehre was arguing with one of the stadium guards, I ran the kickoff back 93 yards for a touchdown. But Tech scored a touchdown in the fourth quarter to tie the game 6–6.

I went on to play some pro football with the Redskins [in 1938], but Georgia was never far away for me. Back then guys in the NFL couldn't also coach in the SEC, but Georgia Tech coach Bill Alexander asked the league to waive that rule, so I got to help coach Butts when he took over in 1939.

I really enjoyed coaching. Probably the most important thing I did as a coach was to talk Frank Sinkwich out of quitting. One day he didn't show up at practice, and coach Butts sent me to the dorm to get him. Frank said he didn't think he had the ability to play in the Southeastern Conference, but he came back, started to work a little harder, and became Georgia's first Heisman Trophy winner in 1942.

I went into the service in 1942, and all during the war I thought about coaching at Georgia. When I came back in 1946, I coached part-time and started selling insurance. By 1956 I decided to go full-time in the insurance business in order to make some money for my family.

But I was lucky. Later in life I got the chance to be the volunteer kicking coach under coach Vince Dooley, and I got to work with some great players. I was also given the honor of being the chairman of the Georgia Student Educational Fund.

All of those things kept me close to Georgia for my entire life, and for that I will always be grateful.

Bill Hartman was an All-American fullback at Georgia in 1937. He served as assistant coach to Wally Butts from 1939 to 1956. He was Georgia's volunteer kicking coach from 1970 to 1994, and he was inducted into the College Football Hall of Fame in 1984.

BILLY HENDERSON

Halfback
1946–1949

Growing up in Macon, Georgia, I had a lot of choices when it came time to go to college. But after I saw Charley Trippi play for the first time, I knew exactly what I wanted to do. I wanted to be a Georgia Bulldog.

In 1945 my high school coach, John Davis, took us to the Georgia-LSU game in Athens. Charley had just gotten out of the service and was going to play his first game in several years. I remember that Georgia didn't do too well that day [losing 32–0]. I read in the papers the next day that some of Georgia's linemen were so impressed with Charley that they started watching him and didn't take time to block. That's how good he was.

Later on that year I was a guest on the Georgia Tech sideline when they played Georgia. What I remember most is a bunch of Tech tacklers trying to get Charley Trippi and him lowering his shoulder and just getting around them. I was hooked. I knew I was going to Georgia.

I remember getting off the bus in Athens in 1946 to start my freshman year. We didn't have doting parents back then. My daddy died when I was eight years old, and my mother had four kids to raise. I pretty much knew that when I got to Georgia that would be it. There would be no going back. I was on my own.

A buddy of mine and I walked to the Milledge Annex, where the football players lived. When we walked in, Weyman Sellers, who I would later coach with, was doing pushups, and somebody was counting for him. When that

7

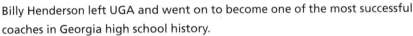

Billy Henderson left UGA and went on to become one of the most successful coaches in Georgia high school history.

guy started counting "85, 86, 87" I turned to my buddy and said, "I think we better go back home." That's when I knew there were already some great athletes there and that things were going to be a lot different from what I was used to in high school.

I learned early on that coach Wallace Butts would always make an example of one freshman to let everybody else know how things were going to be. That year he chose me.

I shall never forget it. I did something wrong during practice, and he asked me to come over and speak to him. While coach Butts was talking to me, I reached down to tie my shoe. The next thing I knew I was flat on my back. He came up under me and knocked me down.

Coach Butts was fanatical about looking you in the eye when he talked to you. And if you didn't look him in the eye or if you were not paying full attention to him, he would let you know it.

I remember an episode one time in the locker room at halftime of a game. During that time he expected every eye to be on him. I was sitting next to Gene Chandler, who was trying to get some mud off of his cleats. Next thing

I knew, coach Butts sprinted at Gene and was all over him. He didn't care who you were—he expected your attention and your respect.

Psychologically, coach Butts knew how to keep his team a little on edge. He never wanted us to get overconfident. One time we were up 40 or 50 to nothing against Furman, and he came into the locker room and kicked the potbellied stove. But we didn't let up and won that game 70–7.

But there was another time in 1947 when coach Butts tried something like that and it didn't work. We had just beaten LSU and things were going pretty good for our team. *Life* magazine came to campus to take a team picture. There was something about it that coach Butts just didn't like, and when the picture was over, he gave us a few choice words and told us to go put our practice gear on. We weren't supposed to practice that day, but we stayed out there until after dark.

That Saturday we went to Kentucky and they wore us out, 26–0. Talk about leaving your game on the practice field! That Kentucky team, by the way, was coached by Paul "Bear" Bryant.

Coach Butts taught me a lot about coaching, and the lessons I learned from him I used as a coach for more than 45 years.

I was a freshman at Georgia in 1946 and had the privilege of playing on a great, undefeated team. My job was to be a backup to Charley Trippi. That was a great honor, given the respect I had for him.

I remember playing the Sugar Bowl in New Orleans against North Carolina and the great Charlie "Choo Choo" Justice. We won [20–10] and when the game was over and we were in the locker room getting cleaned up, a bunch of the guys started putting on their ties. They said they were going to a place called Bourbon Street.

That wasn't for me. I got on a train, went back to Macon, and married my high school sweetheart, Fosky. We moved into an apartment in Athens.

We had another good team in 1948 and went down to play Texas in the Orange Bowl. I remember learning the Texas fight song really well that day, because they beat us pretty badly [41–28].

The 1949 season was really tough [4–6–1]. About the only real memory I have of that season is losing to Georgia Tech 7–6. Bob Durand missed an extra point when we scored the first touchdown, which turned out to be the difference in the game. I don't think Bob went back to Athens. I think he went straight home to Pennsylvania after that. It was a tough, tough loss.

My goal since I was a little boy was to someday play major league baseball. I played a couple years of minor league baseball after I left Georgia in 1950. But by the summer of 1952 I was impatient. I had a young son and decided I couldn't wait on the major league dream to come true. So I got into coaching. Other than going to Georgia, it was the best decision I ever made.

I made a bunch of stops along the way but finally made it back to Athens 30 years ago. I became the head coach at Clarke Central High School, and it was a job I truly loved. We have been in Athens ever since.

The best way to explain how I feel about Georgia is to tell you a story about my son, Johnny, who would later play for the Bulldogs.

When I was coaching in Macon, we would bring a group of kids to Georgia each season to watch the Bulldogs play. Johnny was about 10 or 11 years old and would always like to break away from the crowd and go around the Georgia dressing room. That day when the second half started, I looked around and there was no Johnny. I thought, "What in the world am I going to tell his mother?"

Two or three minutes later Johnny came back screaming at the top of his voice, "Dad, Dad! I just touched Kirby Moore!" Kirby, of course, was Georgia's quarterback at the time.

At that moment, I think Johnny knew that he wanted to someday play for Georgia and be a part of that great tradition. And I remembered that I had felt the same way when I saw Charley Trippi play in 1945. That's how the great Georgia tradition gets passed on from generation to generation.

Being a Bulldog means being unafraid to take on the best competition in the world. And what you learn at Georgia, win or lose, in those four years will help you no matter what you choose as a profession. I wouldn't take anything in the world for that experience.

Billy Henderson left Georgia and went on to become one of the state's most successful high school football coaches, winning three state championships. His son, Johnny, played on Georgia's SEC championship team in 1976.

JOHN RAUCH

Quarterback
1945–1948

MY ENTIRE FOOTBALL CAREER almost never got started. I grew up in Yeaden, Pennsylvania, a suburb of Philadelphia, and back then the first time you ever got a chance to play organized ball was in high school. I had played a bunch in the sandlots and around town and knew I had a chance to make the varsity early.

But when I was 14, a couple of days before the first practice, a doctor gave me an exam and said I couldn't play because I had a heart murmur. My dreams were dashed.

I was in the 11th grade when the football coach at Yeaden decided that he would get a second opinion on my condition. My parents agreed, and that doctor cleared me to play. So I got to play my junior and senior years in high school.

My parents didn't have the money to send me to college, but my coaches were determined to find a place for me to go to school and play ball. I visited Tennessee, but they really didn't seem all that interested.

My life changed when my high school basketball coach, John Naegli, met a Georgia alumnus during a wedding up in Pennsylvania. Harold Hirsch Jr. was a Coca-Cola bottler and his father was a big Georgia booster. In that one meeting, my high school coach convinced Harold Hirsch Jr. that I could be a college football player.

John Rauch started every single game during his four-year career at Georgia.

The next thing I knew, coach Naegli received a train ticket in the mail with a note. The ticket was to Athens, Georgia, and the note said for him to send me down there so that coach Wallace Butts could take a look at me.

Part of me didn't want to go because I didn't know what I was getting into. But I got on that train anyway. It was pretty late when I got to Athens. I got off the train and had no idea where I was or where I was going. I woke up a taxi driver near the station and told him I was here to try out for the Georgia football team.

He knew exactly where to take me. We woke somebody up at the dorm where the football players were living. They gave us some sheets and showed us a room where I could stay. The taxi driver even helped me make up the bed. I tried to pay him but he said, "If you're going to be a Georgia football player, the ride is on me."

For the next three days I just sort of hung out with the guys. I ate at the dorm and even went to a few classes. In the afternoon we would play touch football, and I would be the guy drawing up plays. I had not seen a coach yet.

Finally, on the third day, we were out throwing the ball around, and a car drove up. Three men got out of the car, and one of the guys said, "The short one is coach Butts."

We played for a while longer, and finally coach Butts walked up and asked me who I was. Then I told him the story of how I got the train ticket and how I got to Athens.

That's when he told me that he planned to go to the T formation that fall, and he wanted to show it to me. So he showed me how to take the snap directly from center and some other things. Then we ran some plays while he watched. Finally, coach Butts took me off to the side and asked me about my plans. I told him that my immediate plan was to get back home because I had to graduate from high school in two weeks.

That's when coach Butts told me that if I came to Georgia, I would have a chance to be the starting quarterback that fall. All of his other quarterbacks were going into the service because of the war.

Then he called over J. B. Whitworth, the line coach.

"You go home with Johnny and stay with him until he graduates," coach Butts said. "Then you bring him back."

And that's what he did. We flew back to Philadelphia and coach Whitworth stayed around until I graduated. Then we went back to Athens. The

13

next thing I knew, it was a week before the first game, and I was the starting quarterback. I started the first game against Murray State in 1945 and then started every game for the rest of my career at Georgia.

That was an interesting year to be at Georgia. A lot of guys were coming back from the war. We got Charley Trippi back midway through the season, and it took us a while to teach him the new T formation. Coach Butts took some of the best plays from the T formation and some of the best plays that Trippi ran from the old single-wing and developed quite an offense.

But the 1945 season [9–2] just set the stage for 1946 [11–0] when we went undefeated and beat North Carolina in the Sugar Bowl. Most of the guys on that 1946 team were two or three years older than everybody else. There was a lot of talent on that team—Trippi at left half, John Donaldson at right half, Dick McPhee at fullback, Joe Tereshinski . . . the list could go on and on. There is nothing like ending the season as an undefeated and untied team. That will always be my fondest memory.

In 1947 we still had John Donaldson, and Billy Henderson was coming along, but we just lost too many big-play guys. We ended up losing four games, and that was certainly a letdown from where we had been the year before.

The 1948 team didn't have a lot of stars, but we knew how to play together. We went 9–1 and then got to play Texas in the Orange Bowl. We lost that game, but I couldn't complain. When I left Georgia I was the only player who had ever started every college game, including four straight bowl games. I felt really lucky.

I tried coaching for a while, and I never forgot the lessons I learned from coach Butts. He was way ahead of his time in the passing game. He also believed that you never achieved anything great without paying a price. That philosophy served me well, even if some of my players didn't agree.

I was an assistant at Tulane when Al Davis contacted me at the coaches' convention. He was about to get the Oakland Raiders job and wanted me to come on as an assistant. I didn't know if I wanted the job, but Al turned out to be the most persistent man I've ever met. He could sell refrigerators to Eskimos.

I had been in Oakland three years when I became head coach and had a chance to take the Raiders to the Super Bowl. It also helped that I had a couple of bright young assistants named Bill Walsh and John Madden.

Everything that I ever became in football I owe to Georgia and to coach Butts. Yes, he was a man of many characters and could change very fast, but I always thought that he was pushing me to be better. Some guys just resented that.

He could be as tough as a football coach could be, but each one of us knew that if we were ever in trouble we could go to coach Butts. He did so many good things that nobody ever knew about. There is only one man I respected more, and that was my father.

I've lived in a lot of great places in my life, and even though I was born in Pennsylvania, Athens and the University of Georgia will always feel like home. I never thought I could make it to the Hall of Fame, but I did, and it was because of the Georgia family. It was a team effort and for that I will always be grateful.

From 1945 to 1948, John Rauch started 45 consecutive games for Georgia. He is a former head coach of the Oakland Raiders and Buffalo Bills and was inducted into the College Football Hall of Fame in 2003.

HERB ST. JOHN
Guard
1944–1947

THE WAY I GOT TO GEORGIA was kind of an accident, but I'll tell you what—it was the best accident that ever happened to me.

We moved to Jacksonville, Florida, when I was in the second grade, and I played football at Andrew Jackson Senior High. I was lucky enough to be an All-State player in my junior and senior years.

In 1943, when I was a senior, we invited a team from up North to come down and play us in Jacksonville. Tom Lieb was the coach at Florida back then, and after that game coach Lieb came up to me and said he had seven scholarships left. He said one of them was for me if I wanted to come to Florida. I told him that was exactly what I wanted to do, so I figured I was going to Florida. He said, "Fine," and that he would be in touch with me later.

Not too long after that I got a Christmas card from coach Lieb, but that was the last time I ever heard from him.

Mike Castronis, who went to the same high school as me, was a player at Georgia at the time, and he was home for Christmas. He came over to the house and told me that the coaches at Georgia really wanted me to come up there. So I told Mike, "Fine. Tell them to send me a bus ticket, and I will come."

So they sent me a ticket and I went to Athens. I got off the bus at 4:30 in the afternoon and by 5:00 I was registered in school. The next morning I was in class and on my way.

Herb St. John, a three-time All-SEC guard, almost went to the University of Florida.

Of course, this whole story has a funny ending, because I eventually found out what happened at Florida.

After I got out of Georgia and played a couple years of pro ball, I went back to Jacksonville and decided to get into teaching and coaching. As it turned out, I needed two more courses to get my teaching certificate. I decided to get those courses at the University of Florida.

While I was there, I ran into a Florida coach that I knew and asked him why they never talked to me again after coach Lieb offered the scholarship. As it turned out, they had contacted my draft board and learned that I was going to get drafted in the spring of my freshman year. So they decided not to offer me a scholarship.

Well, they were right. I was in the middle of spring practice my first year when I got my invitation to see Uncle Sam. But when I went down to Camp Blanding to get my physical, they declared me 4-F. So I went back to Georgia and played three more years, plus two more in the pros. I understand some of the Florida coaches caught hell after that happened.

Also in that spring of 1945, I made one of the most important decisions of my life. I was missing my high school sweetheart, Barbara, who was back in Jacksonville. I remember my line coach, J. B. Whitworth, telling me to "go home and marry that girl." So that's what I did, and I brought her back to Georgia with me.

We still feel like the years we spent in Athens were the best days of our lives. We had a great time and didn't worry about anything. We would spend our last dime and didn't worry about where the next one was coming from.

I had a chance to play on some good teams and with some very good players at Georgia. Johnny Rauch was our quarterback and there were other great ones like Dan Edwards and Weyman Sellers.

But for my money, Charley Trippi is the best player I ever saw, played with, or played against. There was nothing on a football field that Charley could not do. And for all the talk about his ability on offense, he was one of the best defensive backs who ever played football at any level.

I remember my sophomore year, in 1945, when Charley came back from the service in time for our game with LSU. We were 4–0 at the time and thought we might win them all. But against LSU I think most of us spent too much time looking at Charley and not enough time blocking. LSU killed us [32–0]. We lost the next week against Alabama but then won the rest of them.

My favorite game in my entire time at Georgia is when we played Alabama in Athens in 1946. Alabama had Harry Gilmer at quarterback. He was known for the "jump" pass and was considered one of the best quarterbacks in the country. But that day we did not allow Gilmer to complete a pass, and we won 14–0. I had something to do with Gilmer having a bad day, so I got a lot of joy out of that.

I guess the person who had the most influence on me at Georgia was coach Wally Butts. On the street, coach Butts could be the finest man you ever wanted to meet. But once he got on that field, he was deadly serious. If you weren't on that field for business, then brother, you were in the wrong place.

But I can honestly say that in my four years there I never heard a cross word from him. What he and coach Whitworth taught me was very important when I decided to become a coach. I would not have had the success I had in life if not for those two men.

Going to Georgia changed my life more than any single thing I can think of. I made a lot of good friends, some in football and some not, who are still my friends today. It was an incredible time in my life, and every year I look forward to getting together with all of the guys who played for coach Butts.

They still call us "Wally's Boys." I'm very proud of that.

Herb St. John was a three-time All-SEC guard and was named All-America in 1946.

19

JOE TERESHINSKI SR.
End
1942, 1945–1946

I GREW UP IN THE WYOMING VALLEY area of Pennsylvania, near Wilkes-Barre. About 20 to 30 miles away, Charley Trippi lived in the town of Pittston. He and I grew up the same way. Our fathers worked in the coal mines, and we both knew that football was our chance to get out. As fate would have it, Charley, me, and two other guys from our area—Andy Dudish and Francis Riofsky—all went to Georgia together.

My contact with Georgia started with a football official named John Bryan. Mr. Bryan worked several of the games I played as a senior, and he took an interest in me. He then introduced me to Mr. Harold Ketron. Mr. Ketron was originally from Clarksdale, Georgia, up in the mountains. He was a captain on the Georgia football team of 1906 and owned the Coca-Cola bottling plant in Wilkes-Barre.

I wasn't very big in high school. The most I ever weighed was about 162 pounds and I was afraid that my lack of size might keep some schools away. I remember the first time coach Wally Butts came to my house for a recruiting visit. It was around Christmas, and he brought coach Bill Hartman with him.

When they arrived I was at the store running an errand for my father, and when I walked into the kitchen my mom told me there were some coaches from Georgia there. I was afraid they would think I was too small, so I went into my room and put on two huge sweaters and then put a big basketball jacket over the top of it so I would look bigger.

Joe Tereshinski's sons (Joe Jr. and Wally) and grandson (Joe III) have all played football for Georgia.

I went into the living room and said hello to coach Butts and coach Hartman. After a while coach Butts asked, "Joe, what do you weigh?" I was going to tell the truth, but before I could say 162 Mr. Ketron, who was also there, jumped in and said 186. I didn't correct him.

When I got to Georgia one of the first things they did was put me on a scale. Sure enough, it said 162. They asked me what happened, because my paperwork said I weighed 186. I told them I got sick and just couldn't put the weight back on.

I remember my first practice because it was very, very hot. Man, that Georgia sun was just beating me down!

In the first scrimmage they put me in at right end, and opposite of me was probably the best player that Georgia had at the time—Tommy Greene from Macon, Georgia. Tommy played defensive tackle and was about 6'3" and 245 pounds. At right end I had to block him on every single play.

When the practice was over, coach Butts walked up to me. He had been watching me from only about 10 or 15 yards away.

He said, "Joe, we were ready to send you to Georgia Military College [a prep school] to put some weight on you. But I watched you on every play during the scrimmage. Anybody who wants to play football as badly as you've shown me . . . well, you can stay here as long as you wish."

Well, that was really all I needed to build up my confidence. I also started eating the good food they served us at the dorm and started gaining some weight. I knew I was in the right place.

We all moved into the Milledge Annex where the football players lived. It seemed like we had about 125 freshmen that year. I will never forget the day when I heard somebody down the hall saying there were some "damn Yankees" living in the dorm.

Some guys finally walked into the room that I was sharing with Trippi. They were nice enough, but when they left one of them said, loud enough for me to hear it, "I wonder how long it will be before he is packing his bag and heading back to Yankeeland?"

Well, of all those freshmen that came in with us, there were only about 14 or so left for the spring of our sophomore year. But I was still there and so was Trippi.

We had a great team in 1942, and I was the second-string right end to Van Davis. George Poschner, the great All-American, played the left end. Now, I played a lot of football, both college and pro, and I'm telling you that Davis and Poschner were the greatest set of ends I ever saw on one football team. Offense. Defense. Covering kicks. Everything. They could do it all. That's a helluva statement, I know, but I really believe it.

I went off to the service in 1943 and didn't make it back to Athens until the end of the 1945 season. But I did get to play against Tulsa in the Oil Bowl. We played that game in Houston and won 20–6.

In 1946 we felt confident that we could have a pretty good football team, and we did. We went undefeated and then went to the Sugar Bowl to play North Carolina and their great back Charlie Justice.

My most vivid memory of that game is that I intercepted a pass and lateralled it back to Dick McPhee. The ball was thrown laterally, but it turned out to be

22

a very disputed play. We won the game 20–10. [Editor's note: Georgia finished the season 11–0.] I was fortunate to have a really good game and make the all-time Sugar Bowl team for the 1940–1950 era. That was a great honor for me.

I know a lot of people have their own stories about coach Butts. But the thing you need to know about coach Butts is that he demanded that you give 100 percent of everything you had in practice, in the game, and in everything you did. And he could tell if you were not giving 100 percent. He would come right up to you and look you straight in the eye. If you were looking elsewhere, he would give you a forearm shiver and knock you to the ground.

He was an actor, too. I remember a game against Furman when we had a big lead at halftime. He was talking and got mad at somebody and kicked a pail of ice. I think it broke his toe, but he never showed it.

I admired coach Butts. He was the greatest coach I ever played for— college or pro. And he would give you the shirt off his back.

Thanks to the great training I got from coach Butts and end coach J. V. Sikes, I was able to play eight years with the Washington Redskins. I coached another five before I started selling automobiles full-time. I was pretty successful at it; I think I sold about eleven thousand cars in 50 years.

23

Everything that I was able to accomplish all goes back to Georgia. I have lived in Bethesda, Maryland, since 1947, and just about everybody I meet has some kind of connection or knows somebody with a connection to Georgia.

Georgia has meant everything to me. I remember growing up near the mines in Pennsylvania and hearing the sound of the ambulance as it raced toward another accident near the shaft. We called it the "Black Mariah" and every time it raced past, we prayed that nobody was dead.

Georgia allowed me to leave that life and start a new one. The best thing I can say about Georgia is that my sons—Wally and Joe—went to school there and played there, and now my grandson—Joe III—is a quarterback there.

In the words of the song, Georgia is our alma mater and we have been true and loyal to thee.

> Joe Tereshinski Sr. was an All-SEC end in 1946 and played on two SEC championship teams [1942, 1946]. Both of his sons, Joe Jr. and Wally, played for Georgia in the seventies. His grandson, Joe Tereshinski III, is a quarterback on the 2004 Bulldog team.

CHARLEY TRIPPI

Halfback
1942, 1945–1946

Growing up in Pennsylvania, I basically had two choices in life. I could find a way to go to college or I could work in the coal mines like my dad.

I saw what the coal mines did to my dad as he tried to support five children. Some days when he got home he would have to lay on the couch for an hour before he could eat dinner. I decided that was never going to happen to me.

The University of Georgia gave me the opportunity to play football and get an education, and it completely changed my life.

As a senior in high school I wasn't recruited all that much. I only weighed 160 pounds. I went to Georgia on a recruiting visit in 1940, but coach Wally Butts had just taken over and I was a little apprehensive about where the program was going.

But when I got back home, I got an invitation and a scholarship to attend LaSalle Military Academy near Long Island, New York. Everything would be paid for, and I would get a chance to develop more as a football player. I told the Georgia coaches that my plan was to go to prep school and then I would enroll at Georgia. It was the smartest thing I ever did.

I went to LaSalle and got heavier and stronger. I also played on a really good team and was named to the All-Metropolitan team in New York. Then the other schools really started paying attention to me.

Charley Trippi is in both the College Football and Pro Football Halls of Fame.

But I had given my word to the Georgia coaches. Also, when I was being recruited, a big Georgia alumnus who worked for Coca-Cola promised me that if I went to Georgia I would always have a job in the summer. I remember graduating from high school on a Friday, and the next Monday morning I was driving a Coca-Cola truck. I was making more money than my dad, who was earning about $90 a month from the WPA. I was making about $25 to $30 a week.

I remember telling my dad about the football scholarship to go to Georgia. He said, "You mean they are going to pay all of your expenses to knock you down?" Of course he was elated, because not many people in my area could afford to go to college.

But I also told him that once I got down there I was not coming back. I had to ride 800 miles on a bus to get to Athens. It took two days, but I thought it was the chance of a lifetime.

When I got to Georgia I really didn't know coach Butts. I had not met him during my recruiting trip, but I certainly knew his reputation. I knew a guy who had tried to play at Georgia and had left. He said, "Buddy, when you go down there it will be like a slaughterhouse." I figured that if they were making the linemen work that hard, I had a chance to be a pretty good back.

I will never forget my freshman year, in 1941. We started out with 65 freshmen, but we ended the year with only 18 scholarship guys and two walk-ons to play the freshman game with Georgia Tech. But I will say this—the guys who were left, you could go to war with. We made a tremendous sacrifice to stay there, and we took some awful beatings.

The 1942 season was a great one for us. I started out playing the same position [tailback] as Frank Sinkwich. He was a great inside runner, but I was a little bit faster on the outside. After making a few token appearances in the first few games, I stayed at tailback and Frankie was moved to fullback, where he went on to win the Heisman Trophy.

The only game we lost all season was to Auburn, when we were ranked No. 1. Auburn was a T formation team, one of the few around, and we didn't know how to stop it. They beat us fair and square, but we still got an invitation to play UCLA in the Rose Bowl.

I was fortunate enough to play in a lot of special games. I played in three bowl games, four college all-star games, and a pair of NFL championship games. But nothing has ever compared to playing in the Rose Bowl.

It's just a special event, and anybody who plays college football has always wanted to play in that game. I can't describe the feeling of stepping on that field for the first time, other than the adrenaline started flowing and I really wanted to play. I remember playing 58 minutes in that game, and we beat UCLA 9–0.

In 1943, like a lot of guys, I went into the service, but I was one of the lucky ones. I got into a good program where I was able to play baseball and football during the war. The services were really competing for talent, and they would move you all over the place. I was finally based in Tampa, at the headquarters, and it was all football. I lived in Clearwater Beach with my family. We would commute in the morning, have practice, have lunch, and go home. That was my job.

I came back to Georgia in the middle of the 1945 season, right before we were going to play LSU in Athens. Coach Butts had gone to the T formation that season, and I didn't know anything about it. I only practiced two days before we had to play LSU. I almost got killed, and we lost 32–0. But believe me, after that I learned what to do in a hurry. Once I got the hang of the offense, I kind of liked it.

27

Going into the 1946 season, we knew we had a chance to have a pretty good team. And once we started winning and got the momentum going, we were hard to stop. I remember beating Alabama and Harry Gilmer in Athens, 14–0. Gilmer was a great quarterback, but I don't think we allowed him to complete a pass that day.

I will always remember the Sugar Bowl, which was my last game for Georgia. We were playing North Carolina and their great running back, Charlie Justice. "Choo Choo" could go the distance any time he touched the ball. He was good enough to beat you by himself.

At halftime we were behind 10–0, and I was really mad. I could see an undefeated season slipping away. I was the captain of the team, so I chased the coaches out of the locker room. I told the players, "If we don't win this ball game, we're going to be characterized as just another football team, even though we won 10 games. What we've done up to this point won't mean a damned thing. Anybody who doesn't think we're going to win then just take your damned uniform off and sit on the bench."

We went back out there and won 20–10 to finish 11–0. It was a great way to go out.

So many people influenced me at Georgia, but I have to start with coach Butts. I learned how to play football when I came to Georgia, and from him I learned the level of commitment you had to give to the game in order to be really successful.

Coach Butts hammered that into me day after day. He would say things like, "Trippi, you're starting to believe everything they write about you." He would never let me get complacent.

I didn't *really* get to know coach Butts until I left college and came back to coach for him. He was awful on the football field because he wanted to win so badly, but he had a big heart. If anybody was in need he came to the rescue. He never let anybody down.

They call us "Wally's Boys," and every year before G-Day [spring game] we try to have a reunion and swap stories. I look forward to that gathering every year.

What does it mean to be a Bulldog? Well, I came to Georgia a poor boy. My first year in Athens I wore Coca-Cola work pants and a T-shirt all the time. That's all I had. But Georgia completely turned my life around. It gave me a chance to excel in football, and I was able to turn that into a very successful career in professional football.

And when my playing days were over I came back to Athens, where I had always had a home, and I was able to enjoy some success in real estate.

It's simple, really. My time at Georgia was the best thing that ever happened to me. That's why I'm still here.

Charley Trippi is still regarded by many as the greatest athlete to ever play football at Georgia. He is in the College Football Hall of Fame, the Pro Football Hall of Fame, the Rose Bowl Hall of Fame, and the Georgia Sports Hall of Fame. In 1946 he was the runner-up for the Heisman Trophy and won the Maxwell Award, which goes to the nation's best college football player. He still resides in Athens.

The
FIFTIES

EDMUND RAYMOND "ZEKE" BRATKOWSKI

Quarterback
1951–1953

I PLAYED AT A SMALL CATHOLIC HIGH SCHOOL in Illinois, located about 30 miles from the campus of the University of Illinois. But as luck would have it, my high school coach, Paul Shebby, coached Charley Trippi when he was in high school in Pittston, Pennsylvania. That's how I got introduced to Georgia.

Back in those days it was OK to work out for the coaches on recruiting visits. In fact, Charley Trippi was there for my workout. I wasn't really a quarterback in high school because we played the old Notre Dame box offense. But I guess coach [Wally] Butts saw something he liked, because the next thing I knew I was on my way to Georgia.

I had never been down South before. When those guys started calling me "a Yankee" I kept thinking, "I don't play for the baseball team." But it was a great experience for me because I hadn't traveled very much at that time.

The transition to college wasn't hard because I didn't have time to think about it. Being a quarterback for coach Butts back then meant you were about as busy as anyone on campus. Because of everything I had to learn on the football field, I never had a class after 1:00 P.M. in my entire time at Georgia. My assignment was to be on the field every afternoon and just throw and throw and throw.

Zeke Bratkowski took the lessons he learned from Wally Butts and played in the NFL for 14 seasons.

It really paid off for me. I have had a lot of important influences on my life, like coach Shebby, coach George Halas, and coach Vince Lombardi. But right up there with them was coach Butts.

Yes, he was a taskmaster, but if he had not made me do all that throwing, there is no way I could have played in the NFL for 14 seasons. Anybody who played for coach Butts didn't realize until he left Georgia what coach Butts did for us in terms of being mentally and physically tough. If you could make it through one of coach Butts' practices, you could do anything.

I remember a time after one of the G-Day games in either 1951 or 1952. I thought we had had a pretty good day throwing the ball. But when the game was over, coach Butts cleared the stadium and said, "We're going to score 20 times from the 25-yard line by running." We did it and had to stay out there until it was almost dark.

I just wish we could have won more games for him. We were 7–4 in 1952, and today that would get you a decent bowl bid. The 1953 season, my last, was really difficult because we won only three games. That season I really felt sorry for him. I was the captain, and after the last game with Georgia Tech [a 28–12 loss] in Atlanta, I stood up and spoke for the team and told him how we cared about him. I just thought he needed to know that we felt bad about the season, too.

Today's kids don't know how tough it was at Georgia back then. A lot of guys had been in World War II, and they loved to pull pranks. We had what we called "Rat Court" for the freshmen every Wednesday night. Each freshman had to run errands and shine shoes for one of the seniors on the team. Every Wednesday they found out if they were a good rat or a bad rat. The bad rats would get some licks from a belt to keep them alert.

We would make guys sit naked on a block of ice for 10 minutes and then make them pick up a marshmallow with the cheeks of their rear ends. Or we would take them out of town, throw their clothes in the bushes, drive off, and make them find their way back to Athens.

We even had something called "Louise Parties," but I don't think I can talk about that here.

Yeah, we did a lot of crazy things, but the day you got to put on your letter jacket with the G on it for the first time . . . man, that was a special day. Winning my first varsity letter and becoming a member of the G-Club is something I will never forget.

There were so many people who helped me. As a senior I led the nation in punting, but the only reason I became a great punter was because Quinton Lumpkin, who was an assistant coach, would play a game called "Pushback." We would get on a field about 200 yards long and keep kicking the ball to each other, trying to push the other one back to the end of the field. Quinton was a great athlete. He would kick the ball over the fence onto Milledge and make me jump the fence to get it.

All the football players lived in the dorm, but the guys from Ohio, Pennsylvania, and the other Northern states would kind of congregate on the third floor. The Southern guys—we called them the blue blazers and khaki pants guys—would be on the lower floors. They wore ties to class. We Northern guys would wear sweatshirts and blue jeans. It was just a different way of life for a lot of us.

But when we got on the field together it didn't matter where we were from—we were a team. I wish we could have won a few more games together. And because of pro football—I played 14 years and coached 26—I haven't gotten back to Athens as much as I would have liked.

But there is no question that my years at Georgia set the stage and gave me the tools that I would need to be successful. It is a great town and a great school. I still feel lucky to have been a part of it and am always proud when people call me a Georgia Bulldog.

Zeke Bratkowski was a three-time All-SEC quarterback who played on three NFL championship teams for the Green Bay Packers.

JOHN CARSON

End
1950, 1952–1953

I LOVED PLAYING FOOTBALL at the University of Georgia, but my first love was always golf. I really didn't have any choice. I grew up in Cabbage-town, a little community in the southeastern part of Atlanta. I lived on a tough little nine-hole course called the James L. Key Golf Course, and I pretty much played every day, so I got to be pretty good at it.

When I wasn't playing golf I caddied. Mama liked that because I was always able to bring home a few extra dollars.

When the time came to go to college, I got more golf scholarship offers than anything else, because at that time I was winning a lot of tournaments. In fact, I never even thought about football until 1947 when the Atlanta school system changed.

They took the two main schools in town and split them up into a bunch of schools and scattered them all around Atlanta. I ended up at Roosevelt High and played on their first-ever football team. Football was completely different from golf, and I kind of liked it and thought I might be good at it, too.

As a senior I was just sort of waiting around to see what the best situation would be for me to play golf and football in college. We were playing in the state basketball tournament in 1949 when coach Wallace Butts and coach Quinton Lumpkin came to see me. My mother was really impressed by coach

John Carson was both an All-American football player and an All-American golfer.

Butts, and she didn't want her boy going very far away from home. So the decision was pretty much made for me. I was off to Georgia.

Coach Butts really didn't like the idea of me playing golf. He thought it took too much time away from football in the off-season, and I had to miss some class time in the spring when I was playing in tournaments. But he finally understood how I felt about golf. If I was sick, I could go off and play golf and get well. That's how much I love the game.

I played a little football in 1950, but then in 1951 I tore up my shoulder and couldn't play at all. I dislocated the shoulder so badly that I had to wear a harness to keep it in place.

I guess the funniest thing—maybe that's not the right word—that happened to me, and the one most folks know about, was in 1952 when we played Auburn in Columbus. We were playing in one of those municipal stadiums built by the Civilian Conservation Corps, and it seemed like it only took a couple of years for those things to get old.

Well, I was sitting on the toilet before the game, and when I went to flush, the hot-water valve busted and sent about six inches of scalding hot water up my rear end. It scalded everything—and I do mean everything.

They had to lay me out on a table because the hot water had literally peeled the skin off of me. It really hurt, but you know coach Butts: there was no such thing as being injured. They put a bunch of Vaseline on me, and off I went.

Despite the pain, I made a long touchdown catch of about 76 or 77 yards from Zeke Bratkowski, and we won the game 13–7. The Auburn guy I beat on the play for the touchdown was Vince Dooley, who would later become a great coach at Georgia.

Later on that day I ended up in the emergency room in a hospital in Newnan. I called coach Lumpkin and told him I was in pretty bad shape. I finally got well, but nothing ever got to me like that again.

In 1953 Zeke and I had a pretty good year, but we didn't win a lot of games and that was tough. I felt bad for coach Butts because he was used to winning and did not handle losing well. But still, that man is tops on my list. Zeke and I had pretty good pro careers and we couldn't have done it without the help of coach Butts.

There were still a lot of fun times. I remember when coach Butts and coach Lumpkin decided they were going to take up golf. Bless their hearts, they just couldn't do it, but it was fun watching them try.

And Dean [William] Tate, God rest his soul, always seemed to be into something. One year he accused me of faking the mumps just to get out of the spring game. I asked Dean Tate, "Have you talked to the doctor? I really have the mumps, and I would like to have children some day, so I'm going to be careful." That Dean Tate was a piece of work.

If you talk to the guys who played in my time, they will tell you they wish we had won more for coach Butts because he deserved it. But Georgia was a special place then, and it still is today. I'm glad I got a chance to go there and be a part of one of the great traditions in college football.

John Carson was an All-American football player in 1953 and an All-American golfer in 1954. He is one of only two Georgia athletes (Herschel Walker is the other) to be named All-America in two sports.

ART DeCARLO

Safety
1950–1952

I GUESS I WAS LIKE A LOT OF PEOPLE my age, because I never really thought too far ahead. I just enjoyed playing sports. I was a captain on my high school football team in Youngstown, Ohio, and I was a starter on the basketball team as well.

I really didn't think about college that much until I finished my sports year, and then I started looking around hoping to get some scholarship help. Heidelberg College and Youngstown University were recruiting in our area, and I thought I would probably end up at one of those schools.

But I had a next-door neighbor, Al Bodine, who was already a player at Georgia. Al was a couple of years older than me and said that he could get me a tryout at Georgia. I thought it might be fun, so I agreed. They sent me a train ticket from Youngstown down to Athens, Georgia, and I was on my way.

I did things a little different than some guys, because my tryout offer came right before school started. So I was in a situation where if I got a scholarship, I knew I was going to stay and enroll in school. If I didn't make it, I figured the folks at Georgia would at least get me back home.

Before I got on the train, I did get a scholarship offer from Heidelberg. It was tempting to just take that offer and not take a chance on what was going to happen at Georgia. But just the idea of going all the way down there excited me—I had never been out of Ohio.

Art DeCarlo went on to play on two NFL championship teams with the Baltimore Colts.

So I went down to Georgia and tried out for coach Quinton Lumpkin. For whatever reason, coach Lumpkin really liked me, and he offered me a scholarship. Both my mother and father had already passed away, so I called back and told some of my relatives that I was going to stay in Athens. From then on, and for the rest of my life, I was a Georgia Bulldog.

We didn't win that many games when I was at Georgia, but I've got a lifetime of memories from my time there.

Zeke Bratkowski was my roommate for a couple of years. He was a great guy and turned out to be a great football player. That's because he really worked at it. Frank Salerno was another roommate of mine. He later became a successful lawyer in Chicago.

We didn't beat Georgia Tech in the three years I was there, and that was a disappointment. But at the same time I always liked and respected Bobby Dodd, the Georgia Tech coach. I played in the College All-Star game as a senior against the Detroit Lions at Chicago's Soldier Field. I made that team because of Bobby Dodd. I remember playing against the Lions so well because they had guys like Bobby Layne, Leon Hart, and Doak Walker. Yes, they beat us, but it was a great experience.

40

I was able to play pro football for many years, and I give a lot of credit for that to coach Butts. He was tough on everyone, including me, but I think coach Butts really liked me. His pass patterns were really the beginning of what's happening now in the NFL. When it came to the passing game, he was really ahead of his time.

Some guys didn't like the fact that coach Butts was so tough on them. He made them work hard, and they had a problem with it. I didn't. I understood where he was coming from. He knew that whatever we chose to do in life, we would have to be willing to work hard at it. So when I got to pro ball I was able to handle everything that they threw at me. I had already been through the toughest part of my career at Georgia.

I was really lucky. I played for the Pittsburgh Steelers in 1953, and then I was in the army for a couple of years. In 1956 I played with the Redskins. We had our training camp at Occidental College in Los Angeles, and I really liked that.

But my big break came in 1957 when I signed with the Baltimore Colts. For the next four years I got to play with the great John Unitas, and he and I became really good friends.

In the pros, Monday is always your day off. And on Mondays we would have a standing golf game with the same four guys: Unitas, me, Don Shinnick, a linebacker from UCLA, and Andy Nelson from Tennessee. We had more fun during those golf games than anything else I have ever done.

I'll tell you a great story about Unitas and our friendship. A while back my daughter called and said she was organizing a charity golf tournament. She asked me to play and asked if I could get Unitas. I said I would try and asked when the tournament was.

"Tomorrow," she said.

I called John and you know what? He was there the next day. That's what kind of friendship we had. I really miss him.

I don't know what the other guys are saying but I can tell you this: Georgia gave more to me than I can ever pay back. It gave me a chance to grow up. Coach Butts and the other coaches taught me how to play football, and from that I was able to make a nice living as a pro and receive a nice pension.

At Georgia I learned that nothing important in life comes your way unless you are willing to pay a price. That's the only way you can ever reach your full potential. Coach Butts and the people at Georgia were determined that every guy on our team should reach his potential, no matter what it was. I think I was really lucky to be at Georgia during their time.

Art DeCarlo was an All-SEC safety at Georgia in 1952. He played on the Baltimore Colts NFL championship teams of 1958 and 1959. He is also the author of the novel *Fumbled Kidnap*.

PAT DYE
Guard/Tackle
1958–1960

YOU COULD SAY THAT THERE was a strong Georgia connection in my family. My mother went to the University of Georgia, and from the earliest time I can remember, we went to Athens all the time to visit my grandparents, who lived there.

My oldest brother, Wayne, went to Georgia in 1953 and played there. Then my next brother, Nat, went in 1955 and did the same. And all of my cousins and other relatives were Georgia people, too. So I guess there were a lot of things pulling me in that direction. The good thing is that I never got any pressure from my immediate family. They were going to let it be my decision.

I didn't want to sign on signing day because my high school, Richmond Academy, was in the state playoffs and we were trying to win a championship. But when it got right down to it, things boiled down to Tennessee, Georgia Tech, and Georgia. Now, I really liked Tennessee, and Georgia Tech was winning under Bobby Dodd. Georgia wasn't winning and hadn't been to a bowl game in several years, and I wasn't necessarily excited about going to a losing program.

Tennessee was far from home, and I was basically just a country boy. So that was out. When it came down to choosing between Georgia and Georgia Tech, I guess you could say that blood is thicker than water. Besides, I came from Blythe, Georgia, and if I had moved to Atlanta it would have been a culture shock, I'm sure.

Pat Dye (right) was an All-American guard at Georgia. He joined with coach Wally Butts (center) and quarterback Fran Tarkenton (left) to lead Georgia to the 1959 SEC championship.

So that's kind of how I picked Georgia, and today I wouldn't take back that decision for anything in the world.

I came to Georgia with a pretty good group of players in 1957. We had guys like Francis Tarkenton, Phil Ashe, Bill Godfrey, and Bobby Walden. It was a special group, and we had a special freshman coach in Quinton

Lumpkin. We weren't intimidated by the varsity and more than held our own when we scrimmaged against them.

The 1958 team was very talented, but it wasn't a team, it was a bunch of individuals. We should have been better. That was my brother's [Nat's] senior year and Theron Sapp's senior year. If you go back and look at the statistics, I'll bet we were better than just about every team we played, but we made too many mistakes. That team had no business going 4–6.

A bunch of us got frustrated with what was going on early in that season and decided to take off to Atlanta to Phil Ashe's house. Francis was with us and some other guys. We thought we would all go to schools somewhere else.

I don't want to get into what we were frustrated about, but needless to say it would have been a mistake for any of us to leave school. I remember calling home to tell Daddy, and he asked me where I was going to go to school. I told him I didn't know. He told me I'd better find a place because "you ain't coming home."

I'm just glad that my brother and coach Lumpkin came and got us. We were only gone one night, but I do think it brought about some changes for the next year.

Nobody thought we were going to be any good in 1959. Nobody but the players, of course. I think we were picked to finish eighth or ninth in the conference.

But things just fell into place that year. First of all, coach [Wally] Butts hired J. B. Whitworth, who had been head coach at Alabama. He had been through the wars and had a lot of experience and maturity. He had a settling effect on the whole group and made us believe we could win.

I'll never forget something that coach Whitworth did on the Wednesday or Thursday before we played our first game with Alabama in 1959. It had a tremendous impact on me, and I remembered it for as long as I was coaching.

Coach Whitworth brought us together during practice and said something like:

"Men, I want to talk about Saturday's game. We're playing against a man [Bear Bryant] who coaches by fear. His coaches are scared of him. His players are scared of him. But the most important thing is the people who play against him are scared of him. We will not fear Alabama come Saturday. We're just as good as they are, and coach Bryant ain't gonna play."

He had us convinced that if we weren't scared of Alabama and coach Bryant then we were going to win the football game. And I really think that 10 or 15 minutes made the difference in our winning or losing. We played a great football game against them and won [17–3].

I ended up working for coach Bryant for nine seasons, and I found out that coach Whitworth was 100 percent right. Part of what made coach Bryant so great was that other teams were completely intimidated by him.

I was involved in college football for 40 years as a player and a coach. I can say that the 1959 Georgia-Auburn game is right up there with the most important ones I've ever been involved with. Nobody got a lot of sleep that week. On Monday we started sitting up late at night at the dorm and talking about the game.

I remember coach Sterling Dupree giving us the scouting report. He had played at Auburn and always liked to scout them. But if we had really listened to him, there was no way we would have thought we could win the game. It seemed like they had an All-American at every position. Jackie Burkett and Zeke Smith and Ken Rice were all great players.

All we knew going into the game was that a win would give us the SEC championship, something that Georgia had not done in a long time [since 1948]. The excitement level before the game was just incredible.

45

It was late in the game and we were still behind 13–7 when Auburn got the ball and tried to run out the clock. Bryant Harvard, a boy from Thomasville, Georgia, was their quarterback, and he ran a naked bootleg back toward me. I didn't take the fake and followed him. For whatever reason, he just dropped the ball—nobody hit him. I fell on the ball. It wasn't really a heroic play on my part.

And here's something I've always wondered about. Bobby Hunt played the biggest part of that game at quarterback, but coach [Shug] Jordan put Bryant in the game at the end. I've always wondered if coach Jordan, being the gentleman he was, wanted to let Bryant run out the clock because he was from Thomasville.

Of course everybody knows the story of how we won the game after that. Francis hit Don Soberdash on a bunch of passes over the middle that got us down there close. Then on fourth down Francis stepped into the huddle and said, "All right, we're going to win the football game."

That's exactly what we did. Francis drew up a play in the huddle to go to Bill Herron and then hit him for the touchdown. We had quite a celebration that night.

We were hoping for good things in 1960, when all of us were seniors, but it just didn't work out that way. We lost some really close games. Coach Whitworth died before that season, and it was really a blow to our team. Then Francis got hurt against Florida. We weren't bad, we just weren't good enough.

But I'll tell you what: it was a fun time to be a student at Georgia. I wouldn't consider myself a great party guy, but I'm not going to tell you I missed them all either. I really enjoyed my time at Georgia.

Of course, I went on to be an assistant coach at Alabama, where I worked for coach Bryant for nine years. Then I was head coach at Auburn for 12 years, and I still make my home in Auburn. All four of my children graduated from Auburn.

But I have to say there ain't a man alive who has more respect for Georgia than I do, and there will always be a place in my heart for Georgia. When you look back on it you're thankful for the opportunity that was given to you. Georgia gave me the foundation that I would live the rest of my life on. And I can't really put into words how grateful I am for that.

Pat Dye was an All-American guard in 1959–1960 and one of three Dye brothers who played for Georgia. Dye won four SEC championships as the head coach at Auburn from 1981 to 1992.

CLAUDE HIPPS

Halfback
1944, 1949–1951

I REMEMBER THE EXACT DAY I got off the bus in Athens—June 6, 1944. Sound familiar? It should.

I remember that as soon as I got off the bus I saw the newspaper rack. The huge headline said, "Allies Invade Normandy!!" It was D-Day. That's why I will never forget it.

My playing career at Georgia was a little different from most. I enrolled in 1944, spent four years in the marines, and then came back to Athens in 1949. I went through a lot and felt like an old man by the time I got back to Athens, but I'll talk more about that a little later.

I was born in Hazelhurst, Georgia, and one of our neighbors was the family of Spec Towns, the great Georgia track star and coach. I didn't know it at the time. I wouldn't know that until later in life, but it goes to show that it is a small world.

Then we moved to Waycross, where I spent all of my high school years.

I guess I was always supposed to go to Georgia. Growing up I had a big picture of Bill Hartman on my wall. When I was a freshman, Vassa Cate came to Waycross as a coach. He was the kind of man I really looked up to. I thought that if coach Cate was the kind of man that Georgia put out, then I would like to go to Georgia, too.

Then when Frank Sinkwich came along and won the Heisman in 1942, I knew that Georgia was the place for me. They sent me a bus ticket to come to Athens. You have to remember that back then, not that many kids could go to college. I think about three or four in my senior class made it. I thought it was the opportunity of a lifetime.

I was lucky enough to make the varsity as a freshman in 1944. I'll never forget playing Florida down in Jacksonville. It was a great thrill because my mom and dad were able to come down from Waycross and watch me play. As luck would have it, I scored my first touchdown as a Bulldog on a 58-yard run against the Gators. My mom and dad were really happy that day.

But I knew my life was about to change. I was going to turn 18 that next April, and I knew I was going to get drafted. Rather than wait on the draft, I wanted to go ahead and enlist so I could control which service I went into. My older brother, Harry, was already in the marines, and he was convinced it was the best part of the service. I always looked up to my big brother and wanted to follow in his footsteps, so my twin brother, Francis, and I both joined the marines that December.

I went to Parris Island for boot camp, then on to Camp LeJeune and Camp Pendleton for training. I was shipped out to Guam, where I joined the Sixth Division, which was training for the possible invasion of Japan.

Then we dropped the bomb and the war ended. I was in the regular marines, so I still had time to serve. But I was really lucky to spend most of the rest of my commitment playing football in various capacities for the service. I played in an All-Star game in China, called the China Bowl, to raise money for Japanese orphans living in China. We played on New Year's Day in Shanghai. It was an incredible experience.

I got out of the service in January of 1949, went home for two days, and on the third day I met with coach Butts in Athens. I moved back into Stegeman Hall, but I really felt old because a lot of the other veterans, like Charley Trippi and Joe Geri, had moved on. But it really worked out fine.

Being an older guy, things didn't affect me like they did the younger guys. Sometimes coach Butts would get to ranting and raving, and I knew he was really just doing it for show. I had been through so much that all I did was put a towel in my mouth so that I didn't make any noise [while trying not to laugh].

Back in those days it seemed like all the coaches coached the same way. They believed that the last player standing always won the game. They would put us through physical practices with no water. Sports medicine wasn't sophisticated like it is today. I thought we left a lot of games on the field because we were so worn out. But I don't really blame coach Butts, because every other coach in the world was doing it the same way.

Claude Hipps, seen here with coach Wally Butts (left), arrived in Athens on D-Day:
June 6, 1944.

I remember in 1950 we had a big win over Maryland [27–7] when they were supposed to challenge for the national championship. We had a really good quarterback in Billy Grant from Valdosta. He was running the team well but then broke his darn leg. We went out to California the next week to play St. Mary's; we were supposed to win. They tied us 7–7.

That was a strange year. We had only one loss [to Alabama] and three ties when it came time to play Georgia Tech. What I remember is that we seemed to spend the whole afternoon down on Tech's end of the field, but we just couldn't get the ball in the end zone. I thought we were the better team that day, but we turned the ball over too much.

In 1951, when I was the captain, we were not the better team. Tech really put it to us [48–6]. Coach Bobby Dodd at Tech was really starting to get on a roll. I didn't like losing to Tech, but 20 years later I got a note from coach Dodd telling me that I had made Georgia Tech's all-opponent team.

But all in all, I loved my days at Georgia. I met my wife, Barbara, when I was a junior, and coach Butts gave us permission to get married. He figured that since I had spent four years in the service I probably knew what I was doing.

I played some pro football [two seasons for the Pittsburgh Steelers] and then got into the snack foods business, where I stayed until I retired for good in 1995.

I'll be 77 in April [2004] and have to rank my days at Georgia as some of the happiest of my life. You look back now and you realize that your character and competitive attitude were formed on the football field and in the classroom at Georgia. Those days taught me that when you're down, you bounce up and keep moving. They taught me that everything in life is not going to be handed to you. You have to earn it.

So what little success I may have had I owe to the people at Georgia. People will always remember that you played at Georgia, and it means a great deal to you.

I was born a Bulldog, and I will always be a Bulldog.

Claude Hipps was the captain of Georgia's 1951 team. That season he led the team in interceptions with six and was first-team All-SEC.

JIMMY ORR
Wide Receiver
1955–1957

I GREW UP IN SENECA, South Carolina, but I guess you could say I was a Georgia fan pretty early in life.

For my 10th birthday I asked my parents to take me to a game in Athens so that I could see Charley Trippi play. That was in 1946, and they took me to see Georgia play Oklahoma A&M—Georgia won 33–13. I still remember everything about that day.

I was always impressed by Georgia. Trippi had kind of been my hero growing up. Plus, they threw the ball a lot, and that was what I was interested in.

I ended up going to Georgia, but I sure took a roundabout way of getting there.

Growing up I played all sports, but I grew to like basketball the most. It wasn't very complicated: basketball is a lot easier on your body than football, and it seemed that in football I got hurt all the time. A lot of basketball was being played among all the textile mills at that time, so you could really play all the time. I was an All-State basketball player at Seneca High School, and I just thought I was better at basketball at that particular stage in my life.

So when I got out of high school I turned down some football scholarships and walked on at Clemson to play basketball. After a semester I transferred to Wake Forest, still hoping to play basketball. I wasn't up there long before I realized that they had a lot of good players and that I really wasn't going to be able to play at that level.

I went back home and tried to figure out what I was going to do next. A family friend, Neal Alford, had gone to Georgia and played a couple of years before getting hurt. He decided to become a trainer. I talked to him about talking to coach [Wally] Butts to see if Georgia had any interest in me as a football player.

I talked to coach Butts and he told me to come on, but he couldn't give me a scholarship. So that's how it all began.

I played freshman ball in 1954, but I will never forget our first game against Ole Miss in Atlanta in 1955. I was like the fifth-string running back and never thought I would get into the game.

But back then there were all these substitution rules that said if you came out early in a quarter, you couldn't go back in until the next quarter. Well, we got caught in a substitution crunch and a couple of guys got hurt, so they had to put me in the game. They threw me a pass for about 50 yards right before halftime, and I caught it and scored a touchdown. We got beat 26–13, but that got me a foothold, and I think it also caught coach Butts' attention.

I'm proud to say that I went on to lead the SEC in receiving that year [with 24 catches] and again in 1957 [with 16 catches]. But what I'm most proud of in those two seasons is that I never dropped a pass.

This is probably a good place to talk about coach Butts and the passing game. Coach Butts had his critics because he ran very tough practices, but the man was way ahead of his time when it came to the passing game. What I learned from him and coach Sterling Dupree made me ready to go when I got to the pros.

I remember when I was a freshman in 1954, we would have these "extra" workouts at the stadium. I'm not sure if they were legal or not. But coach Dupree worked with me and taught me how to run what we called "straight line" patterns and how to break them off at the last second. He and coach Butts taught me a lot of little tricks of the trade, which put me ahead of the competition when I got to the NFL.

In fact, when I was a rookie at Pittsburgh, Buddy Parker, the coach, brought me into his office one day after watching me work out and run some pass patterns. He said, "How did you learn all this?" He said I was far ahead of the other rookies. I told him that was the way they taught football at Georgia. Our passing game at Georgia was really ahead of a lot of pro teams at the time.

Jimmy Orr came to Georgia without a scholarship and went on to lead the SEC in receiving twice in his career.

In my three years at Georgia we only won 10 games. That's not very many, and it's hard to say what the problem was. I've often wondered if it had something to do with the fact that coach Butts ran such tough practices. In the midfifties that might have hurt his recruiting.

But I will always have the memory of the Georgia Tech game in 1957. Man, Tech and coach Bobby Dodd really had it going back then, and they had some really good players. We were 2–7, so nobody really gave us a chance. They had beaten us eight straight games, and the Georgia people were starting to wonder if we were ever going to beat Tech again.

I remember the wind was blowing really hard in Atlanta. It was not a nice day. But we hung in there and had a chance to score a touchdown. We got the ball back around midfield in the third quarter after a fumble. Everybody in the huddle knew how important the drive could be, because we didn't know how many chances we'd get.

Theron Sapp gets the credit for scoring the touchdown to win the game, but I always tell Sapp that the only reason he got any yardage in that drive is that he had to run right off of my blocks. I also bailed him out when I caught a 13-yard pass from Charlie Britt on third-and-12. That gave us the first down we had to have.

54

I'll never forget the touchdown play from the 1-yard line. I was at right end, and the guard and tackle on that side were supposed to block down. I was supposed to kick out the defensive end. The play worked perfectly. Sapp ran right off my tail and scored. We won the game 7–0.

After all that frustration, it was a great way to go out in my final game.

Now a word about Theron Sapp. We give him a hard time because they retired his jersey and named him "The Drought Breaker" because of that one game against Georgia Tech. But let me tell you this: Theron Sapp was one helluva football player. He was second in the SEC in rushing that year to LSU's Jimmy Taylor, even though we had a mediocre football team.

I enjoyed playing pro football because, like I said before, I was ready when I got there. Once you get up there you don't have long to convince them that you can play. I got to play with the greatest quarterback of all time, John Unitas, when I was with the Colts, and I got to be part of a world championship team.

But for me, everything started at Georgia. I not only learned how to play football, I learned how to get along with people. I made friendships that are still with me today. It was one of the most important times of my life. I've had a chance to live all over the country and do a lot of different things, but I will always be a Georgia Bulldog. That never changes.

Jimmy Orr led the SEC in receiving in 1955 and in 1957. In those two seasons Orr never dropped a pass. He went on to have a successful NFL career with the Pittsburgh Steelers and the Baltimore Colts.

THERON SAPP

Halfback
1956–1958

I T'S HARD TO BELIEVE THAT a 1-yard run in one football game could change somebody's entire life, but that's exactly what happened to me after I scored and we beat Georgia Tech 7–0 in 1957. I'm 68 years old now, and I still get letters from people wanting autographs because of that one game.

And it almost never happened.

I had always been a Georgia fan growing up. Back then there was no television, so we listened to the Georgia Bulldogs or the Georgia Tech Yellow Jackets on the radio.

We moved to Macon when I was in the second grade, and my mother worked for Warner Robins at the air force base. I went to Lanier High for boys, which is now Central High School.

As a senior we had a pretty good team. We won the South Georgia championship and ended up playing Grady High in Atlanta for the state championship. Erskine Russell, who would someday be the defensive coordinator at Georgia, was the head coach. They beat us 9–6.

I kind of figured I was going to Georgia, but some other schools like Auburn, South Carolina, and Florida started paying attention to me, so I thought I would listen to what they had to say. I remember that it was the week before the state championship game, and I had gotten a big cut on my chin at practice. I had to go have it stitched up, and when I got home there

Theron Sapp scored the winning touchdown to beat Georgia Tech 7–0 in 1957. That broke Tech's eight-game winning streak and led to Sapp's jersey being retired.

was a bunch of recruiters waiting on me. It was the first day of recruiting. I know there were coaches from South Carolina, Florida, and Georgia there.

Coach Quinton Lumpkin, who was recruiting me for Georgia, met me in the driveway. He just looked at me and said, "You might as well choose to go to Georgia because your mama has already signed your grant-in-aid! But don't tell these other guys that. It will be our secret."

Turned out that coach Lumpkin had gotten there early and done a selling job on my mom. So she made the decision for me. I guess you could say it was the right decision.

But my playing career at Georgia got off to a rocky start. I was in Atlanta where we were having practice for the Georgia High School All-Star game. In the first scrimmage I got hit and knocked up in the air. When I came down I hurt my neck. They took me to the hospital for X-rays. The doctor said nothing was broken so they let me go home, but I still couldn't move my head.

As it turned out, the doctor read the X-rays while they were still wet. I was on my way back to Macon when he looked at them again and noticed that I had three cracked vertebrae. They got in touch with me and told me to go to the hospital in Macon immediately.

At first they put me in traction for four or five days, and then they put me in an entire body cast from the waist up so that I could not move my head. When I was in the hospital coach [Wally] Butts and coach Lumpkin came down to visit me. Coach Butts told me that even if I never played football again, I would still get my scholarship to go to Georgia. That was really something. He didn't have to do that. I told him not to worry. "When I get out of this body cast I will be playing football," I told him.

I started to sit out that fall and not go to school. I didn't want to walk around the campus in that body cast and have people ask me all those questions. But coach Lumpkin convinced me to come and give it a try. He wanted me to go ahead and start blending in with the rest of the guys. I did it, but people were always asking me if I had been in a train wreck or a car wreck.

When I came back to school in 1955, they told me I had to get permission from my doctor to play again. My doctor in Macon wouldn't give it to me. Coach Butts told me that if I were his son I probably wouldn't be playing. I told him I wasn't his son and I was going to give it a shot.

I played on the B team in 1956, but in 1957 I started the first game of the year at fullback against Texas in Atlanta. After that I started 20 straight games.

We weren't in the best frame of mind when we played Georgia Tech in the last game of the 1957 season. We had only won two games that year. We had a chance to beat Auburn the week before but fumbled the ball at the 1-yard line and lost 6–0. Auburn went on to win the national championship.

It seemed like we were in every game that year, but we just didn't get the breaks to come our way. But we were up to play Georgia Tech. They had beaten us eight straight years, and we hadn't scored a touchdown against them in four years.

Driving over to Atlanta from Athens, I told coach Butts, "I've got a good feeling that we're going to win this game. I couldn't sleep at all last night. I felt like a kid on the night before Christmas."

Coach Butts said, "Hell, Sapp, you think we're going to win them all. But I'll tell you this: we are going to play them hard and tough. That much I will promise you."

Well, coach Butts was right. We did play them tough. And on Tech's first or second drive of the second half, I recovered a fumble around the 50-yard line. It was the field position we had been looking for, and we had to take advantage of it.

I can remember every single play of that drive. The big play was when we faced a third-and-12 around the 40-yard line. Charlie Britt hit Jimmy Orr for 13 yards and it gave us a first down at their 27-yard line. Now it was time to go to work.

I carried the ball six straight times down to the 1-yard line. On third down Charlie tried to sneak it in, but he got nothing because Tech put a nine-man line in.

On fourth down the play came in. Somebody said, "Coach Butts said give it to Sapp." I just remember saying, "Yeah, give it to me. Give it to me."

I ran off tackle and the blocking was perfect. I fell into the end zone, and I wanted to jump up and start running out of the back of the end zone.

We still had a lot of football to play, but we hung on and won [7–0]. And when the game ended I couldn't believe it. There was all this hugging and kissing. I couldn't get to the locker room. It was really crazy. It had been so long since Georgia had beaten Tech, and we were having such a tough year.

The next year, 1958, Tech was really laying for us. They had all those great players, like Maxie Baughan, but we beat them again [16–3]. I was named the Most Valuable Player in that game, too. In those two games against Georgia Tech I carried the ball 40 times for 194 yards.

It was after the 1958 game with Tech that some of the Georgia people started talking about retiring my number [40]. I didn't think I should have my jersey retired. That honor belonged to guys like Charley Trippi and Frank Sinkwich. But I wasn't going to tell those people no. They retired my jersey at the next spring game, and it was such an honor.

I guess everybody has their own story about coach Butts, but mine is pretty funny. In 1958 we were playing The Citadel in Athens and beating them pretty good. It was the next to last game of the season, and I was chasing Billy Cannon of LSU for the rushing title in the SEC. Coach Butts took me out of the game when we got the big lead because we had Tech the next week and he didn't want me to get hurt.

Well, I wanted to catch Cannon, so when coach Butts wasn't looking I put myself back in the game. I told Britt that coach Butts said give me the ball. I ran for about 15 yards on the next play, and coach Butts looked up and started screaming, "What the hell is that?"

Coach Butts called timeout and jumped all over me. "Sapp, go sit your butt on the bench and don't get up again unless I call you."

I never did catch Cannon. [Editor's note: Cannon won the SEC rushing title in 1958 with 682 yards. Sapp finished with 635.]

I got a chance to play some pro ball and was on the 1960 NFL championship team with the Philadelphia Eagles. But nothing compares to those five years at Georgia. I remember the panty raids and how Dean [William] Tate would call on the football players to protect the girls. That was a pretty good deal. There were trips to Daytona Beach on spring break. We would take the pigs from the University farm and have a barbecue. I made enough friendships to last a lifetime. I wouldn't trade those years for all the money in the world.

And the Georgia people gave me an honor that has stuck with me for my entire life. When you go to Georgia today you'll see only four retired jerseys: Trippi, Sinkwich, Walker, and Sapp.

One time I was there and I heard somebody say, "Sapp? What did he do?"

I just told him, "Well, he was just somebody they liked."

Theron Sapp was an All-SEC running back in 1957 and 1958. He is one of only four Georgia players (Charley Trippi, Frank Sinkwich, and Herschel Walker are the others) in school history to have his jersey retired.

FRAN TARKENTON

Quarterback
1958–1960

THIS IS HARD FOR ME TO SAY even now, but when I was growing up I really thought I was going to Georgia Tech.

But you have to understand that that was the Bobby Dodd era. Tech was the hot school and the team that everybody wanted to play for. Auburn was probably my second choice.

Yes, I had grown up in Athens. We moved there from Washington, D.C., when I was in the sixth grade. But Georgia didn't really recruit me very hard because they already had two really good quarterbacks—Charlie Britt and Tommy Lewis—who had signed the year before. Those guys could throw the ball better than anybody I ever competed against.

If there is one man responsible for my going to Georgia it was Jim Whatley. He was the baseball coach and the B-team coach for football. I was close to Jim and his wife, Mae. When we moved to Athens, I skipped the sixth grade and went to the seventh grade, where Mae Whatley saved my life. I was young and I didn't want to be there. Coach Whatley was my Little League coach.

By the time I was a senior, I was a confused young man. Frank Broyles was recruiting me hard for Tech. So was coach Dodd. There was an old Georgia Bulldog named Buck Bradberry who was recruiting me for Auburn.

Deep down I knew I wanted to go to Georgia, but I guess I was fighting it. But coach Whatley came over to my house one night and basically flipped the switch. He made me uncover my feelings that I really wanted to go to Georgia. I still thank God that he did.

Let me tell you: the freshman class that I came in with in 1957 was very, very talented. Georgia had been struggling the past few years, but we got Pat Dye and Phil Ashe and a bunch of good old Georgia boys. It didn't take long before we figured out that down the road we might be pretty good.

Freshmen couldn't play back in those days, but I remember that the week before the first game in 1957, we had a full-game scrimmage in Sanford Stadium with the varsity. Our freshman team beat them 14–7. Just think of that. We had a helluva freshman team. We won all of our freshman games, including the one against Tech. Coach Quinton Lumpkin was our freshman coach, and we really bonded with him. That was a special year.

A lot of interesting things happened when I was a sophomore, in 1958. I thought at first they were going to redshirt me, and I really didn't want that. But Charlie Britt ended up as the number one quarterback, Tommy Lewis was number two, and I was number three.

We went to Texas to play them in the first game and got behind 7–0 in the fourth quarter. I got in the game, and at that point I wasn't sure if we had made a first down. We got the ball on the 5-yard line after a punt and drove 95 yards for a touchdown. We went for two and made it to go up 8–7.

But they came right back and scored on us to take the lead 13–8. Coach [Wally] Butts decided to put Charlie back in there and we lost. In a way, I think that hurt Charlie to be put in that situation.

It was a frustrating situation for everybody. I was the new kid on the block, but I really thought I could help the team. Coach Butts started me the next week against Vanderbilt, but I could tell he didn't really want to. I played the first series, but then he put Charlie in to play the rest of the game [Georgia lost 21–14].

After about the fourth game, a bunch of us got fed up. It wasn't that we were unhappy at Georgia or with coach Butts, but the coaching staff, quite frankly, was in turmoil. So one day Pat Dye, Phil Ashe, Bill Godfrey, and I just left and went to Phil Ashe's house in Atlanta. We had made up our minds that we were all going to Florida State.

Of course it didn't turn out that way. Somebody came and got us, and we went back to Athens. That 1958 team finished 4–6, but it really should have been better.

Fran Tarkenton's 13-yard pass to Bill Herron gave Georgia a 14–13 win over Auburn and the 1959 SEC championship.

We had been struggling so much that there was no reason to believe that 1959 would be a special year. But the only bad game we played that year was at South Carolina, when they killed us [30–14]. They just beat the hell out of us and nobody could explain why. It was a wake-up call for that team, and we played well the rest of the year.

There were a lot of guys who made great plays on that team. I remember Charlie Britt returning an interception 100 yards for a touchdown when we beat Florida [21–10]. And when we came back to beat Auburn, Don Soberdash made a bunch of big plays in the winning drive.

People ask me about the touchdown pass to Bill Herron to beat Auburn [14–13] in the game that gave us the SEC championship. The fable is that we drew the play up in the huddle, and the truth is we did exactly that. We were facing a fourth down at the 13-yard line, and this was going to be it.

I can't remember if we called timeout, but I knew I had time to tell everybody what to do. I told Bill to block and down and count "a thousand one, a thousand two, a thousand three, a thousand four." Then I told him to run toward the left corner of the end zone.

Then I told everybody else that we were going to roll right and try to draw the defense toward us. I would do the same count in my head. When I did, I looked and Bill was so wide open it was ridiculous. Thank goodness I just threw it without thinking about it. He caught it for a touchdown, and we won the game and the SEC championship.

I often get asked if I was nervous or if I understood how important that moment was in Georgia football history. The honest answer is that when you're young, you never realize the seriousness of the moment. You never really understand the magnitude of such a play unless you lose, and then it just seems to be a slap across the face.

I played football for 26 years in high school, college, and the pros. I was fortunate to be involved in some special plays, but I get reminded of that one a lot, so I would have to say that it is pretty high on my list.

I was the captain of the 1960 team, and all I can say is that it was a very difficult year. Coach J. B. Whitworth, who was the guy who had really pulled our team together emotionally the year before, died that winter. He was the soul and the coaching catalyst for our team. I think it just took the life out of us.

As it turned out, that would be coach Butts' last year. Coach Butts was a hard man to know, and I can't say that I ever really knew him. But I can say this: the man was a genius when it came to the passing game. He gave me a base in the passing game that allowed me to learn from others in my career, like Norm Van Brocklin.

Coach Butts and I were never close, but I remember that later in my career, when I was playing in New York, I attended the College Football Hall of Fame banquet in the city. I ran into coach Butts at the dinner, and he looked at me and said, "I think you're the best quarterback in football today."

I have to tell you, that was the greatest football compliment I have ever received. I don't think coach Butts ever thought I was going to be a great quarterback when I was at Georgia. For him to take the time to say that to me was pretty special.

I was a lucky guy. After Georgia I got to play for 18 years in the NFL and participate in three Super Bowls. I have been fortunate to have another life in business, which I have enjoyed.

But I always tell people that the four years I spent at Georgia were the foundation to my life. I wasn't a great student, I'll admit that. But being a part of that great university for four years—with all of its traditions—served as the launching pad for everything else I wanted to do.

And the thing about Georgia is that it never leaves you, no matter where you go in life. Athens . . . the Arch . . . the history of Georgia—it's just part of the fiber that is me. Growing up in Athens and being a Bulldog is special. It is part of your soul.

Again, I just thank God that Jim Whatley walked into my living room and told me what to do—and that I did it.

Fran Tarkenton was an All-SEC quarterback in 1959 and 1960 and an All-American in 1960. He played for 18 seasons in the NFL and participated in three Super Bowls. He is a member of both the College Football and Pro Football Halls of Fame. In 1998 he was inducted into the University of Georgia's Circle of Honor.

JIMMY VICKERS

Tackle
1957–1959

I PLAYED MY HIGH SCHOOL BALL in Moultrie, Georgia. I was a little on the small side, and I really didn't know if I was good enough to play college ball. But coach Sterling Dupree came down from Georgia and showed a lot of interest in me. He had grown up in south Georgia, too, and I think he understood that it wasn't always the size of the dog in the fight that mattered—it was the size of the fight in the dog.

Georgia Tech and Auburn showed some interest, but because of coach Dupree, it was Georgia all the way. He wasn't just a good coach; he was a great person and became a dear, dear friend.

There is really no nice way to say it, but we struggled in my sophomore and junior years. In 1957 we only won three games, but at least we beat Georgia Tech and broke the drought. In 1958 we were in every game, but we just couldn't seem to put them away. We only won four times, but we beat Tech again, so that was something to build on.

I was an alternate captain my senior year, in 1959, and I remember we had a lot of team meetings. Don Soberdash was the captain, and he felt the same way I did. We just kept telling the guys, "Hey, we've got to lay it on the line. This is our last time around." It was that sort of thing. We just made up our minds that when something bad happened, we would turn it into something good.

Jimmy Vickers came back to Georgia in 1971 to serve as Vince Dooley's offensive line coach.

We had a really good team in 1959. We dominated Alabama in the first game, 17–3, and that was a fun day for us. J. B. "Ears" Whitworth, our line coach, had been head coach at Alabama before he was replaced by Bear Bryant. And so to handle them the way we did was special.

Every good team has a bad day, and ours was up in Columbia, South Carolina. We lost the game [30–14] because we had a bunch of turnovers. But we remembered what we said in those preseason meetings. We buckled down and found a way to win the rest of them.

Anybody who was on that 1959 team will never forget the win over Auburn. What I remember most was that because of the substitution rules at the time, I couldn't get back into the game when all of the important stuff was happening. I was on the sidelines hollering like everybody else when [Fran] Tarkenton took us down the field and threw the pass to Bill Herron that won the game for us, 14–13.

All I remember is the place going wild. It was really a madhouse. I was on the field when Dean [William] Tate grabbed Bill Godfrey and yelled, "Way to go, Bill!" Now, some of us thought this was funny because it seemed like Dean Tate was always on the football players about something . . . like not going to class or going to the wrong party.

So here was Dean Tate hugging Bill. Bill turned to coach [Quinton] Lumpkin and said, "Coach, ain't folks nice to you when you win." It was a great day. Coach Butts had been struggling for a lot of years, and it was nice to see him win another SEC championship.

After that we got to play in the Orange Bowl and it was quite an experience. Like most of the guys, I had never been to Miami. We flew down there on one of those four-engine clippers, we called them. A lot of guys had never flown before and, believe you me, that was something really different.

We beat a really good Missouri team, 14–0. Looking back, we really had a great defense that year. I know points were hard to come by back then, but in 11 games only one team scored more than 14 points against us, and that was in the loss to South Carolina.

When I got out of school I tried to play in Canada for a year, but I was just too small. I think I was a pretty good college player, but that was about it. I got into coaching and bounced around and finally ended up as the offensive line coach at North Carolina for Bill Dooley. Happily, I had a chance to come back to Georgia in 1971 when Bill's brother, Vince, hired me as his offensive line coach.

After I quit coaching I got into the insurance business and eventually set-tled down in Destin, Florida. I don't get back to Athens as much as I'd like, but I still believe that my time at Georgia was the best four years of my life. And what coach Butts gave me is something I can never repay.

They say coach Butts was a complex man, but he was only complex if you didn't know him. After my freshman year he kind of took me under his wing. He kept some other guys and me on campus that summer to go to school and get ready for the fall. Because of that time, I feel like I knew him as well as anybody.

There was no mystery about Wally Butts. If you laid it on the line for him, he would lay it on the line for you. And to me, that's what it really means to be a Bulldog. When the time comes, like it did in 1959, you've got to be will-ing to lay it on the line for your teammates. And that's exactly what we did.

Jimmy Vickers, an All-SEC tackle in 1959, was also an assistant coach at Georgia from 1971 to 1976.

BOBBY WALDEN

Halfback and Punter
1957–1960

As a senior in high school I was as sure as anything I was headed to Tennessee.

Johnny Majors was the starter up there at halfback, which was a running and passing position in their offense. That was the position that I played, and I could see myself fitting right in that position and taking over for him.

But things changed after I broke my leg. Tennessee backed off and didn't show me any more interest. I was kind of scared because I really didn't know what was going to happen to me. I never thought that much about getting a college scholarship until I was a senior, but I hated to think that I was going to be so close and lose it.

Then one day a letter came in the mail from coach Wally Butts over at Georgia. They had offered me a scholarship, too, but knew I was looking hard at Tennessee. In his letter coach Butts said his scholarship offer was still good, and it would stay good, even if I never played a down of college football.

Well, that was it. That would be the first of many good things that coach Butts would do for me in my life. I had been given a second chance, and I really wanted to make the most of it.

Now, that was a tough time to be going to Georgia. We hadn't been to a bowl game in six or seven years. We had lost eight straight games to Georgia Tech, and that is never a good thing. Coach Butts was starting to feel the heat.

70

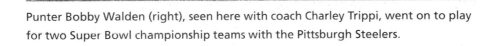

Punter Bobby Walden (right), seen here with coach Charley Trippi, went on to play for two Super Bowl championship teams with the Pittsburgh Steelers.

But as players we were pretty much removed from that kind of stuff. It wasn't like it is now, where everybody knows what's going on, or at the very least they are speculating about it on TV or radio.

I had a lot of fun playing freshman ball in 1957 because I came in with a pretty strong freshman class. Francis Tarkenton was in that group. So was Pat Dye. I'm not going to say that we always beat the varsity when we scrimmaged them, but we certainly held our own. They never ran over us.

We only played three or four freshman games, but at the end of the year we played Georgia Tech in the Scottish Rite game, and that was something really special. Obviously, none of us had ever played in front of that many people before. And the day before, they took us in to see the kids in the hospital; it is something I will never forget.

There's not a whole lot you can say about the 1958 season. We had some pretty good players, like Theron Sapp, who was a senior, but we just couldn't get anything going. We only won like three or four games. [Editor's note: Georgia posted a 4–6 record in 1958.]

I was happy that in 1959 we were able to win another SEC championship for coach Butts. It had been a long time for him, and he deserved it.

But that championship didn't come easy. We had only one slip-up in the season, when we lost at South Carolina [30–14] in a game that I still can't explain. We just weren't ready to play, and they kicked our butts.

We were able to win the rest of them, thanks to some heroics by Francis.

We were trailing Auburn, 13–7, but got the ball back late after Pat Dye recovered a fumble. People often joke that Francis was drawing up plays in the dirt, but that's exactly what happened. He was always changing plays to give the defense a look that they had not seen before, and that's what he did on this play.

It was fourth down and something like 13 yards to go, and this would be our last chance. Francis told me to go down and across the field to my right so that the majority of the defense would come with me. He was right. After I had run my route, I looked over and there was Bill Herron catching the ball for a touchdown. The crowd went absolutely nuts, and we won the game 14–13. You have to give Tarkenton credit—the man knew how to play under pressure.

After we beat Tech [21–14] we finished the season by beating Missouri [14–0] in the Orange Bowl. Georgia football was back on top, where it was supposed to be, but we didn't stay there for long.

We lost some good players from that 1959 team, and we just didn't seem to have enough to get back to the top. We lost to Alabama in the first game [21–6] and then went to Southern California and lost way out there [10–3]. Then things seemed to kind of unravel. At least we beat Tech [7–6]. My senior class could say that we beat Tech four straight years, and that was important.

We had no idea that coach Butts was going to be removed after that season. I was really sad to see it, because I had a great deal of respect for that man. I was scared to death of him when I got to Georgia, but at the same time I loved him. He was a tough guy to play for, but if he told you he was going to do something, he did it. You could count on it. He was tough on the field, but off the field he did so many kind things for people that you never heard about.

When they accused him of working with Bear Bryant to fix a game, I thought that was the most ridiculous thing I had ever heard. It made me extremely mad.

73

As it turned out, I was a pretty lucky guy. I played up in Canada for a couple of years, and after their season I stopped by Minnesota to see Francis, who was with the Vikings. He talked Norm Van Brocklin into signing me, and that began my NFL career. After Van Brocklin got fired, the new coach, Bud Grant, traded me to the Pittsburgh Steelers in 1968. It turned out to be the greatest thing that ever happened to me.

After a couple of years with the Steelers I thought I was going to quit and just hang it up. But then they hired Chuck Noll, who was a great guy. I ended up staying with the Steelers until 1977 and kicked on a couple of Super Bowl teams. That's not too bad for a little boy from Cairo, Georgia.

It's funny: I've been out of football for almost 27 years, and today I still get two or three letters a week from fans. They usually want something signed for their collection. It's nice to be remembered, so I always try to write them back.

But it all began at Georgia, where I learned all the lessons about growing up that I probably wouldn't have learned for a long time if I had stayed at home. One of the main things coach Butts always told us was, "Don't give up. Keep digging and digging and trying, no matter what."

That, and all the friendships I made at Georgia, helped me adjust to professional life. You can't put a money value on that. I've always said that my four years at Georgia were the best of my life, and I still feel that way.

Bobby Walden, "The Big Toe from Cairo," was an All-SEC halfback in 1958 and went on to become an All-Pro punter for the Pittsburgh Steelers. He played on Pittsburgh's Super Bowl champion teams in 1975 and 1976.

The SIXTIES

MIKE CAVAN

Quarterback
1968–1970

Nᴏᴛ ᴀ ᴡʜᴏʟᴇ ʟᴏᴛ ᴏғ ᴘᴇᴏᴘʟᴇ ᴋɴᴏᴡ ᴛʜɪs, but as a senior in high school I actually gave a verbal commitment to coach [Bear] Bryant at Alabama. I wanted to go there and be the next Joe Namath. Coach Bryant looked at me and said, "Son, you will never leave the state. Your daddy won't allow it. The governor won't allow it." I told coach Bryant not to worry about anything. Hey, I was 18 years old, and I thought I could do anything.

Coach Bryant was right, of course. I went to Georgia, and it was the best decision I ever made . . . or I should say . . . had made for me.

When I told my daddy [Jim], I was going to Alabama he didn't get mad, he just said, "No." Now, back then when your daddy said you weren't going to do something, you didn't do it. This was in December of 1966, when you could sign early, so I just bowed my neck up a little and said, "Fine, I'm not going anywhere." And he said, "Fine, but you're not going to Alabama."

I went through Christmas break and through January, and I didn't sign with anybody. Then it dawned on me that Daddy was not going to budge on this particular issue. So I signed with Georgia. Daddy was right. But then again, he was just about always right.

Daddy and I had a different kind of relationship in high school. Not only was he my daddy, but he was also my head football coach. I knew he wanted at least one of his three sons to play at Georgia. My older brother, Jim Jr., went to Georgia Tech, because Georgia was kind of down when he was a senior. My other brother, Pete, was seven or eight years younger than me, and we didn't know if he would be a football player or not. So when it came to going to Georgia, I guess I was the chosen one in the family.

By the way, Pete did turn out to be a very good football player. He went to Alabama. Today, his son plays for Alabama.

It's tough being the son of a head coach, and Jim Cavan was a very good coach. He started me at quarterback in my very first game as a freshman at Robert E. Lee Institute in Thomaston. And that brought about its own set of problems.

I remember my first year at Georgia I was sitting around the dorm with David McKnight, Brad Johnson, and Jake Scott, and we were talking about playing in high school. When I said I started at quarterback as a freshman, McKnight said, "What kind of a dumb coach would start a true freshman at quarterback?"

I said, "My dad."

But Dad and I went through some difficult times together. Because I was a freshman, he felt he had to be really hard on me or the other players wouldn't respect me. In fact, it got so bad that I went to my mom a couple of times and talked about quitting. She said no. She said there were reasons behind this and that I was too young to understand.

Of course when I got older and became a coach myself I did understand. He had to be tougher on me. But things got better later on, and we had some great times together. He died in 1983, and I still miss him a whole lot.

The sixties were a great time to be at Georgia. I really enjoyed my freedom. I was playing freshman ball in 1967, and back then we thought that was a really big deal. At first I didn't handle my freedom all that well because with nobody around telling me what to do, I let my schoolwork slide. I hung myself out there pretty good in the fall quarter, and then somebody got on me. I was OK after that.

In the spring of 1968 I got a chance to compete for the quarterback job. I was going against Paul Gilbert, who was from right here in Athens and a tremendous athlete. Coming out of the spring Paul was a little ahead of me, and he should have been. I wondered if they were going to redshirt me.

But early in the first preseason scrimmage, Paul tore up his knee, and it was obvious that he was going to be out for a while. I knew then that I was going to have the opportunity to move up.

Mike Cavan was the SEC Sophomore of the Year and led the Bulldogs to the 1968 SEC championship.

Coach Dooley is really smart. He knew it would not be the smart thing to let me start the first game against Tennessee. He let me come into the game and get used to it. We had Tennessee beat on the artificial turf in Knoxville, but they came back and tied us 17–17.

Donnie Hampton started the next week against Clemson, but I came in and had a really good game, and we won [31–13]. Then the following week at South Carolina, Donnie started again but threw an interception on the first play of the game.

Coach Dooley put me in, and I responded by throwing five interceptions in the *first half!*

At halftime coach Dooley came up to me and said, "How do you feel?"

I just said, "Coach Dooley, it can't get much worse."

Then he said, "I agree." And he stuck with me.

We came back and won the game [21–20]. I was the starter after that.

I think the 1968 Georgia team was a great, great football team. The guys were really close, and we had a lot of great football players. Jake Scott and Bill Stanfill could have played in any era. They were that good. We had guys like Dennis Hughes at tight end, Kent Lawrence at flanker, and Brad Johnson, who was the best blocking back I have ever seen. Charlie Whittemore was a great receiver. Tommy Lyons, our center, had a really good professional career.

That team averaged almost 200 yards in rushing and 200 yards in passing per game. That kind of offense was unheard of back then!

We went undefeated with a couple of ties, and we beat Auburn to win the SEC championship. We ended up going to the Sugar Bowl. I've heard the stories that some of our guys were upset that we didn't go to the Orange Bowl. We just figured that the Sugar Bowl was willing to take us before the Auburn game, win or lose, and coach Dooley had a tough decision to make. Once I got to be a coach and an administrator, I really understood how tough those decisions are.

I've heard people say that we really didn't care about the game against Arkansas. I don't believe that for a minute. The fact is, Arkansas just lined up and whipped our butts.

And let's get the record straight on one other thing. There have been rumors all these years that me, Brad Johnson, and Jake Scott were out on

79

Bourbon Street at 4:00 in the morning before the game. I can't speak for Brad or Jake, but I was in my room with my roommate, Billy Brice.

Besides, something like that would not have bothered Jake. He was so far ahead of everybody else as a football player.

It's funny. The 1968 SEC championship was the second in three years for Georgia. Those of us in the program then thought we were invincible. We thought it would go on like that forever. In 1969 we found out we were wrong when we went 5–5–1. It was just as bad in 1970 when I was a senior [5–5].

I learned a lot in those two years. They were tough, but they were probably good for me in the long run because they made me grow up. I learned about people. I learned about fans. I learned about the importance of having a veteran offensive line.

I learned that the quarterback gets too much praise when a team wins and too much criticism when they lose. But that's the way it is with quarterbacks, and if you want to play the position at this level, you'd better get used to it.

I was not used to losing. In high school we had always won. It was hell for those two years because everybody was looking at the team and saying it was my fault. I didn't play well, I'll admit it. But we lost a lot of great players after the 1968 season.

Those last two years made me pretty bitter. I was bitter at everybody—at Georgia, at the fans, at coach Dooley. But you learn. I got away from football for a couple of years and realized that it was just life. I just got caught in a bad cycle. I'm happy to say that I put it to rest years ago.

After two years in the real estate business in Athens, I kept feeling myself being pulled back to the game. I wanted to be involved in football again. I asked coach Dooley if I could come back as a graduate assistant. He let me come back and hired me full time two years later. I stayed at Georgia for 13 years, and I was able to stay in coaching for a total of 29 years. Now I'm back in the development office at Georgia, and I love being back in Athens.

I feel like I'm lucky because I've been given a chance to repay Georgia for everything that it has given me. I was away from Athens for 16 years, but when I came back it was like I had never left. The friends you make and the relationships you build at Georgia last a lifetime. They are always with you.

And when you get right down to it, that is what it really means to be a Georgia Bulldog. I had a chance to play on a championship team, and today,

36 years later, I'm still close to a lot of guys on that team. Being a student at Georgia means you are part of this incredible family for the rest of your life. It is a bond with a great university that nobody can ever take away.

I guess Daddy knew that all along.

Mike Cavan was the SEC Sophomore of the Year in 1968 after leading the Bulldogs to the SEC championship. He was an assistant coach at Georgia and later head coach at Valdosta State, East Tennessee State, and SMU.

BOBBY ETTER

Kicker
1964–1966

T HE ONLY REASON I GOT the chance to go to Georgia was sheer luck.

My best friend in high school was Dickie Phillips, a great, great football player who was wanted by every college in the universe. Dickie and his brother, Harry, both played with me at Chattanooga Central and both ended up going to Georgia.

I wasn't a highly recruited athlete. In fact, I wasn't even a lowly recruited athlete. Nobody really wanted me. I played basketball and baseball, and I was the kicker on the football team. But my dad [Red Etter] was the head coach, and I was lucky to play on a really good team.

It was the spring of 1963, and I still hadn't signed with anybody. Georgia had already signed Dickie and Harry. But Bobby Proctor, who recruited that area for Georgia at the time, came up to watch me play baseball. Georgia decided to sign me to a scholarship with the understanding that I would play baseball as well. For me it was a no-brainer, and I jumped on it.

When I signed I didn't know anything about Georgia. I grew up as a Tennessee fan. My brother, Gene, went to Tennessee and had a very good career as a tailback. I had no idea what was in store for me when I got to Athens.

As fate would have it, I arrived at the perfect time. I kicked on the freshman team in 1963, which was the last year of coach Johnny Griffith. That December coach [Vince] Dooley came to Georgia. To be there for his first three years was one of the luckiest things that ever happened to me.

Bobby Etter's touchdown run, after a botched field goal against Florida in 1964, gave the Bulldogs a 14–7 victory.

I didn't know the other coaching staff all that well because as freshmen we had our own coaches. But things definitely felt different once coach Dooley got there. I think a lot of the guys were afraid of coach Dooley at first because they didn't know what to expect. For some reason I wasn't. It might have been because my dad was a coach, but I could always seem to talk to coach Dooley.

I remember that first spring when he got there. Part of the agreement when I signed with Georgia was that I was supposed to play baseball as well. So I went to coach Dooley and asked him if it was all right. He said, "No, I don't want you to play baseball."

So I just accepted that and left.

Later on I started thinking that maybe I had not expressed myself very well. I wanted him to understand that I wasn't going to miss spring football practice in order to play baseball. I was going to do *both*. So I went back to his office and explained myself again. This time he said yes, and I played baseball the rest of my career there. I think coach Dooley was surprised that I came back. Maybe that's why he let me play baseball.

That first season in 1964 was so much fun. We played Alabama and Joe Namath in our very first game, and they beat us bad. But they were one of the best teams in the country. The next week we beat Vanderbilt, and then we tied South Carolina. But you got the sense that every week we were getting better.

Nobody gave us a chance when we went down to Jacksonville to play Florida. But we just kind of hung in there because our defense was really good. The score was tied 7–7 in the fourth quarter, and we drove it to about the 5-yard line. Coach Dooley sent me out to kick the short field goal.

I remember that the ball was on the left hash. Barry Wilson, who would go on to become a coach, was the holder. It was a low snap, and he couldn't hang on to it.

We had a system where if anything went wrong on the snap, we were supposed to yell "Fire!" That way all of the backs would know that they needed to either block or go out for a pass because something had gone wrong on the field goal.

I just picked the ball up and started running around the end. The guys who were coming to block the kick had rushed inside, so I was able to get around them. The films would later show that I faked a pass, but I don't remember it. When it happened, the defensive back hesitated and went back a couple of steps. Barry threw a great block, and it gave me just enough room to get to the corner of the end zone. I dove backward into the end zone, looking like a high jumper doing the Fosbury Flop.

All I remember is that everybody was going crazy. We won 14–7. It all felt like a dream, and today it still doesn't seem quite real. I can't believe that it was 40 years ago.

After we went to the Sun Bowl that year, the excitement level at Georgia was really something going into the 1965 season. We started 4–0 and beat Alabama and Michigan, two highly ranked teams.

I'll never forget the Michigan game. You could tell when the Michigan team came out on the field they didn't think much of us. They were at home in that one hundred thousand–seat stadium, and we were just a bunch of little guys from Georgia. But we won 15–7, and when we got back to Athens, there must have been ten thousand people waiting for us at the airport. [Editor's note: Etter's three field goals were the difference in that 15–7 win over Michigan.]

I really thought we were going to win the SEC championship, but then we went down to Florida State and Bob Taylor broke his leg. Bob was a really good football player, but he never recovered and neither did our team. We finished 6–4.

The 1966 team was very special. It was made up of a lot of guys who played B-team ball early in their careers. But our coaching staff knew how to take these guys and mold them into a great team. I once asked my dad what was the most important thing in coaching, and he said, "Evaluating talent and knowing where they should play." Coach Dooley and his staff were really great at that.

To be on coach Dooley's first SEC championship team was a great honor. We almost won them all, but we struggled down at Miami and lost 7–6. Still, we were there at the start of something big for Georgia.

Back in 2002 I was fortunate enough to be inducted into the Georgia-Florida game's Hall of Fame. I told the folks at the banquet that I figured I came to Georgia at the best possible time. I got to play on his first team, and in my last year we gave coach Dooley his first SEC championship. It was as good an experience as I could ever have.

I've been lucky my entire life. I was lucky that Dickie Phillips was my best friend so that Georgia would take a look at me. I was lucky to be there when

85

one of the greatest coaches in the history of college football took over the program. I was lucky to be a part of a championship team, which is always special. I wanted to be a teacher, and Georgia gave me the education I needed to pursue that dream.

I wouldn't trade anything for the years I spent at Georgia.

Bobby Etter led the SEC in scoring in 1966. He later received his Ph.D. in mathematics from Rice University and became a professor at Sacramento State University. He was inducted into the Georgia-Florida game Hall of Fame in 2002.

STEVE GREER

Defensive Lineman
1967–1969

I GREW UP IN GREER, SOUTH CAROLINA, which is only 40 miles away from Clemson. [Editor's note: The town was named after Steve Greer's great-great-grandfather.] When I was young, people could sit on the hill at Clemson's stadium and watch the football game for only 50 cents. In that area, if you were good enough to play college football everybody just figured that you were going to Clemson or South Carolina.

It was the fall of my senior year and coach Frank Inman came to my practice. My high school coach, Phil Clark, came to me and told me that a guy from Georgia was there to see me. I really didn't know anything about Georgia. I just remembered seeing the road signs to Athens when we would drive down to Atlanta.

Coach Inman invited me and my teammate Steve Woodward to come down for a game. I don't remember what game it was, but I do remember the enthusiasm of the Georgia crowd.

This was the fall of 1964, and that was coach [Vince] Dooley's first year at Georgia. They let us sit along the sideline, and I remember that the other team was driving the ball and had to settle for a field goal. When the Georgia defense came off the field the crowd gave them a standing ovation. I thought, "These people are crazy about football!" It really made an impression on me.

Well, it got down to signing day and Steve Woodward, myself, and Kent Lawrence, another South Carolina boy from Central, were down at Florida on a recruiting visit. I'm pretty sure it was our last one.

On Friday night Florida was really pushing us. Larry Smith, who had been a great player there, was really on us hard and trying to get us to sign. I remember we got back to the room and decided to go home. We had had enough. On that trip back home all three of us decided to go to Georgia.

That freshman class in 1965—the one I came in with—has to be one of the most talented groups of people to come to Georgia. I'm not just talking about football. We had great players—Jake Scott and Bill Stanfill went on to be All-Pros. We also had six lawyers, two judges, and three doctors in that group. Billy Payne was a great football player but became famous for bringing the Olympics to Atlanta. Kent Lawrence became a judge. Happy Dicks is a doctor. Sonny Purdue was a walk-on in that class and became governor of Georgia.

I played freshman ball in 1965, and in the spring of 1966 I got a pretty good scare. I tore up my knee and had to miss the entire 1966 season. Bruce Kemp, a really good running back, got hurt about three days before I did, and we spent the entire season rehabilitating together. I'm not going to kid you, it was hard. Some folks thought I might never make it back, but those people didn't know that I loved to play football more than anything in the world.

I made it back for the 1967 season, but I wasn't very big. Before I got hurt I think I was up to 220 pounds, but after the injury I just couldn't put on any weight. I might have been 205 pounds.

I remember my second game in 1967. We went up to Clemson, and obviously that was an important game to me. I lined up at nose guard for the first play of the game, and opposite of me was a guard named Harry Olszewski. He looked like he was 30 years old. Right before the ball was snapped, he turned to the Clemson lineman next to him and said, "Hey, look, I've got a dad-gum baby in front of me!"

But we won the game, 24–17.

What's funny is that four years later, when I was playing in the Canadian League, I lined up for the first play of the game and there was Olszewski again! He still thought I was a baby!

The 1968 season was really special. We had a couple of ties against Tennessee and Houston, but we won the rest and gave coach Dooley another championship. There was really only one downer on the year.

For his size, All-American Steve Greer is considered to be the best nose guard ever to play at Georgia.

We knew going into the game with Auburn that if we won we would get an invitation to the Orange Bowl. All the guys wanted to go to the Orange Bowl.

We beat Auburn [17–3] to clinch the championship, but on Sunday in the team meeting coach Dooley told us that we were going to the Sugar Bowl. Some of the guys got upset. Jake [Scott] even said something about it in the meeting. But I understand why coach Dooley made the decision he did. We had a chance to go to the Sugar Bowl, win or lose against Auburn, and you just didn't pass up something like that. When I became a coach I understood it even better.

That didn't have anything to do with us losing to Arkansas [16–2] in the Sugar Bowl. They just beat us.

We thought we were going to be pretty good again in 1969, but Jake left early and played in Canada. Dennis Hughes, our really good tight end, got banged up. And we lost a lot of really good players from the year before. Probably the game that sticks out in my mind most is the one with Ole Miss and Archie Manning in Jackson.

Archie was one of the greatest quarterbacks ever to play college football, and he drove us crazy with his ability to scramble. On this particular play I think I had already missed him a couple of times, and then I got off the ground and saw him coming back to me. So I just reached down and hit him with everything I had, right up under the chin.

Somebody later sent me a magazine article where a reporter asked Archie about the hardest he had ever been hit. He said it was from "this little nose guard at Georgia. He hit me so hard he knocked me out, and my teeth hurt for three weeks after that."

This was in the first half, and they had to help Archie get to the locker room. When the third quarter started he still was not on the field. I figured we were in good shape. We had the lead, and their star player had been knocked out of the game.

Sometime in the third quarter I remember we made a good defensive play, but I heard the Ole Miss fans erupting. I look over to the tunnel, and there's Archie running back onto the field. I turned to somebody and said, "Oh, hell. We're in trouble."

Archie came back out and beat us [25–17]. He was one helluva football player.

We were 3–0 before we played Ole Miss, but after that things didn't go all that well. We beat Vanderbilt the next week but lost four out of the last five. We went to the Sun Bowl and probably should have stayed at home. Nebraska wore us out [45–6] with a group of guys that would go on to win the national championship in 1971.

But all in all, I was a lucky guy at Georgia. I got to play for a man like Erk Russell who, for my money, is the best defensive coach who has ever lived. He demanded excellence without screaming. There has never been a greater motivator. If you called up one of coach Russell's players today and asked him to run through a brick wall in a business suit, he'd die trying. That's how much Erk means to us.

Dick Copas took me under his wing as a student. Back then Dick had to do everything for the football players: class scheduling, tutoring, books, study halls. Today they have a building full of people to do that. He made sure I was always doing right. He really took an interest in me. But I remember that if Dick took the palm of his right hand and started rubbing his eye with it, then look out, you were about to be in big trouble.

Coach Dooley gave me the chance to come back and be a part of this great university and this great program. He is a leader of the very best kind.

When I think about what it means to be a Bulldog, I think about the guys I came in with in 1965. All of us who stayed here the whole time still try to keep in touch. If one of those guys calls you in the middle of the night and is in trouble, you are going to be there to help him. You won together and you lost together. You hurt together. You bled together. I know it's a cliché, but it's true. You bond with people when you go through that kind of shared experience.

One of my former players once wrote a poem about what playing at Georgia meant to him. He ended it with the line, "For a Bulldog, by God, I am, and a Bulldog I'll always be."

I think that about sums it up.

Steve Greer was an All-American nose guard and captain of Georgia's 1969 team. He returned to Georgia in 1979 as an assistant coach. In 1996 he was named Georgia's director of football operations.

LEN HAUSS

Center
1961–1963

I GREW UP IN JESUP, GEORGIA, and I guess I was a decent high school football player. I had several offers but really narrowed it down to Georgia, Georgia Tech, and Auburn. To tell you the truth, I kinda halfway wanted to go to Georgia Tech.

In the fall of 1959 my high school was getting ready to play Rossville for the state championship, and at that point the schools were calling my house every night. So I asked the recruiters from those three schools, "Please don't bother me this week. We are getting ready to play for the championship."

Well, Georgia Tech had a recruiter by the name of Dynamite Goodloe, and he was calling my mother every night, which offended me. You have to remember that I was a 17-year-old kid, and from my point of view that was reason enough to eliminate Tech.

I had really been impressed with coach [Ralph] Jordan from Auburn, but back then the old saying was that if you went to college, you should stay in the state where you were going to live.

The other reason I went to Georgia, and really the main reason, was coach J. B. Whitworth. He came to Jesup to see me a number of times, and my family fell in love with him. He was a recruiter without peer. The sad part is that after I signed with Georgia, he died before the start of the next season. His recruiting plus the fact that Georgia was coming off an SEC championship season in 1959 were really the reasons I went to Athens.

Len Hauss played on coach Johnny Griffith's final team in 1963. He went on to play 14 seasons in the NFL.

Coach [Wally] Butts, of course, was the legend back then. I remember the first time he addressed the freshman class on the practice field. Back then the varsity worked out on top of what we called Ag Hill. The freshmen practiced on a field below.

The freshmen worked out a few days before the varsity got there, and coach Butts came down to our practice field to talk to us. He was very impressive.

He said, "Men, we're pretty particular about how we treat our freshmen. We're going to give you time to learn the ropes. We won't bring you up to work with the varsity until we think you're ready."

Coach Butts left and a bunch of us were thinking, "Boy, what a nice guy." We had heard that things were going to be tough under coach Butts.

Well, we got back to our workout at the bottom of the hill while coach Butts was on the top of the hill working with the varsity. About 35 or 40 minutes later we heard this whistle. Then coach Butts started screaming.

"Bring those damned freshmen up here right now!!"

That was the end of the nice-guy stuff.

My freshman class was part of a unique time in Georgia football history. As it turned out, 1960, our freshman year, was coach Butts' last season at Georgia. None of us ever saw it coming. Coach Butts became the athletic director and named Johnny Griffith, the freshman coach, as the head coach.

Over the next three years we won only 10 games. I'm not really sure why we struggled, because we had some really good football players: Larry Rakestraw, Mickey Babb, Don Porterfield, Pete Case. We had a bunch of them.

One of the problems had to be on the coaching staff. We had some great coaches on that staff—John Gregory, Jim Posey, and Charley Trippi to name a few—and coach Griffith kept the entire coaching staff in place. I have to believe that four or five guys on that staff thought they should have been the head coach instead of Johnny Griffith. It made for a most tumultuous situation.

Then in 1963 came charges that coach Butts had been part of fixing a game with Alabama in 1962. There was a lot going on at that time. There seemed to be turmoil right from the get-go after Johnny Griffith was named the head coach.

But there were some fun moments. I remember in 1963 we went down to Miami and beat them [31–14]. Miami had a great quarterback named George Mira, but Larry Rakestraw really put Mira to shame that day.

Later in my career some scouts told me that they had been at that game to see some other guys, but they thought I had an outstanding day against Miami. It was because Larry threw so often that day and so I had plenty of chances to show that I was a pretty good pass blocker. Based on that the Redskins took an extra look and drafted me.

Like I said, my freshman class went through a strange time. After our senior season, in 1963, coach Griffith was let go. We didn't see that coming either, but back then guys didn't really talk about or think about what was going to happen to the head coach. It wasn't like it is now.

We didn't win a whole lot of games during my time at Georgia, but there is no question that what I learned there made it possible for me to play 14 years in the NFL. I really believe those of us who played through those lean years became tougher men. And that kind of toughness helped no matter what profession we went into.

When I think about what it means to be a Bulldog, I go back to something that happened in my rookie year with the Redskins. We were up in training camp in Pennsylvania, and I've often told people that I was so scared that it was three weeks before I spoke to anybody.

Sam Huff had just been traded from the Giants to the Redskins. Sam Huff is a legend and one of the greatest linebackers to ever play this game.

We were doing one-on-one drills, and when it came my turn I was the center and Huff was the linebacker. The first time we met, Huff knocked me on my rear.

Well, the next time Huff was up, I broke in line in front of a couple of guys because I wanted another shot at him. I whispered in the quarterback's ear that we were going to change the count and go on the first sound. The time before, Sam knew what the count was.

So we went on the first sound, and I knocked Huff on his rear. Everybody cheered. A lot of those guys didn't like Sam because he was so good.

Huff got up and said, "That's the way, Hauss. There's an old Georgia Bulldog. I never knew a Georgia Bulldog in my career who wouldn't knock you on your butt."

Then I heard one of the coaches say, "All those guys from Georgia are always tough."

So here is a Hall of Fame player and a legend like Sam Huff thinking I am tough because I'm a Georgia Bulldog. And there are coaches who, because I'm a Georgia Bulldog, think I'm tough. That meant something to me then, and it still means something to me today. That's why I will always be a Bulldog.

95

Len Hauss played 14 years with the Washington Redskins (1964–1977) and was All-Pro five times. He is listed among the 70 greatest Redskins players of all time.

PAT HODGSON

End
1963–1965

It would have taken a lot for me to go anywhere other than Georgia. My grandfather [Morton Hodgson] was Georgia's first four-year letterman in 1908. My father [Hutch] played there in 1933. I lived in Athens when I was young.

But to tell you the truth, I didn't know if I was big enough to play major college football. In my senior year at Westminster I was really thinking about smaller schools. Out on the recruiting trail, I would meet guys like Preston Ridlehuber from Gainesville. Preston could have gone anywhere, but he was thinking that if you were going to a state school, you probably should go to the one in your own state. So when I got the opportunity to go to Georgia, I grabbed it.

The fall of 1962 was an interesting time to be at Georgia. The old traditions such as the silver helmets and the silver britches were still there. But coach [Wally] Butts had left and coach [Johnny] Griffith had taken over, and none of us really knew what was going to happen.

The summer between my freshman and sophomore years brought the scandal involving coach Butts, Bear Bryant, and the *Saturday Evening Post*. There always seemed to be something brewing.

I was a sophomore in 1963 and was backing up Mickey Babb when we played our first game with Alabama. Joe Namath and those guys came up to Athens and kicked us pretty good [32–7].

Pat Hodgson's father (Hutch) and grandfather (Morton) played football at the University of Georgia.

Later in the year I got a chance to start in the game at Miami. Larry Rakestraw was having a great day, and I got a chance to catch a lot of balls. [Editor's note: Hodgson caught eight passes for 192 yards as Georgia won 31–14.] I think the coaches started to notice me after that.

That football team had a lot of really good players, but for whatever reason, we just couldn't win many games. There were a lot of internal things coach Griffith had to deal with. There were a number of guys on the staff that he inherited who thought they should have been the head coach. There was not a lot of loyalty because of it. It was just a nutty year.

I was among that first group of players that got to meet coach [Vince] Dooley on the day he was introduced in Athens in December of 1963. Right away we learned that things were going to be very, very different.

First of all, coach Dooley hired one of the best coaching staffs I have ever seen. Guys like Bill Dooley and Erk Russell and Hootie Ingram, along with Ken Cooper, who stayed from the old staff. You could tell in spring practice that things were going to be different. Yeah, it was tough, but when you made mistakes you still got coached.

In 1964 we opened up with Alabama again, and they killed us again [31–3]. But this time our coaches watched the film and saw some good things. They saw some changes we could make to get better. We went on to have a pretty good year and went to the Sun Bowl to beat Texas Tech. After everything Georgia football had gone though by that time, you would have thought we had won the world championship. What a time it was!

Things were starting to change around Georgia. People started getting excited about football again. The whole atmosphere around Athens changed.

In 1965 we started the season by playing Alabama again, but this time things felt different. I remember standing at the end of the field getting ready for the game. We looked at Alabama's players, and they didn't look any bigger than us. I think every guy on our team knew that we could beat them if we didn't make too many mistakes.

We jumped on top early, but then Alabama bounced back and went ahead of us, 17–10.

We got the ball back, and what happened next changed my life forever, I can tell you that.

People still talk about the flea flicker play that we ran that day to beat Alabama. What I remember most is that we had tried to run the thing in practice for two weeks and it would never work. I was supposed to run a little curl pattern, catch the ball, and then lateral it back to Bob Taylor, who was trailing the play. But in practice I would always drop the ball or miss the lateral or something.

Needless to say I was pretty nervous when our quarterback, Kirby Moore, called the play. All I could think was, "Catch it, then find Bob."

I remember the ball coming my way and the ball hitting my hands. People said my knee was down, but I just juggled the ball a little bit to give folks some controversy to talk about. As the ball hit my hands I saw Bob coming. I flipped the ball in his direction and hit the ground.

All I remember after that is the roar. I got off the ground and looked as Bob was running down the field for a touchdown. The sound was unlike anything I had ever heard. It came in thundering waves.

After the score everybody knew we would be going for two, and unlike a lot of teams, we had practiced a two-point play. It was just a little flood pattern where we put a lot of receivers in one area. In the huddle, Kirby looked at me and said, "Get open in the back of the end zone. I'm coming to you."

Well, that's exactly what happened. Kirby rolled out to his right, and I found a little hole. Kirby always threw these wounded ducks, and it seemed like it took forever for the ball to get there. But I grabbed it. We won the game [18–17]. What an incredible feeling it was!

A couple of weeks later we went to Michigan and nobody gave us a chance up there. In those days we flew out of Athens in a couple of props—Martin 404s, I believe—to Ann Arbor. We actually had to stop in Nashville to refuel!

We got up there, and the night before the game both teams ended up at the same movie theater. We're all standing in line to get popcorn, and we catch Michigan's players looking at us. We could tell they were thinking, "What high school do you guys play for?"

It was about 75 degrees that day in Ann Arbor, and for a while they ran over us. But as the game went on, we kind of got our rhythm and ended up beating them 15–7.

Landing back in Athens was one of the most unbelievable experiences of my life. There were thousands and thousands of people at the airport. They later told us that before we arrived, the people surrounded an incoming plane and shouted, "Damn good team! Damn good team!"

A little lady then walked out and said, "Wrong damn plane! Wrong damn plane!"

That game and the Alabama game were the highlights of the year. We went down to Florida State, and Bob Taylor got hurt. We were a good team, but we just weren't that deep.

But for the guys who were seniors with me those last two years at Georgia, they were an incredible experience.

I was one of the lucky ones who got to continue the experience. After I graduated I worked in business for a couple of years but found that I missed football. So coach Dooley brought me on as a freshman coach in 1968. I would stay in coaching for 28 years, and 9 of those years I got to spend at Georgia.

There are so many great memories. Dr. Boyd McWhorter was a wonderful influence on me. Dean [William] Tate was a legend. They would send us to a movie the night before a game, and sometimes we would cut up a little bit. I can still hear Dean Tate's voice: "Mr. Hodgson, have coach Castronis call me in the morning."

Those traditions at Georgia have been the building blocks not only for my life, but for many members of my family. My father and my grandfather both went to Georgia and walked the same paths that I did. They went to class in the same buildings. I'm proud to say that both of my sons chose to go to Georgia.

Athens is just a special town that draws you back. It has an ambiance that is hard to describe. You have to walk Between the Hedges. You have to go to the Varsity and get a hot dog.

My grandfather wrote a song called "Going Back to Athens Town" that is still played at the football games today. He understood then what we all understand now. The University of Georgia is a special place, and we are all lucky to be a part of it.

Before every game now they roll a film clip of great plays in Georgia football history. On that film clip you'll see the flea flicker play against Alabama in 1965. That play happened over 38 years ago and people are still talking about it today.

Each generation of Georgia people has one of those special moments. It is the thing that binds all of the generations together. My grandfather, my father, myself, and my sons. We have all been Bulldogs. How could anything be better than that?

Pat Hodgson was an All-SEC tight end in 1965. He was an assistant coach at Georgia for nine seasons (1968–1970 and 1972–1977).

JOHN KASAY

Offensive Guard
1964–1966

A LOT OF PEOPLE HAVE ASKED ME WHY I have never left the University of Georgia. I tell them that I'm still in Athens for the exact same reason I came here 42 years ago—I care about the people.

From the moment I got off that plane in 1962, I could tell that Georgia was a unique place. The camaraderie of the guys who play and work here and of the people in this town is something that I have never found anywhere else. Plus, I was working for a man [Vince Dooley] I liked and respected. If I had ever left Georgia I would have missed out on some of the best times in my life.

When I was coming along in Johnstown, Pennsylvania, we had a guy named Doc who taught us how to be good coaches. He believed in getting deeply involved in our lives and helping us to become better men. So when I became a coach, that is how I thought I was supposed to do it.

I think six or eight of my former players have told me that they have named their children after me. I am really humbled by that. I think I gave them as much of myself as I could. It's just that when I went into the living room of a recruit and told his mama we were going to take care of her son, I felt an obligation to do it. What that meant back then was that if the young man needed emotional support, he was going to get it. If he needed to have his butt kicked, he was going to get that, too.

That feeling probably kept me from doing some other things in life that I probably should have done. But when I would sign one I usually said to myself, "Well, I'm here for another four years." I had made a commitment to that kid and his parents. I couldn't just take the next job that came along.

But if I had ever left Georgia, I hate to think about some of the things I would have missed.

I lived in McWhorter Hall [the school's athletic dormitory] for 12 years. It was the damnedest and most unique experience of my life. I thought I was pretty worldly, but those guys taught me some things I would have never even thought about. It gave me the chance to get involved in the lives of some people that I still care about. Guys like:

- Mike Cavan, who was the perfect position coach for Herschel Walker. Mike was one of those guys who knew how to keep a staff loose, and he knew how to use Herschel's talent and not wear him out.

- Mac McWhorter, who literally worked his way into becoming an All-SEC guard. He wanted to be a great football player, and I took it personally when it came to helping him get there. He is one of the most positive people I have ever been around.

- Troy Sadowski was a little immature when he got to Georgia, but you could tell that he had the stuff to be a good player if he worked at it. I had some of my old weights in a storage area at McWhorter and gave them to him. He left here as an All-American, but I don't think I ever got those weights back.

- Kendall Keith wanted to quit any number of times. One day we were running at practice, and he just ran right out the gate toward McWhorter Hall. I saw him and chased him down. He said, "I don't want to do this anymore." I told him that I wouldn't let him quit. I used to check on him about once an hour so he'd never have time to pack and leave. He finally broke through and was an All-SEC player for us in 1971. [Editor's note: Kendall Keith named his son after John Kasay.] He went on to get a master's degree, and now he is a high school principal.

- I don't know how many times we had to go get Moonpie [Wilson] after he had quit. He told me he wanted to be a carpenter. I pointed out to him that he was too damned big to be a carpenter. He wouldn't be able to walk through the studs of a house, which are only 13 inches apart. He went on to be an All-American and played in the pros for a dozen years.

John Kasay became a graduate assistant coach after his playing days at Georgia ended in 1966. He is still at Georgia today as an employee of the UGA Athletic Association.

103

I don't have any illusions that I helped these guys become great football players. I think the thing I did was give them help beyond football. I think they named their children after me because they knew I cared enough about them to do what was necessary off the field. I wanted each and every one of them to succeed and graduate. Like I said, I took it personally.

If I had left Georgia I would have probably missed out on the great 1980 season. I would have missed out on watching Herschel Walker do the little things that made him great. I remember day after day walking down the hall 30 minutes before the players' meeting, and there was Herschel, already dressed and ready to go. Man, that guy was special. I would have hated to miss that.

One of the reasons so many guys tell you they love this place is that they had a pretty common experience. That is due to the stability of the athletic program, and that stability is because of coach Dooley. He has been the constant through all the years. He may have stopped coaching in 1988, but he has always been here. And I think that gives most Georgia players the sense that this is their home.

I think the best example I can give you of what it means to be a Bulldog was the reaction of Georgia's players after the untimely death of Royce Smith back in January (2004). The day we learned about it, I probably got 15 or 20 phone calls from his teammates wanting to make sure that I knew. And I was totally amazed at the number of his teammates who attended his funeral down in Statesboro. It must have been 45 or 50. A lot of these men had not seen Royce since they last played together 32 years ago! That means something.

Bottom line: I never felt I could be as happy somewhere else as I was at Georgia. And if I couldn't be as happy somewhere else, why would I be stupid enough to leave? I would have hated to do that to myself. I wouldn't trade when and what I did if I knew I could start over right now. The experience that I had with the guys that I coached and the guys I came along with was the best in the world.

Shoot, I wouldn't trade the memories I have for all the rice in China.

John Kasay was a starting guard on Georgia's 1966 SEC championship team. But Kasay earned his greatest distinction as Georgia's longtime strength and conditioning coach and as the resident manager of McWhorter Hall, the school's athletic dormitory. Today, 42 years after he came to Georgia from Johnstown, Pennsylvania, Kasay remains on the UGA athletics staff as an assistant manager of facilities. At least six former Georgia players have named one of their children after Kasay. His son, John Kasay Jr., was a placekicker at Georgia from 1987 to 1990.

TOMMY LAWHORNE

Linebacker
1965–1967

EARLY IN MY LIFE I WAS TAUGHT that one of the secrets of success was to take the opportunities you had and apply yourself to them as much as you possibly could. You should never put any limits on yourself because of where you are from or what your background might be.

Given my background, I probably shouldn't have been a successful college football player. My high school team was 1–9 and I was not a highly recruited athlete. I grew up in tiny Sylvester, Georgia, and some might say that I shouldn't have been able to go from there to one of the top medical schools in the country.

But thanks to the University of Georgia, I was able to do both of those things.

I always loved Georgia growing up, and I had already committed to go to Georgia in the fall of 1963 when coach [Vince] Dooley was hired. I never thought about changing my mind.

But that first fall in 1964 was a very long one for me. I took about 17 hours that first quarter because I pretty much knew that I wanted to go to medical school. There were lots of labs and lots of extra studying to do.

Freshmen didn't play back then, and we were kind of fodder for the varsity. I'd finish up practice about 7:00 P.M., have to hustle to eat, and then get to the library where I would stay all night. There were a couple of times when I said to myself, "I don't know if I can do this." I wanted to do both, but if it came down to a decision, I was going to let football go.

Tommy Lawhorne was the valedictorian of the 1968 senior class at Georgia.

106

But I loved the game and just wanted to play. So I kept plugging along and finally got through that first fall, but it was no fun, I can tell you that.

The following spring practice I went to my position coach, John Donaldson. We called him "Hubba, Hubba" because that was one of his favorite sayings. I was a quarterback in high school, but they moved me to wing back. I was the number three wing back, and it really didn't look like I was going to get a chance to play. I sure didn't want to get redshirted, because I knew I wasn't going to stay more than four years because of medical school.

So in the summer of 1965 I decided to get serious about working out. I ran every day, and before the summer was over, I put on about 20 pounds of muscle and got up to about 205. I was ready.

About 10 days before our first game with Alabama one of our best linebackers got hurt, so they asked me to play linebacker. They put me into a scrimmage on the Saturday before the game, and I had a pretty good day. The next thing I knew, the coaches were telling me that I was going to start against Alabama. I was scared to death.

But coach Erk Russell, our defensive coordinator, knew what to do. To me he is the greatest motivator who has ever lived. Coach Russell came up and put his arm around my shoulder. He was chewing on his cigar. He said, "Tommy, you're going to start Saturday against the national champions.

You're starting at linebacker, and I don't know of anybody in the world I would rather have starting for me than you."

Well, of course he was lying, but after that I was really jacked up to play. If my grandmother had been wearing an Alabama helmet I would have said, "Look out, Granny, here it comes."

We probably didn't have any business beating Alabama that day [18–17]. They were the defending national champions. We had about 20 really good football players. They had about 50. But the game was on national television, so we got a few more rest breaks than in a normal game. I just remember how good it felt to win a game that big.

That 1965 team started 4–0, and early in the year we were good enough to play with anybody in the country. But like I said, we didn't have any depth. Bob Taylor got hurt down in Tallahassee, and we had a hard time getting it back together.

The 1966 team was a very good one. I was a junior, but I remember we had some very strong seniors, like George Patton. We also had some very talented sophomores, like Bill Stanfill and Billy Payne. What I remember most is the only game we lost, which was to Miami, 7–6. We missed a couple of chances to kick field goals, and I believe the boy that scored Miami's touchdown was from College Park, Georgia.

That was my junior year, and I missed some games due to injury. I went ahead and applied to medical school and got accepted. I was thinking about leaving for med school early and not playing as a senior in 1967. But we had a lot of guys coming back off that 1966 team, and I thought we had a chance to win another championship. I decided I really wanted to be a part of it.

I really don't know why, but that 1967 team just didn't play as hungry as we did the year before.

My most vivid memory is a painful one. We went to Houston and played on a Friday night. I was running a fever of about 104 because I had an abscess on my tailbone. I was really miserable. On the night before the game Dr. Butch Mulherin asked me if I wanted him to drain that thing, and I told him I had to get some relief.

So Lee Daniel grabbed one of my arms and Billy Payne grabbed the other to hold me still. Somebody else grabbed my legs. Dr. Mulherin sprayed some ethyl chloride on that thing and proceeded to go to work. I couldn't go to the movie with the team that night, but the next day I felt great. They made me a little donut to protect that area, and I went out and had one of my best games of the season.

Unfortunately, we lost the game, 15–14, when Paul Gipson scored the winning touchdown. Larry Kohn and I got our signals crossed, and we both took the same guy on the play, so Gipson went in untouched for the score.

We finished the season 7–3 and went to the Liberty Bowl, but I didn't go with the team to Memphis. I stayed in Atlanta for the final interviews for the Rhodes Scholarship. After the interviews I flew on a private plane and got to the stadium in time to put on my uniform, warm up a little, and then play the game.

It was not a great day. Earlier in the afternoon I found out that I didn't win the Rhodes Scholarship. Then I went out to play my last game for Georgia, and we lost to North Carolina State, 14–7.

Still, good things were ahead. I was honored to be named valedictorian of the senior class at Georgia. It was something special to give the valedictory address at graduation.

I went on to medical school at Johns Hopkins, where there were a lot of students from Ivy League schools. I took pride in knowing that I was as well prepared as any of them for medical school.

I spent 10 years at Johns Hopkins, gave a couple of years to Uncle Sam, and then came back to Columbus, Georgia, to practice my craft.

Those four years at Georgia made several major impacts on my life. The greatest impact was meeting a little girl from Jonesboro named Susan. She is the mother of my children and my best friend.

The second impact: it was Georgia that spurred me on to be the best I could be. It took me from a little rural town in Georgia to one of the most prestigious medical institutions in the world.

And finally, Georgia gave me friendships that have lasted forever. Playing football together is like going through boot camp together. You never forget those guys. I still talk to one teammate about three times a week. Guys like Bruce Yawn and Jack Davis will always be with me.

At Georgia you go from wanting to be an adult to actually having to become an adult. It was the best possible training I could have had. That's why Georgia will always be a special place to me.

Tommy Lawhorne was the valedictorian of the 1968 senior class at the University of Georgia. He attended medical school at Johns Hopkins. Today he has his own surgical practice in Columbus, Georgia.

KENT LAWRENCE

Flanker
1966–1968

How I got to Georgia is a pretty unusual story. I grew up near Clemson, South Carolina. My older brother went to Clemson. My younger brother ended up going to Clemson. My high school idol growing up was Jimmy Howard, the son of Frank Howard, Clemson's legendary football coach.

I played some of my Little League football games at Memorial Stadium in Clemson. So everything I experienced when I was growing up said that I should probably go to Clemson.

Truth be told, I was really looking hard at Tennessee. I was being recruited for both football and track, and back then Tennessee had the premier college track program in the country. Tennessee was also recruiting a great sprinter by the name of Richmond Flowers from Alabama to play football and run track. Richmond and I were two of the top high school sprinters in the country, and I finally met him when we ran against each other in the Florida Relays.

Richmond and I got to know each other. Chuck Rhoe, the Tennessee track coach, made it clear that he wanted both of us. I had a good visit to Tennessee, and it was reasonably close to home. Doug Dickey was the football coach, and I liked and respected him. So at that point I was probably leaning to Tennessee.

But right after that I made my first visit to Georgia, and a funny story goes with that visit.

The visit was on a Saturday, and the night before we had played Greer High School in the state playoffs. They had a player named Steve Greer who was a legend in South Carolina high school football. Steve was a great, great player.

Well, we beat them, and as the final seconds wound down I looked across the line and saw Steve. Now, I had never met him before, but he was screaming at us because he was really upset because his team was about to lose. Well, I decided to give a little bit of it right back to him. As soon as the game was over, I think he started looking for me, but I ducked into the locker room.

The next morning we were in Athens, and when we arrived, coach [Frank] Inman took me and my parents upstairs to meet coach Dooley. As soon as we walked in the door coach Dooley said, "Well, I guess you know these people."

It was Steve Greer and his parents.

After that Steve and I got to be good friends, and we started going on recruiting visits together. We decided at the same time that we were both going to Georgia. And that brings me to another interesting story.

Steve and I went on our last recruiting visit together down to Florida. Steve Woodward, who was Greer's teammate, went with us. They flew us down on a Thursday night, and we weren't there long before we decided that we really didn't like it. So we got a car Friday night and started driving home.

We stopped in Macon and bought an Atlanta paper. In the paper was a story about how Georgia was signing all these great players and putting together a super recruiting class. The signing period had just started. So we got back in the car and started driving again.

I'm not sure how it happened, but somewhere between Macon and Athens the three of us all decided that we were going to Georgia. We all liked it there, and coach Dooley had really impressed me and my parents. It was about 1:00 in the morning when we got to Athens, so we stopped at a Gulf Station outside of town and called coach Inman's house.

Mrs. Inman answered the phone and said, "Where in the world are you guys?" She said coach Inman and coach [Sam] Mrvos were already in Greer looking for us. She said they had already signed three other South Carolina players—Pat Rodrique and Steve Farnsworth from Greenville and Wayne Byrd from Florence.

So we called Greer's house and sure enough coach Inman and coach Mrvos were there. So we kept driving, and they dropped me off at Clemson and went on to Greer's house. They signed Greer and Woodward at about 4:30

Kent Lawrence, one of the fastest men ever to play at Georgia, is now a judge in Athens.

in the morning. Then they came to my house and signed me at 6:30 in the morning. And that's how the top six players in the state of South Carolina ended up going to Georgia in 1965.

We played freshman ball back in those days, but I hardly got into the games at all. I played some against Georgia Tech in the Scottish Rite game and had a reasonably good game. I think that caught the eye of some of the varsity coaches.

My sophomore season, in 1966, I was second-team tailback to Randy Wheeler, who was a senior, going into the first game with Mississippi State. Unfortunately, Randy got injured in the first quarter and never completely recovered. It was my first game, and we won [20–17]. You never forget that.

The next week we went up to Roanoke to play Virginia Military Institute, and I had some decent plays there. [Editor's note: Lawrence returned a kickoff 87 yards for a touchdown against VMI in a 43–7 win.] Then I just kind of built from that.

What I remember most about the 1966 season, of course, is giving coach Dooley his first SEC championship. He had only been at Georgia three years, but every year the program got better and better. We beat Georgia Tech when they were undefeated and headed toward the Orange Bowl. And we beat Florida in the year that Steve Spurrier won the Heisman Trophy. All in all you'd have to say that was a pretty great year, and that team was as close as any team I've ever been on.

It's hard to say what happened in 1967. That team just never jelled. Richard Trapp of Florida made a long run against us, and they beat us. Things just never seemed to click.

Some people say that the 1968 Georgia team was as talented as any team we've had. I don't know that I would argue with that. Any team that has Jake Scott and Bill Stanfill has to be good. And we had some new young talent, like Mike Cavan at quarterback and Dennis Hughes at tight end.

We had a couple of ties against Tennessee and Houston, but we went undefeated and won another SEC championship. We ended up going to the Sugar Bowl and playing Arkansas, and that day, on offense at least, we just didn't play well at all and got beat [16–2]. I did not play well because I was seeing some defenses I had not seen all season. It was a tough way to go out.

I tried pro football for a while. I enjoyed traveling and meeting people, but it was a business. I was probably a bit naïve, but it just didn't give me the satisfaction I got from my college experience or my high school experience.

So I came back to Athens and got into law enforcement. I worked for the district attorney's office as a special investigator and then became the chief of police in Clarke County at the tender age of 25. Then I decided I wanted to go to law school. In 1985 I got the opportunity to be a judge, and I've been doing it ever since.

There is really no way to measure what I've gotten from playing football at the University of Georgia. It taught me discipline. It taught me about work ethic. It taught me about the team concept and a commitment to the task at hand. All those lessons have carried over into my professional life.

And what I'm doing now allows me to give back to a community that has given so much to me. Georgia gave me the opportunity to leave home and go to college. It gave me a chance to make personal relationships that are still a big part of my life today. Georgia opened doors for me that otherwise never would have been open.

I look at the University of Georgia as a family. In 1965 Georgia invited me to be a part of its family. I have been grateful ever since.

Kent Lawrence was an All-SEC flanker in 1968 and was later inducted into the Cotton Bowl Hall of Fame. He went on to become a state court judge in Clarke County, Georgia.

TOMMY LYONS

Center
1968–1970

W HEN I LOOK BACK ON MY LIFE it is amazing, all the twists and turns that occurred to make me end up at Georgia.

I grew up in Atlanta, and really the only thing pulling me to Georgia was my good friend Bruce Kemp, who was also my across-the-street neighbor. He went to Georgia a year ahead of me.

My dad went to Georgia Tech to play football, and when I was a kid we went to Tech games all the time. They had been sending me tickets and sideline passes for years, but when it came time for recruiting they really didn't do much. I don't know if they just assumed I was going to Tech or not. Back then people said that if Bobby Dodd comes to see you, then it's a done deal— you're going to Tech. I just didn't feel that way.

I looked all around, and actually I was being recruited well by Tennessee. But the coach who was recruiting me for Tennessee was killed in an automobile accident that fall. [Editor's note: On October 18, 1965, Tennessee assistant coaches Bill Majors, Charley Rash, and Bob Jones were killed when their car collided with a train in West Knoxville.]

After that the next recruiter from Tennessee was Vince Gibson. He was an older, down-home guy—just the opposite of the younger guys who had been recruiting me. Tennessee was a hot program back then, but after that it sort of fell by the wayside.

That's how I ended up at Georgia, which has been a really positive thing in my life.

I started at Georgia playing offensive and defensive end, but I wasn't really getting on the field. I played freshman ball in 1966, which was fun. We couldn't play on the varsity, so we would dress up and sit in the stands for home games and act like regular students. I liked it.

I got redshirted in 1967, and at the time I thought it was pretty crappy. The only really fun thing I got to do was make the trip to the Liberty Bowl with the varsity. Tommy Lawhorne, a senior, was my roommate, and that trip was something special. I'll always remember it because Tommy had to stay in Georgia to interview for the Rhodes Scholarship and come to Memphis later than the rest of the team. He was a brilliant guy who was going to be the valedictorian of the senior class and go on to medical school.

I remember when he walked back in after the trip, the first thing he said was, "I'm not going to get it."

I was floored. I believe the Rhodes was at that time one-third scholarship, one-third leadership, and one-third athletics. Well, Tommy was the captain of the football team, an All-SEC linebacker, the president of the senior class, and he was going to be the valedictorian. How does he not get that award? I guess the judging panel had never heard a guy from Sylvester, Georgia, talk.

It was the spring of 1968 when one of the coaches came to me and said that there was one position open—at center. He said if I wanted it, they would put me there and see if I could keep it. After two years of basically doing nothing, I just wanted to get on the field. I would stay in that position for the next three years.

The 1968 team at Georgia had to be one of the most balanced teams that coach [Vince] Dooley ever had. That team was so good offensively that we made it our goal to run at least 85 to 88 plays a game. To do that, the center had to get the huddle together quickly, get up to the ball, and snap it. It was my job to keep that offense moving fast, because if we ran under 80 plays in the game the coaches wouldn't be very happy with me.

Along those lines, my most embarrassing moment at Georgia came in a game against Kentucky. I rushed up to the line, and when I got there I noticed the ball was wet. When that happens the lead official is supposed to get you a new ball. Instead he said, "Turn it over." I did and it was wet on

116

After a successful pro career, Tommy Lyons went on to become one of the nation's leading doctors in the field of obstetrics.

that side, too. I told him I wanted a dry ball, and he said, "Snap it anyway." When I didn't, we got a delay of game penalty, and I was furious.

Well, not too long after that, we ran a running play and I came near that official. I never touched him, but I did sort of swipe my elbow in his direction. They penalized me 15 yards and threw me out of the game. I went off and, needless to say, coach Dooley was not happy with me at all.

We played some incredible teams that year. Houston came to Athens with a bunch of studs. We were lucky to tie them [10–10]. That team was so good that they had a guy named Riley Odoms who just brought in the plays and then left the huddle! Riley Odoms turned out to be one of the best tight ends to ever play the game.

We played Tennessee on that AstroTurf in Knoxville when it was incredibly hot. I think the line on that game was Georgia plus 36. I'm not a betting man, but I knew that Tennessee was not 36 points better than us. They tied us [17–17], but we should have beat them.

At the end of the year they told us that we had a choice between the Sugar Bowl and the Orange Bowl. They laid it all out for us. I didn't think there was any doubt. Everybody I talked to wanted to go to the Orange Bowl and enjoy Miami. We voted, but then they announced that we had chosen the *Sugar* Bowl. We just looked around and scratched our heads and said, "What?"

It was obviously one of those things where a deal had been made. I'm sure it was a better financial package. Sure, some guys were really mad, but that's not why we lost to Arkansas in the Sugar Bowl. We just didn't play very well, and they were better than they were ranked.

In 1969 we really thought we were going to make another run at the SEC championship. We started 5–1, and then the bottom just fell out. A bunch of people got hurt. I got hurt against Tennessee. We lost three out of the next four and tied the other one.

Then we go to the Sun Bowl to play Nebraska. I had hurt my knee late in the year, so I was in a cast and couldn't play. Well, Nebraska had an All-American nose tackle named Ken Geddes who was big and as quick as a cat. And he would play right on top of the center. The guy who replaced me— Mike Lopatka—had a habit that when he snapped the ball, his head would dip. That was all Geddes needed. He was in our backfield all day. That was a

117

long day and pretty painful to watch. [Editor's note: Georgia lost to Nebraska 45–6.]

To be perfectly honest about it, in 1970 we just weren't that good. Mike Cavan and Paul Gilbert shared the quarterback job, and that didn't seem to be a perfect situation. We finished 5–5. They asked us if we wanted to go to a bowl game, and we said no. We had had enough.

But we did have one great moment when we went down to Auburn. Nobody gave us a chance to win that game. Auburn had Pat Sullivan and Terry Beasley, and the game was going to be on national television. Back then that was a pretty big deal.

I remember we had our little walk-through practice down there on the day before the game. It was like the Keystone Kops. We couldn't do anything right. I remember thinking that we were going to get killed.

But something changed on the day of the game. On one side of the locker room were the offensive players, with the defense on the other side. I think a set of lockers was between the two groups.

Frank Inman, the offensive coordinator, was talking to us while Erk Russell was on the other side of the room talking to the defense. Well, coach Inman was not the most inspiring guy in the world. Suddenly I looked around the room and discovered that all of us on offense were listening to Erk. Coach Inman, to his credit, realized what was going on and stopped talking, and we all listened to Erk, who could fire up the boys like nobody else.

They didn't need to open the door to the locker room. We just went out and blistered them from the start. They were never in the game. It was a great win [31–17]. I just wish we hadn't lost to Tech in the last game, which is always awful.

I guess I am one of the lucky ones. I got a chance to play pro football for a number of years and get my medical degree at the same time. I had been playing football my whole life, and I was curious to know if I could mix it up with the big boys. At Denver I was in the right place at the right time. In the NFL, once they find an offensive lineman who can get the job done, it's hard for a young guy to beat him out.

Then, after football, I was able to move into another phase of my life that I really enjoy. Not a lot of guys have been able to say that, I know.

A lot of nice things have happened to me in my life, and I have to say that playing football at Georgia was one of the major things that affected me. As a kid growing up in the South, I worshipped the guys who played. And to eventually become one of them was a dream come true.

The amazing thing was that when I moved back to Athens from Denver it was like I had never left. The people, then and now, treat you with the same kindness and generosity as they did when you played ball.

Georgia is a great university that certainly prepared me for anything I wanted to do from an academic standpoint. I think there are six or eight guys I played with who are now doctors.

Today, I'm basically a surgeon and, for some patients, the last stop for their problems. At those times you sit in the operating room and you realize there is no one you can call. It's just you.

That's one of the lessons that football at Georgia taught me. I feel like the Georgia people are my extended family. I'm grateful for the opportunity that they provided me. And let's don't forget, it was fun, too. I really had a great time.

119

Dr. Tom Lyons was an All-American center in 1969 and 1970. He earned his medical degree while playing for the Denver Broncos of the NFL. He received the NCAA Silver Anniversary Award for distinguished achievement in 1996. He is a member of the Georgia Sports Hall of Fame and the University of Georgia Circle of Honor. Today he is one of the nation's leading physicians in the field of obstetrics and gynecology.

KIRBY MOORE

Quarterback
1965–1967

To tell you the truth, it was pretty late in my high school career before I even thought about playing college football. I was a much better baseball player growing up in Dothan, Alabama. I had a chance to sign a baseball contract coming out of high school, and I really thought that was where I was headed.

Very few schools were recruiting me for football, but that changed after my senior season, when I was named All-State in football.

One of the recruiters that started showing up was Big Jim Whatley, who was also the Georgia baseball coach. Coach Whatley, recruiting my area of Alabama for the football team, started watching me, and we got to know each other. He was a big influence on my decision to finally go to Georgia. There was also a Georgia recruiter in my area named John Turner McAllister. Back then there were no limits on how many times a recruiter could come see you, and John Turner became like a family member.

I almost went to Auburn, but I visited Georgia twice, and I remember that on one of those visits somebody—it might have been Frank Inman—said, "We need young men like you at Georgia. You have a place here."

I don't know why, but that really clicked with me. I was an Alabama boy, but at that time Bear Bryant really had a rough reputation. The word was that you really had to be tough to play for him. I didn't see myself as somebody who wanted to play for Bear Bryant, so I picked Georgia.

Quarterback Kirby Moore was the triggerman on one of the most famous plays in Georgia history—the "flea flicker," which upset Alabama 18–17 in 1965.

I got to Georgia in the fall of 1963, and that was an interesting time to be a part of the football program. Johnny Griffith was the head coach, and Georgia was losing. But when you're a high school senior you figure you can do anything. I felt like I could be a part of turning the program around.

I remember a few things about 1963. I remember playing in a freshman game against Florida and Steve Spurrier and getting the stew beat out of us. And I remember when the rumors started that coach Griffith might be on his way out. It wasn't like it is now with all the talk radio. We might have heard something once or twice, but as players we were just too busy with being students to think a whole lot about what was going to happen to the head coach.

There were a bunch of guys from Alabama on that team, and when we found out that coach [Vince] Dooley was coming from Auburn to be the head coach, it was up to us to find out what the real deal was with him. We had read the newspapers, but we started calling home to find out everything we could. We didn't find out much. All my friends said was that coach Dooley was tough and that we had better buckle up our chin straps when he got there.

It wasn't long before everybody got the word that things were going to be a lot different. The first meeting we ever had with one of the new coaches was with Bill Dooley, coach Dooley's brother, who was going to be the offensive coordinator. Now, coach Bill was only about 26 years old, not much older than some of our seniors.

Coach Bill called a meeting for 4:00 P.M. over at Stegeman Hall. Now, we had some senior guys from Pennsylvania like Jim Wilson and Ray Rismiller, and they were kind of used to doing things their way. Some of them came in a little late, and coach Bill just lit into us.

He told us that if we couldn't be on time that we would get to take part in a thing called "opportunity" and that this "opportunity period" would take place at 5:30 in the morning. He said we would learn the significance of being on time. Then he said, "We will run you until your tongues hang out! Do I make myself perfectly clear?"

When we walked out of the room a bunch of us looked at each other and went, "Oh, God!"

But we weren't late anymore.

Coach Dooley was a former marine, and that first spring practice was like boot camp and he was the drill sergeant. I had a horrible spring. Coach

Dooley was a very fundamental coach, and I didn't know anything about the fundamentals of playing quarterback. I threw a lot in high school, but I threw sidearm, underhand, whatever it took. I really couldn't do the basics, so coach Dooley decided to redshirt me for the 1964 season.

I was really disappointed and almost quit. I wanted to play baseball, but coach Dooley wouldn't let me do it because I would miss spring practice. So I went to coach Dooley and told him I was thinking about quitting.

He convinced me to stick around a little longer because he thought I had a chance to be the first-team punter the next season. He told me I was giving up an opportunity to be our starting punter, and that was a great way to go to college. I thought about it and realized that he was right. Besides, if I was just the punter, maybe I could play baseball, too.

It's hard to say why, but after that my whole attitude changed. The next day I was running the scout team against the varsity, and we almost beat them. As the fall went on, I started having more success against the varsity, and I started thinking, "Well, maybe I can play here."

I didn't play in 1964, but I have two vivid memories of that season as a redshirt player.

123

We were at Alabama for coach Dooley's first game. Now, can you imagine a more difficult situation for your first game as a head coach? You're playing Alabama, coached by Bear Bryant, in Tuscaloosa. Joe Namath is the quarterback. Talk about nervous. There were guys throwing up all over the locker room.

Here comes coach Dooley right before the game, and I was expecting him to give this impassioned speech. He stood up and pointed his finger and said, "Men, let's go."

That was it. But that was coach Dooley. He figured his team was prepared, so a big speech wasn't necessary. Of course, Alabama killed us, 31–3.

Later that year we were playing Kentucky at home. We had just lost a tough game to Florida State [17–14], who had a really great team, but you could tell people were starting to get excited about our program. I will never forget this: Kentucky scored a touchdown, but our defense had fought so hard that the crowd at Georgia gave them a standing ovation. Those of us on the sidelines looked at each other and couldn't believe it. I really believe that from that point on, we knew something special was happening with Georgia football.

That spring I began to make my move, and I was able to win the backup job to Preston Ridlehuber, a senior.

We had complete first and second teams, so Preston and I kind of shared the position. I loved it, but Preston hated it. He was a senior and didn't want to come out of the game. We had a great relationship, but we were different. I wasn't expecting to play all the time, and he was. I didn't blame him for being mad, but it was funny when I would come into the game and he would leave. Preston would be mumbling all kinds of things under his breath. He was a great football player, though.

People like to talk about the 1965 Alabama game and the flea flicker play that won the game. What people don't remember is that Preston pulled a muscle in that game and couldn't play anymore, so I got to play a lot more than I thought I would.

I've told this story many times, but when the flea flicker play came in I really didn't believe it. A lot of times guys would bring in plays from the sidelines, and they would get all excited because they were in the game and forget the play by the time they got to the huddle.

I don't remember who brought in the play, but my first response was, "C'mon, he didn't call that. Tell me the play."

He said, "No, it's right. Coach Dooley said run the flea flicker!"

So I looked around the huddle and said, "All right, guys. Remember that thing we ran that never worked in practice? We're going to run it. Flea flicker!"

It's not a very complicated play to explain; it's just hard to execute. Pat Hodgson was supposed to go down about 10 yards and do a little curl. I was supposed to hit him with the pass. Our running back, Bob Taylor, was supposed to run out to Pat's right a few yards and stay behind him. When the defense closes in on Pat, he's supposed to lateral the ball to Bob. If it works perfectly, Bob's supposed to have a clear path.

On the snap I dropped straight back and saw that Pat was open. As soon as I let the ball go I got creamed, so that's my out when people ask me if Pat's knees were on the ground. By the time I got up, Bob was running free down the sideline for the touchdown.

That was a great play, but we were still behind 17–16. The offense stayed on the field because we knew we were going for two. Here again is where I have to give coach Dooley credit for preparation. We had a specific two-point play that we had run in practice time after time. So when the time came, we knew exactly what we had to do.

The play called for me to roll to my right, and then I had about four options on where to throw the ball. In practice I noticed that as I rolled to my right, the defense would always forget about Pat Hodgson in the back of the end zone. There always seemed to be a hole back there where I could throw it. So in the huddle I told him, "Pat, I'm coming back to you."

That's exactly what happened, and we won the game [18–17].

I'll tell you something funny about that play. Several years ago we were asked to do a reenactment during one of the home football games against Alabama. Bob, Pat, and I were more nervous about that than when we actually played Alabama back in 1965. Before the game the three of us went to an elementary school in Athens and practiced for about two hours! Now that was pressure!

The other great memory of 1965, of course, was the Michigan game when we went up there and beat them 15–7. I remember the Michigan band making fun of us as we were getting ready to take the field. One of them said, "Hey, look, they brought a high school team up here to play our guys!" That was a sweet win.

On the way back to Athens I was sitting up front with the pilots when we looked down and saw the thousands of cars that were on the way to the airport to meet us. That whole weekend was one of my favorite times at Georgia.

It's funny, the 1965 team was probably good enough to win the SEC, but we got wiped out by injuries. We won the championship in 1966 with a great team, filled with a bunch of great guys. I'm sure there was no team in the country that had a better pair of tackles than our guys, Bill Stanfill and George Patton.

The 1967 team was just as talented, but it seemed we lost all the close games. We lost by one point [15–14] at Houston, and then the next week Florida kicked a late field goal to beat us 17–16. The next few days after that loss were probably the lowest point of my athletic career. I really felt that I had let everybody down and was shouldering that burden when practice started on Monday. I had a lousy attitude about everything.

Finally coach John Donaldson came up to me and said, "You and I need to walk and we need to talk."

We started walking underneath the Coliseum and talking and he said, "You need to get this off your shoulders."

At that point, I'll admit that I cried like a baby. I told him I felt responsible for us losing. He put his arms around me and made me feel better, like a father would. I got it all out of my system.

We went on to finish with a couple of big wins. We beat Auburn [17–0] and Georgia Tech [21–14], which is always a great way to finish. I remember playing the Liberty Bowl with a lot of back pain because of a hit I had taken against Georgia Tech. We lost to North Carolina State [14–7], when Jim Donnan was the quarterback.

I almost went back to Georgia as a graduate assistant for coach Dooley, but I was living in Macon at the time and had a chance to stay there and go to law school. That's what I did, and I have been in Macon ever since.

I get asked a lot what playing football at Georgia meant to me. There is really no way you can measure it. As a former player, I've had opportunities to sit with governors and heads of large corporations—they want to talk to you as much as you want to talk to them. So when it came time to get a job, I was very comfortable in that kind of situation. Being a Bulldog has opened up a whole lot of doors for me.

Being a student at Georgia is an experience that impacts the rest of your life. I can go anywhere in this state and there will be somebody in the room who remembers the flea flicker play in 1965 against Alabama. And there are people who want me to represent them because they remember me as the "old Georgia football player."

There is this bond with my teammates and to the Georgia people that is hard to describe. Whenever I see Bob Taylor or Pat Hodgson we hug, and it's like we've only been apart for a short while. It's hard to believe that the play against Alabama happened over 38 years ago.

Because of that one play, Bob, Pat, and myself are going to be linked together forever. That is a very special feeling. We all shared an incredible moment in time that will live as long as people talk about Georgia football. That's pretty neat.

126

Kirby Moore was the captain of Georgia's 1967 team. He went on after football to become a successful attorney in Macon, Georgia.

GEORGE PATTON

Defensive Tackle
1964–1966

I GREW UP IN TUSCUMBIA, ALABAMA, where I was a quarterback trying to follow in the footsteps of my two brothers. [Editor's note: Patton's brother, Jim, played on Alabama's 1961 national championship team.] I was a slow quarterback with a strong arm, who could throw it a long way. Back then, though, everybody ran the ball all the time, so there weren't a whole lot of teams looking for a quarterback with no foot speed.

My brothers helped me look around to see if I could maybe get a partial scholarship. Alabama wanted me to play center, and Ole Miss wanted me to play tackle. But I was hardheaded—I thought I could still play quarterback.

There were a couple of guys who lived near me that were Georgia supporters, and I found out that they sent some film over to the coaching staff in Athens. Next thing I knew, Georgia sent over Spec Towns and Bobby Towns to talk to me and my teammate Vance Evans. They were really after Vance, because he was a good player.

They invited us over to Georgia to look around. We met coach [Johnny] Griffith. We talked, and before Vance and I left we got scholarship offers. Vance said he liked Georgia. Nobody else was recruiting me, so it was kind of a no-brainer. That's how I ended up at Georgia.

When I got to Georgia in the fall of 1962, I was at least the number six quarterback on the depth chart. I was on the freshman team in 1962, and in 1963 I was redshirted and basically played quarterback on the B-team. I don't think the coaches had any idea what to do with me. I didn't know if I was ever going to get on the field.

But in the spring of 1964 coach [Vince] Dooley came. He and his staff started moving players around to different positions trying to get the best athletes on the field. They tried me at end but quickly found out that I had hands of stone.

Then one day coach Dooley said, "What about defensive tackle?" That decision would change my football life.

They put me in at defensive tackle, and I immediately did well. Everybody was lean and quick back in those days, and teams depended more on speed than on size. I found that being a former quarterback helped me anticipate the play, and being a good athlete allowed me to slide through all those big linemen trying to block me and make the play. It wasn't long before I realized I had found a home.

A lot of stories have been told about coach Dooley's first year at Georgia in 1964. He and that coaching staff did a lot of really good things to help us win. The biggest thing they did, I think, was see things in players that other coaches didn't see. I didn't know that I could be a good defensive tackle, but they did.

128

When we went to Alabama in 1964, coach Dooley's first game, I was convinced we were going to win. They had us so well prepared. Well, Alabama clobbered us [31–3] and showed us what a good team really was. But coach Dooley convinced us that if we kept working, we could be a good team. He made some adjustments, and that team got better as the year went along.

The next year, when Alabama came to our place, we were ready. Coach Dooley told us that if we played hard, we could play with anybody. I was lucky enough to pick off a tipped pass and run it back for a touchdown. [Editor's note: Patton intercepted a Steve Sloan pass, which was tipped by Jiggy Smaha, and ran it 55 yards to give Georgia a 10–0 lead.]

I never knew the flea flicker pass against Alabama was coming. I just remember standing on the sidelines and looking up when Pat [Hodgson] pitched the ball back to Bob Taylor. I thought, "Where in the world did that come from?"

But I knew the answer. It came from the imagination of coach Dooley, who had made our guys work on that play earlier in the week. Then we went for two and made it to win 18–17. For an Alabama boy, that was mighty sweet.

George Patton was a high school quarterback who became an All-American defensive tackle for the Bulldogs.

My other great memory of 1965 is when we went to Michigan and played up there in front of one hundred thousand people. I remember being in the tunnel with all those people yelling and screaming at us. We really wondered what we were getting into.

When we won the game [15–7], it really made those people get quiet. I remember Edgar Chandler, our great offensive tackle, blocking their big All-American defensive tackle [William Yearby]. When that game was over Edgar was just beat to death. He was bloody. I thought Edgar was just great that day.

I really thought that team was good enough to win the SEC, but down at Florida State two weeks later, Bob Taylor, our great running back, broke his leg. That was a killer for our team, and I think we lost four of the next six games to finish 6–4.

In 1966 we knew we were going to have a pretty good team. There were a lot of seniors, like me, who had been through the wars. And we had some really talented sophomores like Bill Stanfill and Billy Payne.

We were 4–0 when we went down to Miami and lost 7–6 in a game we really should have won. The year before we were 4–0 when we lost to Florida State, and that started a downhill slide. I could tell coach Dooley was concerned that the same thing might happen again.

130

The following Monday we were practicing in Stegeman Hall because it was raining, and coach Dooley took me up into the stands to talk. He said, "George, we're not going to allow this to happen again, are we?"

I promised him that this team was not going to fall apart. We had too many good players.

We kept winning, and we made it down to Auburn, where a win would give us the SEC championship. We played a lousy first half and were behind 13–0. We got close to their end zone a couple of times and fumbled. I was sure that coach Dooley was going to chew us out at halftime.

But all coach Dooley did was say, "We've made all the mistakes we can make, so let's turn it around."

And that's exactly what we did. The seniors took over that game at halftime and inspired the sophomores to step it up. We came back and won [21–13] and gave coach Dooley his first SEC championship. That was a great day.

The thing I still get asked about the most is playing quarterback at the end of the Cotton Bowl. I didn't know it was going to happen. After we beat Georgia Tech, I read in the paper that coach Dooley had considered it but didn't do it. I never thought about it again.

We were beating SMU pretty good in the Cotton Bowl, and after the last defensive series coach Dooley grabbed my jersey as I was coming off the field. "George, go back in there and play quarterback," he told me. I thought he was kidding. He was not.

I got in the huddle and told the guys that they were going to let me play quarterback. Everybody just smiled. I hadn't taken a snap from center in three years, so I decided to get into the shotgun. I told the receivers to run as far and as fast as they could and I was going to throw it.

Well, we did that for three plays, and fortunately I just overthrew my guys and nobody intercepted it. I think the SMU players thought we were making fun of them, because on fourth down I ran the ball, and a bunch of those guys jumped on me and started hitting me with their fists in the pileup. I tried to tell them that the team was honoring me by allowing me to play quarterback one last time. Later that night we had a banquet and got it straightened out.

That was a long time ago, but hardly a day goes by that I don't talk to somebody who saw it on television or who was at the game.

I'm 59 years old now, and it's hard to imagine what my life would have been like if I hadn't gotten the opportunity to play at Georgia. It's one of those things that seem to impact you every day of your life. No matter where I go, there is somebody who saw me play or went to school with me. All those friends and contacts have opened so many doors for me.

Today, I still go back to the games, and people remember me. And the guys that you played with become your extended family. We're close, because it was really beating the odds for our group of guys to win a championship.

In my life I went from thinking I wouldn't even get a college scholarship to being an All-American. It is hard to believe when I look back on it. But it was Georgia that gave me the opportunity to succeed.

131

George Patton, a three-time All-SEC player, was captain of Georgia's 1966 SEC championship team. He was an All-American in 1965 and 1966. Today Patton lives in Lilburn, Georgia.

BILLY PAYNE

Flanker
1966–1968

IOFTEN TELL PEOPLE THAT I probably had the easiest job of anybody who has ever played at Georgia.

As a sophomore, I was a tight end playing next to Edgar Chandler, the great All-American tackle. Edgar was so good that he would block everybody in his area and leave the leftovers for me.

As a senior I was a defensive end and played next to Bill Stanfill, who won the Outland Trophy at defensive tackle. Bill would occupy all the blockers and leave me free to make a play now and then. And if I messed up, I had Jake Scott, another All-American, behind me at safety. It's hard not to be good when you have that many great players around you. What an experience that was!

Because my dad [Porter Payne] was a great player at Georgia, I guess people always assumed that's where I would go to school. I remember going with my dad when he was an official and worked Georgia's scrimmages. I would sit in coach [Wally] Butts' lap and do all the things a young kid could do at practice.

But when you're young and pretty cocky you think you need to make your own way. I went through the whole recruiting process to the very end. I went through a stretch in my own mind when I was looking at anywhere *but* Georgia. I have to give credit to my dad—he never said he wanted me to go to Georgia. He was going to let me make up my own mind.

Billy Payne (right), pictured here as a baby with his father in 1948, and again when he became a player in 1968 (above), brought the 1996 Summer Olympics to Atlanta.

So I went just about everywhere on recruiting visits. The two schools that really attracted me were Florida and Auburn. Part of the reason was that the two guys who recruited me for those respective schools were friends and former teammates of my dad's—Rabbit Smith at Florida and Buck Bradberry at Auburn.

Buck was a wonderful man and really had a way of making the kids he was recruiting feel important. I grew very attached to him. I think I was very close to going to Auburn, but at the end of the day I had to sit down and evaluate the situation.

The truth was I had grown up totally associated with Georgia. Finally, I had to admit to myself that that was where my heart was.

The freshman class of 1965 was coach [Vince] Dooley's first full recruiting class, and it was very good. In fact, there was a lot of talk early on about how good that class was. I remember the coaches put us in a scrimmage against the varsity a week before they opened up with Alabama—and we kicked their butts in that scrimmage. Our defense stopped the varsity every time. I thoroughly enjoyed playing freshman ball.

When we were sophomores, in 1966, we thought we had a chance to be a pretty good team. There were a lot of seniors who had come up through the ranks combined with a bunch of talented sophomores like Stanfill and Scott. Plus, coach Dooley and his staff taught the fundamentals in such a way as to allow average players to be very good on Saturday. It was obvious that the Georgia program was taking a step forward and doing it very quickly.

We made a lot of great memories in 1966. The only game we lost was down at Miami [7–6]. But what I remember most about that game is that my backup at tight end—a guy named Wayne Ingle from Conyers, Georgia—broke his neck on the opening kickoff. Then they came to me and said I had to cover kickoffs for the rest of the game.

Of course who can ever forget us kicking [Steve] Spurrier's butt the year he won the Heisman Trophy! [Editor's note: Georgia won the game in Jacksonville 27–10.] It was one of those days where everything was clicking. If you go back and look at that film you'll see that between George Patton and Bill Stanfill, Spurrier never had a chance to set up all day. It was total domination by those two guys. Stanfill put it in a different gear that day.

To this day I can't explain why we didn't have a better year in 1967 [when Georgia went 7–4]. I remember going to the Astrodome to play Houston, who had one of the greatest sets of running backs I had ever seen. They were so fast we were all left looking around and wondering, "What is this?"

We played that game on AstroTurf, and early in the game I got the crap knocked out of me and hit my head on that hard turf. It really rang my bell, and for several series I was just standing around because I didn't know where I was. Finally, Edgar Chandler started screaming at me to wake up. I told him I couldn't remember the play.

He screamed at me, "Dammit, Billy! We've only got three plays! Just block the guy in front of you!"

Before the 1968 season coach Dooley brought me into his office for one of his "talks."

He said, "Billy, you're one of the best all-around players that I've ever had at Georgia."

Then he paused.

"But you're not particularly outstanding at anything." He meant it as a compliment, I think.

That was coach Dooley's way of telling me that he wanted me to move from tight end to defensive end. There were a couple of good reasons for this. We had been hit hard at defensive end by graduation. Also we had a good young guy at tight end named Dennis Hughes who was better than me. I was a team player and just wanted to play, so I made the move.

135

Like I said earlier, when I made that move I found myself next to Bill Stanfill with Jake Scott behind me. How can it get any better than that?

I think the 1968 Georgia team was one of the most balanced that coach Dooley ever had. We went undefeated during the regular season but had a couple ties to Tennessee and Houston.

The Tennessee game [17–17] should never have been a tie. My old Atlanta neighbor Bubba Wyche was the quarterback of that team, and I got to sack him a couple of times. But Tennessee trapped a pass in the end zone that was ruled complete. We should have won that football game.

I guess we were lucky to tie Houston [10–10]. Like the year before, they were running all up and down the field. Coach [Erk] Russell was giving us hell for getting blocked. Shoot, even if we didn't get blocked, we couldn't outrun them to the corner.

Still, we had a chance to tie the game late with a field goal. I'll never forget when our kicker, Jim McCullough, was getting ready to go on the field for the kick. Coach Dooley grabbed him by the helmet and said, "You've been on scholarship for three years, and it's time for you to earn it! Now get in there and make that kick!"

We were horrified, thinking it would make Jim nervous. But he made the kick, and we tied the game.

A lot has been made of our trip to the Sugar Bowl, where we lost to Arkansas [16–2]. I just remember that we talked coach Dooley into going down there several days earlier than normal as a reward to the seniors. About 80 percent of our top 22 players were married, and we were able to take our wives.

On that trip we had about $100 per diem that would allow us to charge food to the hotel room. We would go out to these official banquets and then come back late at night and order fudge sundaes and shrimp cocktails until the money ran out. I think all of us gained about five pounds that week.

Sure, I hated losing my last game because we didn't play very well, but in no way did that take away from the incredible experience I had at Georgia. I went back and coached with coach Dooley for a couple of years while I went through law school. Coach Dooley put me on as a graduate assistant, and that really helped Martha and me through those lean early years.

I can honestly say that my four years as a football player at Georgia had a very significant impact on my life. I came from a disciplined family, and my dad was always persistent in saying that you have to earn your own way. He also always said that no matter how good you think you are, there is always somebody better. The only way that you can compete with those people is to work harder than they do.

That was the philosophy I took to Georgia, and I built on it with what I learned by playing for coach Dooley. I picked up a lot of life's lessons while watching the way that coach Dooley coached the game. My dad was right and coach Dooley was right: those who make the greatest sacrifices and work the hardest are going to have the greatest successes in life . . . athletically and otherwise.

Those lessons are still with me today.

136

Billy Payne was an All-SEC defensive end in 1968. A graduate of the UGA law school, Payne went on to become the president and CEO of the 1996 Olympic Games in Atlanta.

PRESTON RIDLEHUBER

Quarterback
1963–1965

I GREW UP IN GAINESVILLE, GEORGIA, and there seemed to be all kinds of things pulling me when it came time to go to college. And very few of them were pulling me toward Georgia.

I was fortunate to play in one of the greatest high school programs of all time, for coach Graham Hixon. I think in my four years there something like 24 guys got full scholarships to play football. Coach Hixon was an Auburn man, but he never tried to guide any of us in any direction. He was just there to answer questions about the recruiting process.

When I was a young player, two of my best buddies were Billy Lothridge and Billy Martin, two great players who went on to Georgia Tech. I was only a sophomore when I started tagging along on recruiting visits with them. I used to pretend that the schools were really recruiting me, but I knew better.

When I was a junior, coaches started recruiting me pretty heavily. Auburn had shown a lot of interest. Clemson and Georgia were there, too. And then came the phone calls from Alabama.

I'll never forget the summer before my senior year, in 1961. I was one of a group of guys who were invited to Tuscaloosa on a recruiting visit. When I got there I was taken to a hotel and ushered into a meeting facility with coach [Bear] Bryant and the rest of the coaching staff. There were 21 players in that room. After a while, coach Bryant asked the rest of the coaches to leave. The door closed, and we were alone with *the man*. And when coach Bryant talked, everybody listened.

"There were 22 guys invited to this meeting and 21 of you made it. As of right now every one of you in this room have scholarships to play at Alabama. And if you come, we will win national championships," he said.

I didn't make any kind of commitment at that time, but later in the summer when we started practice, Paul Bryant Jr. came and stayed at my house and would go to the practices. Alabama was really showing a lot of interest in me.

I'll never forget this story. One day during that same preseason practice, an Auburn recruiter came by to see me. At that time Paul Bryant Jr. was still staying at my house. As soon as the Auburn recruiter walked into the office, coach Hixon introduced him to Bryant.

The Auburn recruiter got so mad and flustered. You could see it in his face. He had to leave a little while after that because he just didn't know how to handle it.

The next day coach Mike Castronis of Georgia came over and the exact same thing happened. Coach Hixon immediately introduced coach Mike to Paul Bryant Jr.

Coach Mike just stuck out his hand and smiled and said, "The Cub!!" It was a totally different reaction, and it made an impression on me.

I narrowed it down to Alabama, Clemson, and Georgia. Then one day I got a call from the little airport in Gainesville. A plane was coming in and the people on it wanted me to pick them up. It was Pat Trammell, who was going to be Alabama's quarterback that fall, and one of the coaches. They had just come from Cleveland, Tennessee, where they had signed Steve Sloan, who was considered the number one prospect in the country. They said that while they were out they wanted to see if they could come by and sign me, too.

Well, I thought about that. They had just signed the best quarterback in the country in Steve Sloan. They had a freshman in their program named Joe Namath, and I knew how good he was. Needless to say, I didn't sign that day.

I was being pulled in all kinds of directions. Finally, I sat down with coach Hixon, and he said, "Where are you going to live when you graduate?"

I told him that I would probably live in Atlanta. Then he said, "Then why would you go to school in Alabama?"

His point was that the contacts that would help me in my future life would be made in college. He was right, of course. So I called coach [Johnny] Griffith and coach Mike and let them know that I was coming.

138

Preston Ridlehuber (right), seen here with fellow quarterback Lynn Hughes, had to say no to Alabama's Bear Bryant before enrolling at Georgia in 1962.

Let me tell you this, the hardest thing I've ever had to do in my life was, as an 18-year-old kid, to call Bear Bryant and tell him I wasn't coming to Alabama.

As it turned out, coach Bryant was true to his word when he told us guys in high school that he was going to win national championships. Alabama won a national championship in 1961, when I was a senior, and he won two more in 1964 and 1965.

I don't know what it was like for other guys, but I was young and naïve and ill-prepared to play college ball. The rigors of going to school kind of overwhelmed me. I was on probation after the first quarter of school.

I played freshman ball in 1962 and made it to the varsity as a sophomore in 1963, which was coach Griffith's last year as the head coach. I don't know why we didn't win more games, because we really had some good football players. I was a backup to Larry Rakestraw, who was a helluva quarterback.

I'll never forget the day that coach Griffith got fired. We had to be at the old Stegeman Hall for a 3:00 P.M. meeting, but we had already heard what was going on. When we got there coach Griffith told us that Joel Eaves was coming in as athletic director to replace coach Butts and that he was leaving as head coach. He wished us well.

140

I was leaning up against a door in the back of the room thinking, "What is going on here?" I was just a sophomore wondering what in the world I had gotten myself into.

Coach Griffith was still talking when I heard a knock on the door behind me. It was one of the athletic department secretaries. She told me to round up about four other players and come with her. She said, "We're going to meet the new football coach."

I said, "You've got to be kidding me!!"

We went over to the Continuing Education Center, and the athletic board was finishing up their meeting. We saw one of the members we knew, and I asked him, "Who is the new coach?"

He said, "Vince Dooley."

I said, "Who is Vince Dooley?"

So we went in to meet coach Dooley and my first impression was that he wasn't much older than us. But it quickly became clear that things were getting ready to change around Georgia football.

I remember one day I was talking to coach Castronis about some off-season workout schedules. I was sitting on the corner of his desk, which was something I had always done. Coach Dooley walked by the door, took about two steps past, and then came back in and chewed my butt out for sitting on the desk.

Another time we had a meeting scheduled for 4:00 P.M. A bunch of us were playing basketball and then walked into the meeting room at about 3:55 P.M. Coach Dooley's brother, Bill, was the offensive coordinator and was running the meeting. At 4:00 sharp he closed and locked the door, leaving the guys who had gotten there late outside.

Then he lit into us.

"When I call a meeting, or if anybody calls a meeting, and it is scheduled to start at 4:00, then it will start at 4:00 . . . not 4:05!"

He chewed our butts for about 10 minutes. We got the message. Nobody was late after that.

There are so many great memories of my last two years at Georgia. We got worn out [31–3] in coach Dooley's first game against Alabama, but I think the staff learned something there. They worked us so hard in preseason that it took several games before we got our legs back under us. The next season coach Dooley told us to come back in shape, and we wouldn't work so hard. That showed me that coach Dooley was really smart, and it paid off for us.

141

Going into the 1965 season, I thought we were going to have a good team. I remember picture day and listening to coach Dooley getting interviewed. He was saying that he didn't know if we were any good . . . you know, the stuff coach Dooley always says.

Well, when they got around to me I said, "We've got to win two out of our first three, and I think we can win all three." Our first three games were with Alabama, the defending national champs, Vanderbilt, and Michigan on the road. Coach Dooley heard that and almost fell out of his chair. But I had confidence in my teammates.

We did beat Alabama [18–17] thanks to the flea flicker play. That was a great win, but the one that sticks with me is when we went to Michigan. I'm telling you, we had everybody in the South pulling for us when we went up there.

Kim King, who was the quarterback at Georgia Tech, told me he was on the field playing somebody during our Michigan game. He was in the huddle, and he heard the crowd counting down "5 . . . 4 . . . 3 . . . 2 . . . 1." Kim said he thought he was losing his mind but found out later that the people at Grant Field were listening to the Georgia game on the radio. That's how big that win [15–7] was for everybody in the South.

I remember that Dean [William] Tate told me about being in Athens at the end of that game. He told me that as Ed Thilenius counted down the final seconds on the radio, he stepped outside and could hear the game all over town. Nobody was on the street.

And when the game was over, the town exploded. Campus security kept calling Dean Tate because guys were riding up and down the street with kegs of beer in their truck. Dean Tate just told the police to leave them alone and make sure they didn't hurt anybody.

We flew back in a couple of those old prop planes, and the pilot decided to buzz the city right down Lumpkin Street. Then we headed toward the airport. We looked down, and the road between Athens and the airport was absolutely jammed.

The only weakness on that 1965 team was that we didn't have depth. When Bob Taylor broke his leg down at Florida State, things started to get tough. Against Auburn, we fumbled on the 1-yard line [in a 21–19 loss]. Against Florida, [Steve] Spurrier beat us with a couple of long passes. If we had won those games, we would've had a pretty good year and gone to a decent bowl.

In those two years we set the stage. The next year coach Dooley won his first SEC championship, and I like to believe we helped get his program started.

Looking back on it now, I can't imagine having gone to school anywhere other than Georgia. There is no way I can measure what Georgia gave to me. I'm 60 years old, and I can still go to any town in this state and meet somebody I went to school with. I made some lifelong contacts and friends who are still with me today.

I was lucky enough to play pro football and to have some success in business, but something always kept drawing me back to Georgia. It has always been a very important part of my life.

I remember what Mr. Bulldog, Herschel Scott, used to say: if you're very good and say your prayers at night, when you die God will let you go to Athens. That's the way I feel about Georgia. I was blessed the day I became a Bulldog.

Preston Ridlehuber was the MVP of the 1964 Sun Bowl. Today Ridlehuber is in private business and lives in St. Mary's, Florida.

BILL STANFILL

Defensive Tackle
1966–1968

I'LL NEVER FORGET THE DAY I signed my scholarship to go to Georgia. I was recruited by a bunch of schools, but pretty quickly I narrowed it down to three: Auburn, Georgia, and Florida State.

Yeah, coach [Ray] Graves at Florida did call. But I told him in no uncertain terms that I had no interest in becoming a Gator. Never did care much for the Gators, but I'll talk more about that later.

When it came down to signing time in December, I decided on Georgia. I liked the Auburn coaches and Florida State had some good offers on the table. But I was a Georgia boy, and that's where I figured I should go to school.

I called coach Sterling Dupree and coach [Vince] Dooley, and they came to my house. I signed my scholarship on coach Dooley's back while Hal Herring, the Auburn defensive coordinator who was recruiting me, sat in the living room and watched. He told me he wanted to see it with his own eyes, and then he left.

Georgia has had a bunch of good recruiting classes, but the group of guys I came in with in 1965 had to be one of the best. Not only did we have a lot of great football players, but we had some quality people who went on to become doctors and lawyers and successful politicians. And before we were done we also won a couple of SEC championships.

I was a freshman in 1965 and couldn't play on the varsity. I just remember that Jake Scott was my roommate. Now, that was an experience. Jake may have been the single greatest athlete to ever play at Georgia. He could do everything on a football field. He was very intelligent, but he didn't like school. As a result he wasn't eligible in 1966 when the rest of us finally got a chance to play. They had to redshirt him.

A lot of great things happened in 1966, my sophomore year, but my fondest memory of that year—and probably my whole college career—was when we went to Jacksonville to play Florida. I was hurt, and I wasn't really supposed to play. It was the night before the game, and I was rooming with George Patton. There was a knock on the door; it was coach Dooley and the team doctor. I'm thinking, "Uh-oh, what's going on here?"

Well, I always said that coach Dooley was a miracle worker when it came to injuries. The next day, I was in the game playing Florida, and the Super Gator—that's what we called Steve Spurrier—was their quarterback.

They led us 10–3 at halftime, and all they had to do was beat us to win the SEC championship. But in the second half we took that boy to the woodshed and won [27–10]. That was a great day.

Next we went on down to Auburn where we clinched coach Dooley's first SEC championship. Then we got to play Georgia Tech when they were undefeated in coach Bobby Dodd's last year. Tech had already accepted a bid to play Florida in the Orange Bowl. And we beat both of them.

I'm proud to say that in my three years we never lost to Tech, and we never lost to Auburn. We beat Florida twice.

In 1967 I thought we had a pretty good team, but we lost some close games. We lost to Houston by a point and we lost to the Gators by a point. What I most remember about that Florida game was their All-American tailback, Larry Smith. During the game I hit him with a flipper and knocked him out. The Florida media called it a cheap shot and were raising all kinds of noise.

The next week coach Dooley brought me into his office. He said, "Bill, it was not a cheap shot, but let's try to quiet this media down somewhat. I want you to write Larry Smith and apologize to him."

I thought he was kidding. I told coach Dooley that was the way he taught us to play the game—tough and physical. Finally he said that he would write the letter, but he wanted me to sign it. And I did. I didn't understand it at the time, but as I got older I appreciated what coach Dooley was trying to do.

In 1968 we had a helluva team. We started out the season with a tie against Tennessee on that damned rug in Knoxville. Man, I hated that AstroTurf; it was like playing on a pool table. I got a strawberry on my leg that turned into

Bill Stanfill won the Outland Trophy at Georgia in 1968 and went on
to a great career with the Miami Dolphins.

a staph infection. I had boils up and down my leg and had to go to the
hospital several times to get IVs. That's how bad it was.

We had a couple of ties, but we won the rest of them. We beat Florida
again. We beat Auburn again and clinched another championship. And we
beat Tech again.

The only downer was the bowl game. Some of the guys were let down
because they thought we were going to the Orange Bowl. Instead we went to
the Sugar Bowl and played Arkansas. I heard all the stories about guys being on
Bourbon Street the night before the game, but I don't think it's true. I was married and in my hotel room with my wife. Arkansas just beat us [16–2].

For the record, I don't like New Orleans. I lost a Super Bowl there, too. [Editor's note: Miami lost to Dallas 24–3 in Super Bowl VI on January 16, 1972.]

There were so many funny things that happened off the field when the game was over. I guess it's safe to talk about them now—at least the statute of limitations has passed.

At the end of the Georgia-Florida game in 1966, people went pretty crazy. I hit old Spurrier so many times that people kept coming up to me wanting to show their gratitude. By the time I got to the locker room, I looked down and my helmet was full of money. One guy actually tried to buy my helmet from me, but I figured I'd better not do that.

In 1968 we were down in Jacksonville playing Florida in a monsoon. We got up something like 35–0 at halftime. After the first possession of the second half, the coaches told the first-team defense that we were through for the day. So a bunch of us got our Gatorade cups and stood by the fence while the Georgia fans filled them up with liquor. Then we would stand on top of the bench so nobody could look down into the cups while we enjoyed ourselves.

I had a great experience at Georgia. It prepared me for the NFL and it prepared me for life after the NFL.

Quite frankly, when I first got there I thought coach Dooley was out of his mind. But as I got a little older, I realized where he was coming from and what he was trying to get us to do. He was trying to shape us, not only as football players but as men. When you're young you just don't understand or appreciate that.

I was lucky. In my career I got to play for three great coaches: Vince Dooley, Erk Russell, and Don Shula. It doesn't get any better than that.

It's funny. I had to give up a lot to play football. I played four years at Georgia and eight years in the NFL. I have four discs fused in my neck. I have one bad disc in my lower back. In January of 2001 I had my left hip replaced. In November of that same year I had my right hip replaced. In 2003, for the first time in a long time, I was finally pain free.

And you know what? If I were 18 years old right now, I would be glad to do it all over again. That's how much I loved going to Georgia.

Bill Stanfill was the 1968 Outland Trophy winner. He played on the Miami Dolphins Super Bowl champion teams of 1972 and 1973. He was inducted into the College Football Hall of Fame in 1998. Today he lives in Leesburg, Georgia, where he is a real estate broker.

BOB TAYLOR

Running Back
1963–1965

I WASN'T A VERY BIG HIGH SCHOOL FOOTBALL PLAYER, and as a result, nobody really wanted me. My high school coach, Oliver Hunnicutt, was a Georgia man, and he had sent a number of boys to Georgia over the years. Coach Hunnicutt talked it over with my dad and then told me to walk on at Georgia and see what would happen. My dad would pay my way, and we would just hope for the best.

That was the fall of 1962, and somehow I managed to make the freshman team. Then the following spring I made the varsity as a member of the second team. And that's when I got my scholarship. Let me tell you what, that was a proud day.

It's hard to explain why we couldn't win at Georgia in 1962 and 1963. I think the world of all those coaches we had back then, but things just didn't seem to work. I remember the summer of 1963 we went up to north Georgia to one of those places where they had a boys school. We stayed up there for three weeks and had two-a-days. It was bad news.

It seemed like the coaches thought that the more you ran and hit hard, the better football team you would be. It wasn't a fun experience, and we didn't win a lot of games when I was a sophomore in 1963. [Editor's note: The Georgia team of 1963 had a record of 4–5–1.]

I'll never forget the first meeting we had with coach [Vince] Dooley in December of 1963. A notice was put on the bulletin board at Lipscomb Hall, which is where we were living. It said that we would be meeting with coach Dooley over at Stegeman Hall at 6:00.

Some of us arrived about a minute late, and I was one of them. When we got there the door was shut and locked. Coach Dooley let us mill around a little outside and finally let us in.

Coach Dooley said that everybody who was late had to write their name down on a piece of paper. Then he told us to be at the practice field at 4:30 the next morning with our running shoes on. We had to run about 30 or 40 100-yard dashes. I have never been so tired in my life, but we were never late again.

After that the players started talking in the dorm amongst ourselves. It was obvious that things were going to be a lot different under coach Dooley. He meant business, and he meant to win. Discipline was going to be the name of the game.

There were a lot of great memories in coach Dooley's first season, in 1964, but the game I remember most was one that we lost. Florida State had a great team with quarterback Steve Tensi and receiver Fred Biletnikoff. They beat us [17–14] but just barely. We beat them everywhere but on the scoreboard. They knew it and we knew it. Coach Dooley called it one of our greatest games, and I think that proved to everybody that we were going to be winners in the future.

The trip to the Sun Bowl that year was incredible. People were so excited because it had been so long since Georgia went to a bowl game. The game was in El Paso, and we played Texas Tech. They had Donny Anderson, who would go on to sign a big contract and be a star with the Green Bay Packers. I just remember that we won the game [7–0] and that while we were in El Paso they let us go across the border to Juarez a couple of times. What a great trip!

When 1965 rolled around we were ready to be a good football team. The guys reported back to Athens in shape, and we had great two-a-day practices. Alabama was coming to Athens as the defending national champions for the first game. Man, was Athens excited!

Joe Namath had gone to the AFL, but Alabama had another great player, Steve Sloan, as their quarterback. We jumped on top of them early, but then they jumped back ahead of us, 17–10, in the fourth quarter.

I remember the day that coach Dooley put in the flea flicker play during practice. Some of us kind of thought it was a joke. It looked like something that you would run in grade school. It was a play you'd draw up on the grass to fool people. And it never, ever worked in practice. So I never thought we would run it in a game!

Bob Taylor scored the winning touchdown against Alabama in 1965, but his football career came to an end several weeks later against Florida State.

But there we were, fighting to stay in the game with Alabama, and our quarterback, Kirby Moore, came into the huddle and called flea flicker left. I couldn't believe it, and a bunch of the other guys couldn't believe it either.

But Kirby said, "Calm down. Calm down. It's that play we couldn't run in practice. We've got to make it work now."

My job was pretty simple. Kirby was supposed to throw the ball to Pat Hodgson, who would do a little curl route. I would trail right behind the play, and when the defense collapsed on Pat, he would toss the ball back to me.

I have never seen anything unfold so perfectly. I don't know if Pat's knee was on the ground or not, but the ball came right to me. When I got it I was near the Alabama sideline and there was nobody between me and the Alabama goal line. I was thinking, "Lord, Taylor, please don't fall down." I didn't think my legs would carry me that far, but they did.

Of course, coach Dooley called for the two-point conversion, and we made it to win the game. It's hard to believe that was 38 years ago. People never get tired of talking about that play, and I'm glad because I never get tired of talking about it either.

Then came time to go up to Michigan. I have a lot of great memories from that game. It was obvious from the stuff we were reading on our bulletin board that the Michigan players didn't think much of us. And neither did the crowd. When we went out for the coin toss there were one hundred thousand folks in that stadium!

Michigan beat us up pretty good in the first half, but then coach Dooley gave one of the best halftime speeches I've ever heard.

He said that they were faster, but we were quicker.

He said they were stronger, but we were tougher.

He said they were bigger on the outside, but we were bigger on the inside because we had bigger heart.

Then he took the rest of the coaches and left the locker room. He said, "When y'all are ready to play football then come on down."

Well, we sat there for a couple of minutes and looked at each other and then went out there and beat those people bad [15–7]. I still think that was one of the greatest days in Georgia history.

We were 4–0 and ranked No. 4 in the nation when we went down to Florida State. Just like the year before, they had a really good football team. We were staying with them pretty good at halftime. But on the second or third play of the third quarter, I started to run a power sweep. Somebody hit me right below the knee, and the second I got hit, I knew I was gone.

I went back and looked at the films; when I planted my right foot, somebody just hit me in the perfect place, and both bones below the knee snapped. I never played football again.

I've heard people say that our season turned bad because I got hurt. I don't believe that. We had a lot of guys who could take my place, but we had a lot of injuries other than mine. I sure wish that team could have stayed healthy. We might have been able to win the SEC championship.

It took a while for my leg to heal. They had to set it twice before it finally stayed in place.

It took a lot longer for me to heal on the inside. It took me several years to really get over it. In fact, I had to grow up to get over it. I just couldn't understand that when we had such a great team . . . why in the world would something like that happen to me? But when you grow up, you understand that things happen for a reason. It was just my time to stop playing. I had to get on with the rest of my life.

I went to work for the Monroe shock absorbers company and stayed with them for 30 years. I was in sales but eventually became the motivational speaker for the company. Thanks to my experiences at Georgia, I could talk about the meaning of teamwork and preparation and persistence. I could talk about bouncing back from adversity. I had lived it.

Being a football player at Georgia helped me in my life and in my career in so many ways. I was shy when I got there in 1962, and the four years I spent there made me a much better person.

There are no relationships quite like the ones you have with your teammates. A bunch of us try to get together to play golf in the spring, and it is a really special time. We tell the same stories we've told a hundred times before, but to us, they never get old.

I was proud to be a Bulldog then, and I'm proud to be a Bulldog now. Because once you're a Bulldog, it stays with you the rest of your life.

151

Bob Taylor was leading the SEC in rushing in 1965 when he suffered a broken leg in the fifth game of the season against Florida State. He never played football again. Today Taylor is retired and lives in LaGrange, Georgia.

JIM WILSON

Tackle
1962–1964

IT'S FUNNY HOW LITTLE THINGS that don't seem that important at the time really change the entire direction of your life.

I was born with a bad back, and when I was young my family was told not to let me play contact sports. But when I was 10 years old I saw the movie *Jim Thorpe, All-American*. Burt Lancaster played the lead role. That was in 1951, and from that moment on, that's what I wanted to be. I wanted to be a running back, and I wanted to be an All-American.

I grew up just outside of Pittsburgh and went to a very small high school. We only had 32 guys on the football team. Coach Wally Butts really liked to recruit guys from Pennsylvania, guys like Frank Sinkwich from McKees Rock, Charley Trippi from Pittston, and Johnny Rauch, who was from the eastern part of the state.

Not a whole lot of people were recruiting me, but coach Johnny Griffith, who was the freshman coach at Georgia, came up to see me. I was a big kid who liked to work out, and I was a running back. I went down to Georgia and just fell in love with the place. It was an easy decision for me.

I was a freshman in 1960 and came in with a helluva class. Guys like Len Hauss, Larry Rakestraw, and Mickey Babb came in with me and were really good players.

I wasn't there long before the coaches wanted to move me to center. Charley Trippi, the running backs coach, said I ran the ball like a wild

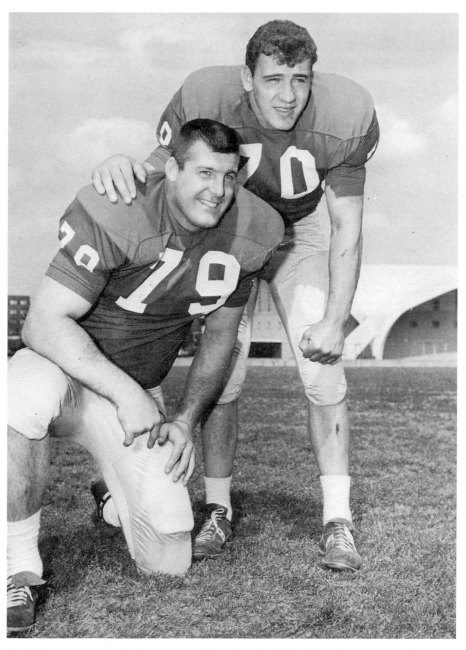

Jim Wilson was a senior lineman on Vince Dooley's first Georgia team in 1964. Wilson (left), seen here with teammate Ray Rissmiller, went on to become a professional wrestler.

Indian, but nobody could stop me from the 5-yard line on in—not even the varsity defense.

I got so disappointed that I left Georgia, and the next summer I went to Tulsa, thinking I'd get a chance to play there. Tulsa had recruited me out of high school, and they were putting together a great program. They had guys like Jerry Rhome at quarterback and Howard Twilley at wide receiver. They were going to let me play running back and linebacker.

Coach Butts and Charley Trippi started talking to my parents and telling them that they would not give me a release to go to Tulsa. Finally, the coaches at Tulsa brought me in and said if Georgia wouldn't grant a release, they weren't going to fight it. They couldn't afford to have a stink going on. So I went back to Georgia and redshirted the 1961 season.

In that redshirt season I made up my mind that I was going to build myself up and learn how to play the line. I built myself up from about 225 to 255 pounds. I was ready to play.

Those next two years [1962 and 1963] were pretty tough. Johnny Griffith was the head coach by that time, but it was hard to follow a legend like coach Butts.

And back in those days coaches thought that the harder they worked you and the more you hit, the better the team you would be on Saturday. I think they know better now. Every day at practice was like a street fight to see who wanted to play. They would sign a ton of guys and sort of weed a bunch of them out. I really think we left some of our best football on the practice field.

I didn't really get to know Johnny Griffith until after I had left Georgia. He was such a gracious man, who was really put in a difficult situation. He had a hard time at Georgia because there was almost no way he could succeed. It was so sad when he passed away a while back.

But then came coach [Vince] Dooley and the difference was night and day. He established discipline immediately. No cutting classes. No being late for meetings. I was in the group that got to run at 5:00 in the morning because we were late for the first team meeting.

I was in the perfect situation. I was the only guy they let play both ways, which meant I got to play for Erk Russell on defense and Bill Dooley, Vince's brother, on offense. Both were great guys and great coaches with a lot of enthusiasm. The best thing of all was their teaching. They worked us hard, but they were always teaching us how to be better football players. It was really great.

I was drafted as a future in the NFL, and because I was in my fifth year at school I could have left. But I was one of 14 seniors on that team, and all of us got together and decided that we were willing to make the commitment to win. I wanted to finish what I had started at Georgia, because as soon as coach Dooley got there you could tell this was going to be something special.

Yeah, we lost our first game to Alabama [31–3]. Joe Namath was the quarterback, and I remember playing against Joe in an eighth-grade basketball game. He was from Beaver Falls, just up the river from where I lived.

But we ended up having a great year and went to a bowl game, which was terrific.

I went on to play pro football for a while. I was with the Rams when George Allen was the coach. He put me back at tackle after another coach had switched me to guard. I loved it, but I also had to go against Deacon Jones every day in practice. I got a quick indoctrination on how to play tackle in the NFL.

I was also in professional wrestling for a while. I had always been a closet fan growing up. I got pushed out of that business before I was ready, but that's another story for another time.

I look back on my time at Georgia and realize that those five years meant everything to me. I went there as a boy and left as a man. I came there in coach Butts' last year and left in coach Dooley's first year. I was a part of the team that laid the foundation for what Vince did there, and to me, that meant more than being an All-American.

I have so much admiration and respect for coach Dooley. What he and the other coaches taught me were lessons I'll carry in my heart as long as I live.

It's about the team. You win as a team. You lose as a team, no matter what. That's the bottom line for me. To me, that's what it means to be a Bulldog.

Jim Wilson was an All-American tackle in 1964. After four years in the NFL, Wilson went on to become a successful professional wrestler. He was inducted into the Georgia State Sports Hall of Fame in 2001. Today Wilson lives in Evans, Georgia, where he is in private business.

The SEVENTIES

DICKY CLARK
Defensive End
1974–1976

I GREW UP A TREMENDOUS ALABAMA FAN. I went to a lot of the Alabama games when they were the dominant team in the SEC. That's where my dad wanted me to go.

But there were a lot of things pulling me to Georgia. One of my best friends was a trainer down there, and I had some other friends in Athens. I was a quarterback, and Andy Johnson, Georgia's starting quarterback, was going to graduate after my freshman year in 1973. I was from Rossville, up in north Georgia, and figured that going to an in-state school would benefit me down the road.

Doc Ayers recruited me, and Doc was a really great fellow. He got me a job working for a blind lawyer by the name of Bill Love in Ringgold, Georgia. I was his chauffeur and his eyes as he carried on a full-fledged law practice. Bill was a big Georgia guy, and he and I got to be very close.

There were a lot of little things like that pulling me to Georgia, so I signed. I don't think my dad spoke to me for a month after that.

I wasn't the only quarterback to come to Georgia in 1973. Ray Goff and Matt Robinson also came in. Ray got bumped up to the varsity while Matt and I played on the junior varsity.

I entered my sophomore season, in 1974, as the starting quarterback. We beat Oregon State in the opener, but then we went to Jackson and lost to

Dicky Clark came to Georgia as a quarterback, but left as an All-SEC defensive end. He was a Georgia assistant coach for 15 seasons.

Mississippi State. I remember after that game coach Bill Pace, our offensive coordinator, came to me and said, "You're still our number one quarterback, but we're going to let Matt play a little bit and see what happens." What happened was that Matt played the rest of the year. It looked like I was out of a job.

I stood on the sidelines the rest of the year, so I was standing for that horrible game against Georgia Tech in 1974. It was icy cold, it was raining, and the wind was blowing. I can easily say that it was the coldest I have ever been in my life. At halftime my socks were literally frozen, so I took them off and asked the equipment manager for some fresh ones. He said, "Only the guys who are playing get dry socks."

I went over to my roommate, Stan Tedder, and I said, "Stan, let's quit." I was so miserable I really thought about quitting right there.

Erk Russell [Georgia's defensive coordinator], of course, coached the entire game in a short-sleeve shirt.

I didn't quit, but I also didn't know what was going to happen to me. Then that spring Erk came to see me. We had really struggled the year before on defense. "We need some people to come up and help, and we think you can," Erk told me.

You have to understand how the players felt about Erk Russell. He is the greatest motivator I have ever seen. And when coach Russell asked you to do something, you really wanted to do it. If he had asked me to play nose guard, I would have given it a shot.

I just wanted to play, and they convinced me that I could get on the field by playing defense and that it would be the best thing for the team. So I said fine. Sure, it was tough giving up on being a quarterback; that's what I had always been. But like I said, I wanted to play.

In a sense, I was really lucky. Nine out of ten teams we played at the time ran an option offense. As a former quarterback, I could read the option because I had run it so many times. I almost always knew where the ball was. So that was a good position for me at a good time. At 215 pounds, I never could have played defensive end against the kind of power offenses they run today.

The 1975 season was the start of the Junkyard Dawgs on defense. Erk was trying to come up with a catchy name to describe what was a pretty scrawny defense. None of us were really big. I think Ronnie Swoopes [at 245 pounds] was the biggest guy we had, and the rest of us barely got to 200 pounds. But we were tough, and we were pretty smart.

I didn't start the first game against Pittsburgh. I didn't really get to play a lot until the second game with Mississippi State, when the guy ahead of me got hurt. Ironically, I had lost the quarterback job against Mississippi State the year before, but this would be the day I would win a job at defensive end.

I don't remember what the score was, but it was close. [Editor's note: At this moment in the game Georgia led 7–6.] I just remember that Swoopes hit a pass, and I picked it off and ran 71 yards for a touchdown. We won the game [28–6], and I got the SEC Lineman of the Week award. I was the starter after that.

After that the Junkyard Dawg mania took off. Yeah, we gave up lots of yardage that year, but we tended to tighten up when teams got near the goal. The perfect example of that was the game with Florida. They ran up and down the field with that great offense, but we held them to one touchdown. The problem was that it didn't seem like our offense was ever going to score on them—until the great Appleby-to-Washington touchdown play. Once we got the lead in that game, we knew we were going to win.

Before the 1976 season a bunch of guys shaved their heads as a sign of unity. But not this old boy. I told the guys that I liked dating and I liked my hair. Besides, my mama told me I had some ugly scars on my head—at least that was my excuse.

161

A lot of great things happened that season; best of all, we won the SEC championship. But for me, the greatest moment will always be when we beat Alabama 21–0 in Athens. Unless you were there, you can't understand what it was like in Athens and what that city went through. The excitement was in the air all week, because we knew we were good enough to beat them. Alabama had been dominating the SEC for years, and we just controlled them.

They basically had to shut down the whole town after the game. It was the most excited after a win that I have ever been.

We went on to beat Florida and then clinched the SEC championship down at Auburn. There is nothing like being on a championship team. It is something that stays with you the rest of your life.

I was lucky because I got to come back to Georgia as an assistant coach and stayed with it for 15 years. But when Ray [Goff] got fired in 1995, I had to decide if I wanted to go somewhere else and be an assistant or stay in Athens and work with a ministry [Fellowship of Christian Athletes] that I had always loved. That's why I'm still here.

The things you go through as an athlete and a student at Georgia are things that stick with you forever.

I remember after I had played my last game in the Sugar Bowl against Pittsburgh, our president, Dr. Fred Davison, came up to me as I was taking off my uniform. He said, "Dicky, I want you to know something. If you take the same effort and desire, time, and dedication that you put into football and put it into whatever you do in life, you will be successful."

Then he walked off, but I have never forgotten that moment.

I got to know coach Dooley much better after I quit playing for him and started working for him as a coach, and he has been a very influential person in my life.

Coach Jim Pyburn was my position coach, and he was tough. You had to toe the line when you played for coach Pyburn. He didn't let you get away with anything, and that was a lesson I took with me when I became a coach.

And what can you say about Erk? Everybody called coach Russell a tough guy, but the biggest myth about him is that he was a screamer. I don't ever remember him raising his voice. He was always teaching. He had the ability to say exactly the right thing at exactly the right time to get the most out of you.

The greatest thing I learned at Georgia was about a group of guys working together to reach a common goal. And we did that with the championship of 1976. A lot of us have gone our own ways, but when I see a teammate I don't think, "Here's a guy I used to know." It's, "Here is a dear friend." It may have been 10 years since we talked, but we can pick up right where we left off. It's like we've been together the whole time.

Those lessons and those kind of relationships are what Georgia gave me. And you can't put a value on that.

Dicky Clark was an All-SEC defensive end and the defensive captain of Georgia's 1976 SEC championship team. He was an assistant coach at Georgia for 15 seasons (1981–1995).

GEORGE COLLINS

Guard
1975–1977

W HEN I WAS GROWING UP, it never occurred to me that I would go to college anyplace other than Georgia. I never thought I would play college football, but I figured I'd go to college, and I was always a Georgia fan.

I remember playing middle school basketball in 1968, and right after the game I had to rush out to the car to check the score of the Georgia-Florida game. When I got a little older I remember sitting in the dove fields and listening to Georgia games on the radio. That's how big of a Bulldog I was when I was young.

Now, there was some wavering when I got to be a senior in high school and the recruiters started coming to my house. Wayne McDuffie of Florida State was the first to visit me. Little did I know that when I was a senior at Georgia he would be my offensive line coach. Jerry Glanville came over from Georgia Tech.

I had a really good friend who was also being recruited, and we thought about going to the same school. But when he said he was going to sign with Florida, I said no way. I told him that if he went to Tech I'd *think* about it. But there was no way that I was going to be a Gator.

The toughest thing I had to face was being recruited by Alabama. You have to remember that in the seventies Alabama was on a roll. They were winning the SEC championship every year. Coach Bear Bryant was getting just about every player he wanted.

I went over to Tuscaloosa to watch Alabama practice, and while it was going on, a manager tapped me on the shoulder and said, "Coach Bryant wants you in the tower."

You have to think about this: a little boy from Warner Robins, Georgia, standing in the tower watching practice with coach Bryant—just me and him. He didn't say a whole lot, but at one point he looked at me and said, "Son, we want you here at Alabama." Now that's tough.

But in the end it was my upbringing. I knew I was going to live in Georgia after college, and the way I was brought up, if you're going to live in Georgia, then you should be a Bulldog.

Steve Dennis was a really good player from Macon, and he and I were on some recruiting trips together. I found out that Steve had decided to go to Georgia. Not much later coach Jimmy Vickers, who was recruiting me for Georgia, called and asked if I was ready to sign. I told coach Vickers that when he came to Macon to sign Steve just to come over and sign me, too. And that's how it happened.

I was a freshman in 1974, and back then freshmen were sort of apart from the varsity. We practiced against the varsity as the scout team and played a few freshman games. My only real memory of 1974 is the awful weather on the day we played Georgia Tech in Athens. I'm sure that was the coldest I have ever been. My girlfriend came up, and we tried to stay dry under a piece of plastic. We didn't. And it really didn't help that Georgia Tech was putting it to us. [Editor's note: Georgia lost that game 34–14.]

I was a sophomore in 1975, but I really expected to get redshirted. But we had some injuries and some academic casualties, and the next thing I knew, I was being moved from guard to tight end. I was the second tight end behind Richard Appleby. I got to play a pretty good bit because coach [Vince] Dooley liked to go with two tight ends and run the ball, especially since we had a great offensive line.

The only bad thing about playing tight end was that I couldn't weigh more than 225 pounds, so I actually had to watch what I ate. That would kill me on Thursday nights at the dorm when we had pizza.

The first week I went to practice as a tight end, Richard Appleby and Gene Washington stopped me before I went on the field. They said, "You can't go out there looking like that. You can't look like an offensive lineman if you're going to play tight end!"

So they made me put some tape on my shoes and spat them up a little bit. They showed me the ropes of how to get open as a receiver. Not that it did

George Collins was an All-American guard in 1977 and was a member of Georgia's 1976 SEC championship team.

any good, because all I did was block. I remember one time in practice they threw me a ball and I caught it. Coach Dooley was so amazed that he ended practice right there.

Everybody remembers the great end-around play—Appleby to Washington—that we used to beat Florida. What people don't know is that we were actually in a two-tight-end formation on that play, and we had never practiced that play in that formation. But Florida was putting so many guys up on the line of scrimmage, the coaches decided we needed another tight end to give Richard time to throw the ball. So I got to be a part of that great play.

What I remember most was after we scored, we got the ball back and had a chance to run out the clock. That's when I first heard the term "Fire Drill" about the Georgia-Florida game. The Florida fans were leaving that stadium so fast that we called it a fire drill. It was really great being in that huddle and watching all of those Gators pour out of that place.

I have one more great memory about 1975. We had a big tackle on that team, Steve Wilson. We called him the Hulk. One night before a game Steve and I were wrestling on the floor, and he twisted my nose and left a big red ring around it. Well, we won the next day. So after that, every night before the game Steve would come in and want to twist my nose.

This went on for several weeks, and finally one Friday night I told my roommate, Mark Farriba, that Steve was not going to get me. We were going to double-team him.

Well, the next day I played with a red ring on my nose—and a black eye. Steve Wilson was a man, but he was also a good buddy.

We went on and played in the Cotton Bowl that season. After that they moved me to guard, and I could eat again!

There's a lot I could say about the 1976 team. We won an SEC championship, and the ring I have is very important to me. I only wear it on special occasions, when I dress up.

But every guy who played on that team will remember the Alabama game in Athens for as long as he lives. I remember everything about that week. I remember that when we went to the stadium on Friday to work out, people were already on the tracks putting their "game face" on. Just seeing that sent chills through my body.

I will never forget the bus ride from the Coliseum to the stadium. It was wall-to-wall people, and they were ready to play. Then we walked down those steps to the locker room with people screaming. When that was over, coach [Erk] Russell said, "If you're not ready to play now, you'll never be ready."

Of course we were ready to play, and we beat Alabama bad [21–0]. The town went wild, and they had to shut down Milledge Avenue. There has never been another day like it in Athens.

We beat Florida again, even though we fell behind 27–13. The great thing about our team was that we never panicked. We knew that if we just kept running our offense, we could take control of the game. Yeah, we got a little luck on the "Fourth and Dumb" play by Florida [see page 137], but once we took control of that game there was nothing they could do.

Another of my favorite memories is going to Auburn and clinching the SEC championship. Ray Goff, our quarterback, was hurt and couldn't throw. So we just lined up and said, "Here we come!"

After winning the championship in 1976, it was tough to go through 1977. [Editor's note: Georgia went 5–6 in 1977, coach Vince Dooley's only losing season in 25 years as coach.] It seems like we led the nation in turnovers, and we went through something like five quarterbacks because of injuries. Plus, we lost a lot of great players from the year before. We were undermanned a little.

Still, I had a great four years at Georgia. There were so many people who had a positive influence on me. Coach Dooley had a big impact on me because of his character and integrity. When I became a coach, I tried to emulate his way of doing things.

And let me say something about coach John Kasay, our strength and conditioning coach. He lived in the dorm and was really close to us, and I learned from him that if you're going to do something, then do it right. If your workout is at 7:00 A.M., then you don't walk in at 7:00 A.M. You go to work at 7:00 A.M. If you're supposed to do 10 reps, then do 10 good ones. If coach Kasay was going to be a part of something, then he was going to do it right. That's a lesson I've carried with me my entire life.

I was very lucky and got to play seven years of pro ball. I was a college coach for a while, and now I'm a high school coach. As I look back on my life, I realize how fortunate I was to be at Georgia. God blessed me with some talent, but he also put the right people in place to teach me the lessons I would need to be a man.

When you ask me what it means to be a Bulldog, I think of this: right now I'm 48 years old, but if I were in trouble, I could pick up the phone and call John Kasay or one of my teammates and they would be there for me, no questions asked. That's what being a Bulldog means to me.

167

George Collins was Georgia's offensive captain in 1977 and was named an All-American guard that same season. Today, he is an assistant football coach at Houston County High School.

RAY GOFF

Quarterback
1973–1976

I GREW UP PLAYING ALL KINDS OF SPORTS, and I really had no choice but to love them. My dad played for the Yankees until he broke his ankle really badly and had to quit. So he came back to Moultrie, Georgia, and became a recreation director. If I wanted to be near him, I needed to be in sports. I played everything—football, basketball, baseball, tennis, and swimming. I did it all, and I really loved it.

To be perfectly honest about it, I didn't know a whole lot about college football when I was young. I remember that Georgia Tech had an assistant coach named Dynamite Goodloe. My grandparents ran a hotel in Moultrie, and every time coach Goodloe would come to Moultrie for recruiting he would stay with my grandparents. I got to know him and learned about Georgia Tech, but I didn't know anything about the University of Georgia.

In the fall of 1965 I was 10 years old and my parents took me down to Tallahassee to watch Bob Taylor and Georgia play Florida State. I wasn't really paying attention. I thought we were going to see Georgia Tech play. When I found out it was Georgia and not Tech, I cried. I didn't enjoy the game because I really did not know what Georgia was all about.

The next memory I have of Georgia wasn't until Thanksgiving night of 1971. Georgia was playing at Georgia Tech. That night, Andy Johnson, who was the Georgia quarterback, led them on a long drive at the end of the game, and Jimmy Poulos went over the top for the winning touchdown. I

Ray Goff, the SEC Player of the Year in 1976, was Georgia's head coach from 1989 to 1995.

liked that game, and I liked Andy Johnson. That was one of the reasons I went to Georgia.

I also have to give credit to the guy who recruited me, Pat Hodgson. He was a big influence on me. First of all, he convinced me that if I came to Georgia, they were going to throw the football. What he didn't tell me was that most of the throwing would take place in pregame warm-ups and at halftime.

Turns out that didn't matter. I was a pretty decent passer in high school. Not great, but decent. But once I got to Georgia, I couldn't throw it a lick.

My first year, in 1973, I figured I'd just be working with the rest of the freshmen, but one day I was working against the varsity and ran an option play. I kept the ball and ran about 40 or 50 yards for a touchdown. The next thing I knew, I was moved up to the varsity as the number three quarterback. I sat on the bench for the whole year because Andy Johnson, the guy I really liked, was a senior that year.

Coming out of the spring of 1974, I was still number three on the depth chart behind Dicky Clark, who was number one, and Matt Robinson, who was number two. I didn't know what kind of future I had at Georgia. Unfortunately, we weren't a very good team that year. We had some good players, but it just didn't seem like we were all headed in the same direction.

There's a funny story about our opening game with Oregon State. They were coached by Dee Andros, the man called "The Great Pumpkin," and they were terrible the year before. I can still hear coach [Vince] Dooley telling us, "Men, they've got the best onside kicking team in the country."

We looked around and said to ourselves, "Who is this guy kidding?"

Well, we get up real big, and it looks like we've got the game under control, but then Oregon State scores. They try an onside kick and get it. Then they score again. They try another onside kick. They get it and score again. Then they try another onside kick and get it. But time finally ran out, and we won 48–35.

From that point on, I started to believe whatever coach Dooley said about an opponent.

That year ended badly. We lost to Georgia Tech on the most miserable day I can ever remember. It was the coldest I've ever been in my life. Nobody wanted to go into the game. It was embarrassing, because they beat us so badly [34–14].

Then we went down to the Tangerine Bowl and they [Miami of Ohio] beat us pretty badly, too [21–10], and we finished with a 6–6 record. I've known coach Dooley a long time, but that is the maddest I have ever seen him after a game.

He said, "Men, this spring we are going to find out who wants to play football."

I was a player and a coach for 21 years at Georgia, and I promise you, the spring of 1975 was the roughest spring I was ever around at Georgia. But we did find out who wanted to play football, and it would help us for the next two years.

In 1975 we had a great offensive line, and we really committed to running the ball and being physical. I came out of that killer spring as the starting quarterback. We lost our first game against Pittsburgh [19–9] in Tony Dorsett's junior year. They were pretty good. Then at halftime we were behind Mississippi State [6–0] in Athens. I hadn't done a whole lot in either game, and I figured I was about to lose my job.

But that day against Mississippi State, my mother started a tradition for our family. She left at halftime of that game, and we came back to win 28–6. I had a long touchdown pass in that comeback. My mom was superstitious, so for every game over the next two years she would leave at halftime. We lost only four more games the entire time I was at Georgia.

Everybody likes to talk about the "shoestring" play that we ran against Vanderbilt that year. We really have to give credit to coach Jimmy Vickers for that play. He noticed on film that on defense Vanderbilt would always huddle right next to the ball and hold hands. So he came up with this play and explained it to me.

171

He said, "The first thing you're going to do, Ray, is run a sweep outside the hash mark, and nobody is going to block for you."

I really didn't like that idea at all.

I was supposed to run outside the hash but not go out of bounds. The official would then put the ball on the hash mark, and that's where Vandy would huddle. I was supposed to then walk over to the ball and lean down like I was tying my shoe. While all this was going on, Gene Washington was across the field, lined up behind our offensive line. I was supposed to just lean down and shovel the ball to him, and he would have a convoy to the goal line.

It was early in the game, and we weren't playing all that well. We were up 7–3 when the shoestring play was called. I did my job and ran the sweep with no blocking and, of course, they killed me. The official put the ball down, and sure enough, Vanderbilt got in a huddle and held hands. When I knelt down next to the ball, one of the Vandy players asked me what I was doing.

I said, "Nothing," and shoveled the ball to Gene. He went into the end zone and nobody ever touched him.

We tried a variation of that play in the Cotton Bowl against Arkansas, but that time it didn't work. We were ahead 10–3 and Gene was supposed to take the ball from me and hand it on a reverse to Richard Appleby, our tight end. I was an eligible receiver, and he was supposed to throw it back to me. But the ball was fumbled and Arkansas recovered. They knocked in a touchdown right before the half and tied the game at 10–10. We lost the momentum and never got it back. They killed us 31–10.

But in 1976 we knew we were going to have a good team. We had a bunch of great offensive linemen, like Joel Parrish and Mike Wilson—we called them Cowboy and Moonpie. We had Al Pollard and Kevin McLee in the backfield and a bunch of great receivers. We were really good on offense.

That summer I arrived at practice and noticed that a bunch of guys had shaved their heads. Moonpie started it when he didn't like a haircut he had gotten, and it just sort of caught on. All of the offensive linemen were doing it, and when you're the quarterback, you better do what your offensive line says. So I shaved mine too.

I'll never forget that when the number of guys with shaved heads got to be about 20, coach Erk Russell, who had always been bald, took a picture with all of us. He had copies made and signed it, "May you always be A Head!"

There are a lot of great memories from 1976, but I'll tell you this: I've spent most of my life in Athens, but I've never seen the town the way it was for the Alabama game that year. And it's never been that way since.

The buildup to the game was phenomenal. On Wednesday people were already riding up and down Milledge Avenue honking their horns. I get goose bumps just talking about it right now. When we went to the stadium on Friday to work out, there were several hundred people already on the tracks drinking and getting ready.

That was the game when the biggest challenge was getting off the bus and getting into the stadium. The fans had our bus surrounded. We had tear-away jerseys on, and a bunch of us got our jerseys torn off just getting off the bus. I told somebody that I wanted to stay out there with these folks, because they were going to have some fun!

We beat Alabama 21–0, and I believe it was the first time that Bear Bryant had been shut out in 66 consecutive games. [Editor's note: It had actually been 69 consecutive games.] We dominated the second half because our defense just whipped their butts. Coach Russell did a great job.

Let me say a word here about coach Erk Russell. I have incredible respect for coach Dooley, but coach Russell was the guy that people would die for. It didn't matter if you were on offense, defense, whatever. I remember when my playing days were over at Georgia, coach Russell wrote a letter to my mom and dad telling them how much he had enjoyed our association. And I was on offense! I know he did the same for a lot of other players, but it meant a lot to me.

I guess the highlight for me that year was when we went to play Florida. They had to beat us to win the SEC championship. We fell behind 27–13 at halftime, but nobody ever hollered or screamed. We knew we could win the game. On our second possession we drove about 80 yards to make it 27–20. Florida got the ball back, and then came the play that became known as "Fourth and Dumb." [Editor's note: Facing a fourth and inches at his own 29-yard line, Florida coach Doug Dickey elected to go for the first down. Florida's Earl Carr ran a sweep to the left and was tackled for no gain by Georgia's Johnny Henderson. Georgia took possession and immediately scored to tie the game at 27–27.]

173

From that point on, they couldn't stop us. It was kind of a dream game for me. I completed five passes on five attempts, and two of them were for touchdowns. [Editor's note: Ray Goff threw for two touchdowns and ran for three more touchdowns. For his efforts he was inducted into the Georgia-Florida game Hall of Fame.]

If Florida was the dream game for me, then Georgia Tech was almost the nightmare.

Before the game I popped off in the press about how Georgia Tech wasn't really a big rival anymore. I thought Florida and Auburn were our biggest rivals. As soon as that paper hit the street I was in coach Dooley's office, where he proceeded to tell me why Georgia Tech is our biggest rival of all. At the time I sort of halfway believed him.

Tech played really well that day. In some ways they outplayed us, but at the end it was 10–10 and we were driving with about four minutes left. Then yours truly fumbled the ball. I was angry and upset because I thought I had just cost us a shot at the national championship. We were 9–1 and were going to play Pitt in the Sugar Bowl, and we had heard that we had a shot if we beat

Pittsburgh. But now I was convinced we were going to tie. I have never thrown a helmet in my life, but I threw mine into the hedge as we came off the field.

On the very next play there was a fumble and Bill Krug came out of the pile with the ball. We got the ball and a chance to win! I had to go rumbling through the hedge looking for my helmet. We moved the ball into position, and Allan Leavitt kicked a field goal to beat them 13–10. I can still remember looking up on the scoreboard that said 0:07 left when he kicked it through.

That was a very happy occasion for me, and from that day on I always understood the importance of beating Georgia Tech. Never again did I forget that Tech was our number one rival.

Well, we didn't beat Pittsburgh in the Sugar Bowl because they were one of the two best college football teams I've ever seen. The other one was the Pittsburgh team we played in 1980 when I was coaching at South Carolina.

It was disappointing to go out on a losing note, but I can't complain. I was able to come back to Georgia in 1981 as an assistant and was then named head coach when coach Dooley retired after the 1988 season.

People ask me if I am bitter about the way things ended for me at Georgia. [Editor's note: Ray Goff was fired as Georgia's head coach after the 1995 season.] I'm really not. I'm not mad at anyone.

I enjoy what I do today. I have a great relationship with my kids that I might not have had if I had continued to coach.

When kids who played for me call me and ask my advice, I realize I have made a difference in their lives. That's all that matters to me. I wasn't the best coach Georgia ever had, but I wasn't the worst, either. I can look in the mirror and know that I gave that job everything I had, and I always did what I thought was right for the University of Georgia.

I still love Georgia and that will never change.

174

Ray Goff was the 1976 SEC Player of the Year and captain of Georgia's 1976 SEC championship team. He was Georgia's head coach from 1989 to 1995.

GLYNN HARRISON

Running Back
1973–1975

I GUESS I WAS LIKE ANY OTHER cocky high school senior when I came to Georgia in the fall of 1972. The way they recruit you, they make it sound like they can't live without you, so I expected to play right away. But when I got to Georgia there were some great running backs already there, like Jimmy Poulos, Horace King, and Bob Burns. I realized early on that I was going to have to wait my turn.

Growing up I was kind of a Georgia Tech guy. We were in Atlanta, and my dad really liked Tech, so that was the school that I followed for a while. But Frank Pancoast recruited me for Georgia, and I really liked him. And it just made sense to me that if you were going to live in this state, then if you had a chance you should play for the big state university. It just felt right for me.

As a freshman I was one of about three first-year guys they let play in the first game against Baylor. After that they put us back with the freshmen for the rest of the year.

When I was a sophomore in 1973, I spent most of the season on special teams. I remember that I was supposed to start as the number one punt returner in the first game against Pittsburgh, and right at game time they nixed the idea and put a senior in there. Needless to say, I wasn't really happy about that.

Then in the fourth game we went to Alabama, and they finally put me in. I had about a 30-yard return to set up a touchdown. [Editor's note: Harrison's 33-yard punt return set up a touchdown that gave Georgia a 14–13 lead. Georgia lost the game 28–14.] That was really the first highlight of my college career, and I got to return punts for the rest of the season. I was named the Special Teams Player of the Year for the 1973 season.

My only other big memory of that year is when we went down to Tennessee and beat them [35–31]. I remember that early in that game Eddie Brown of Tennessee ran a punt back 80 yards for a touchdown. That's the loudest I have ever heard a stadium, but they got pretty quiet after we scored late to beat them.

In 1974 I finally got to play a lot at running back, and we had a pretty good offense. However, we got into a situation where we had to outscore everybody, because the defense was struggling. I remember that we almost got tied by Vanderbilt at homecoming, and we had to drive the length of the field at the end of the game to win [38–31].

I remember playing against Houston at home. They were the biggest, most physical team I had ever seen. They looked like a pro team. They jumped on top of us and we came back, but we could never seem to get over the hump and lost [31–24]. They were really good.

Everybody remembers how badly that season ended. We lost to Tech [34-14] in the worst weather day in history. At least that's what I think. I was miserable. There must have been six inches of water on the field, and they were kicking our tails pretty good. Then we played Miami of Ohio in the Tangerine Bowl, but we were not prepared to play a team that good. We finished 6–6 and for Georgia that was unacceptable.

When the Tangerine Bowl was over, one thing became pretty clear: there was going to be a lot riding on the 1975 season. I was going to be a senior, and I sure didn't want to go through another year like that. Coach Dooley was feeling it because we had gone three seasons with pretty average results. It was time to go to work.

I'm not sure what I expected going into the 1975 season. I knew we were going to be good on offense again, because we had a great offensive line coming back, but there hadn't been a whole lot of changes on the defense, and that was where we had struggled. But I also sensed an attitude among the seniors that we weren't going to let the bad stuff happen again.

We really only had a couple of bad games in 1975. We lost to Pittsburgh [19–9] even though we held Tony Dorsett pretty much in check. They were pretty good.

My worst memory is the trip to Ole Miss [a 28–13 loss]. Everything just kind of fell apart in that game. I reinjured a shoulder that I had hurt the week before against Clemson and had to miss the rest of the game. Allan Leavitt,

176

"Glidin'" Glynn Harrison was one of the most elusive runners ever to play for the Bulldogs.

our place kicker, also got hurt. We were playing on AstroTurf, and it was really hot. We fumbled on the 1-yard line, which gave them some momentum, and we never got it back.

Because of my hurt shoulder, I had to miss the next week's game at Vanderbilt. In fact, it was the only full game I ever missed. I stayed back in Athens and listened to it on the radio. I knew the shoestring play was coming, I just didn't know when. I laughed when it worked. [Editor's note: See chapter on Ray Goff for a description of the shoestring play.]

The Florida game in 1975 [10–7] was the biggest upset I have ever been involved in. We were outmanned by them on both sides of the ball. When I look back on that game, I think they really should have blown us out. But they didn't, and that game means as much to me now as any I played in.

I was on the field for the Appleby-to-Washington touchdown. My job was to take a fake handoff from Matt [Robinson] and try to get somebody to tackle me. I was supposed to occupy a defender to give Richard [Appleby] time to throw the ball. After I made my fake I looked up and saw the ball in the air. Gene [Washington] was way behind the defense, and when he caught it I knew nobody was going to catch him.

Then we played Tech and got up on them 28–0 at halftime and 42–0 in the second half. I remember a fumble rolling across a guy's back and Lawrence Craft picking it off and running it back for a touchdown. We weren't that much better than Tech, but things just got rolling for us.

The Cotton Bowl against Arkansas was two different games. In the first game we got up 10–0, and we were pretty much dominating things. Then they tied it 10–10 right before halftime, and it was like they put locks on the doors, because we didn't come out for the second half. They killed us [31–10].

Still, the seniors on that team finished up with a good season. We got things turned around, and the year after we were gone, the Bulldogs won an SEC championship. I like to think we got that started for them.

I played a little pro football [for the Kansas City Chiefs], but it was never the same. Playing college football is really fun, and it is a special time in your life.

There is no question that playing football and going to school at Georgia has had its benefits. I'm still recognized by some people, but I know it's ancient history now. Still, playing football is a discipline you can't get anywhere else. It was good for me to have that structure. And playing football gives you a fraternity—a brotherhood that you will have all of your life.

That's what Georgia gave me, and I will always feel lucky that I had the chance to go through that experience with a great group of guys.

"Glidin'" Glynn Harrison was an All-SEC running back and the captain of Georgia's 1975 team. Today Harrison is a businessman who lives in Watkinsville, Georgia.

RANDY JOHNSON

Guard
1973–1975

I AM THE CLASSIC EXAMPLE of how going to a place like Georgia can turn somebody's life around.

When I came to Georgia in 1971, I wasn't much of a student. I didn't know anything about hard work. I didn't know how to work out properly to become a better football player, and at one point I even quit the team.

When I left Georgia I was an All-American, and I eventually got my degree and became a teacher. None of that would have been possible without the help of the people I met at Georgia. Sometimes when I look back it's hard to believe that all those things really happened to me.

For a lot of reasons, I got off to a pretty rough start at Georgia. I didn't care a whole lot about school. I was married when I got there. I stayed in the dorm for two quarters before I brought my wife down. I just had a hard time getting adjusted to college life.

After my freshman season, in 1971, I came back for two-a-day practices in the summer of 1972. I went to the morning practice on the first day and decided I was going to quit before the afternoon practice. I had a good-paying summer job back in Lindale, so I was going to go home and do that.

As I was walking out the door to go home, I saw coach [Vince] Dooley walking in. I told him what I was going to do, and he started talking to me about the opportunities I would be giving up if I left. He made some good points, but I was too stubborn and left anyway.

I lasted about six weeks, and then I went back to Athens to ask coach Dooley for another chance. He told me that he'd give me another chance, but then he said, "Quite frankly, I don't think you're going to make it." We still get a good laugh about that today.

I came back during the 1972 season and practiced for two weeks on the scout team. Then I had an emergency appendectomy, which kept me out for the rest of the year. I took a redshirt so I would have three years of eligibility left.

Things finally began to start looking up for me in 1973. I was a second-string guard and still not in really good shape when we went up to Tennessee. That game really got my career started, I think. We won the game [35–31] when Andy Johnson picked up a loose ball and ran it in for a touchdown. The next day in the paper there was a picture of me and Chris Hammond blocking. I'm in the linebacker's chest, and his feet are about six inches off the ground, and our back is running right off of us. After that game I became a starter and stayed a starter for the rest of my career.

The 1974 season was a nightmare year for us [6–6] that I hope everybody has forgotten by now.

In 1975 we came close to winning an SEC championship but slipped up. We lost our first game to Pittsburgh [19–9], which was a better team than most of us thought. We had to reevaluate a lot of things after that loss.

We lost at Ole Miss [28–13] in a game where everything that could go wrong did go wrong. Allan Leavitt hurt his leg, and I had to kick off. I had done it in high school and could usually get the ball to the 5-yard line. I was really excited when the game began, probably too excited. My first kickoff hit one of the up men for Ole Miss right in the chest. In fact, Butch Box almost recovered the ball for us. If Butch had recovered, I'm sure I would have been a hero. As it was, my place-kicking career was over at that point.

Nobody gave us a chance to beat Florida, but I went into that game thinking that there was no way that we were going to lose. That was just the way we felt about that game back then. Once Richard Appleby hit Gene Washington to give us the lead, the fun really began. I remember being on the field when we were running out the clock. We were smiling at each other in the huddle and reminding each other not to jump and create a penalty. What a great feeling!

Then in the Georgia Tech game, I finally got my chance to do what every lineman lives for—carry the football! Coach Bill Pace put in the "Randy

Randy Johnson quit college football for six weeks as a sophomore, but came back and left Georgia as an All-American guard.

Rooskie" play, where I would pull and pretend to run into Ray Goff, our quarterback. I would bend over like the wind had been knocked out of me, and Ray would give me the ball and keep running in the other direction. Then I take off running.

The play worked except for one thing: Richard Appleby, our tight end, was supposed to run at the defensive back on that side and block his vision. Instead, Richard blocked on the outside, and the defensive back saw me. I only gained six yards. I always think how neat it would have been to score a touchdown on national TV!

I always tell people that I left Georgia in 1975 and finally graduated in 1984, and that was possible because of coach Dooley. After playing pro football for a while, I thought the world owed me a living. I quickly found out how wrong I was about that. So I went back to school to get my degree, and coach Dooley found a way to put me back on scholarship for a year. I don't know how he did it, and I never asked. All I know is that when I needed some help, he gave it to me.

Because of that I will love that man with all my heart for as long as I live; I owe him everything that I have. I got my degree and I have been a teacher for over 20 years.

And the thing is, coach Dooley never asked for anything in return. To me, that's what being a Bulldog is all about. When you're a Bulldog you're part of a big family that looks out for each other when times get tough. Coach Dooley and Georgia gave me discipline at a time when I really needed it. I will always be grateful for that.

Randy Johnson was an All-American guard in 1975. He played for the Seattle Seahawks and the Tampa Bay Buccaneers. Today he is a teacher living in Lindale, Georgia.

HORACE KING

Running Back
1972—1974

I DIDN'T THINK OF MYSELF as a pioneer when I signed to play football at Georgia in 1971. There were five of us—Richard Appleby and Clarence Pope, who were my teammates at Clarke-Central, and Larry West, Chuck Kinnebrew, and myself.

I remember not too long after we got to Georgia, Loran Smith wrote a story and called us "pioneers" because we were the first African-American men to play football at Georgia. I remember swelling up with pride because then I understood the importance of what we were doing.

For a while, though, I didn't know if I was going to Georgia. It was coming down to the last days of the signing period, and I was getting ready to go visit Michigan State. I thought that was where I wanted to go.

Coach Mike Castronis was recruiting me for Georgia, and it was decided that we would all have a meeting. Appleby was there with me. Our assistant principal, Walter Allen, got involved. We all sat down and decided to put everything on the table.

My main issue was that I didn't want to be a token person on campus or be considered unique or special when it came to being a football player. I wanted to be a member of a team. That's all. I wanted to go somewhere to play football and to get an education.

So in the final minutes the discussion came down to this: would I go to school at Georgia and give it a shot? Then my mom reminded me that if I went off to play football someplace far away, she would never get to see me play. That weighed on my mind a little bit.

Finally, I looked at Richard and said, "I'll go if you go." It was just like that. I signed first and then Richard signed. Then they signed Clarence Pope, and that told me they were serious about bringing us there to play football.

I'm sure there were a lot of discussions going on behind the scenes in the community that I didn't know about. There were some people—some of them were my high school teammates—who said that I didn't want to go to Georgia. [Editor's note: King's teammates were trying to tell him that, as the first black player at Georgia, he would be uncomfortable. The campus had very few black students and had not been integrated for very long.] I shared that with my mother and she said, "They are not recruiting them. They are recruiting you."

It turned out to be one of the greatest decisions I ever made. Even though I went there with some concerns and doubts about how real my opportunity would be at Georgia, things just fell into place.

Yes, there was some talk about what it was going to be like when we went on the road to certain places in the South. But Georgia had a trainer named Squab Jones who had been there forever. He knew my family. Squab had ridden on all those same buses, and if he could do it and survive, why couldn't I?

I came in with a great freshman class in 1971. Guys like Barry Collier and Dan Spivey were great athletes. Randy Johnson could do things athletically that I'm not sure I could do.

Coach John Donaldson was our freshman coach, and every day he would come to practice ready to go. His favorite saying was "Hubba, Hubba." And what that meant was, "Men, let's get to work." He had a great influence on me, and he really got us ready for varsity ball.

Billy Payne was my first position coach at Georgia as a running back. He had a very strong influence on me and was very demanding. I had to do things right. He was always in my ear. He held me accountable and responsible for being the best football player I could be. You could tell then that he was a special person.

Now, I'm not trying to say that everything was perfect. Getting comfortable and getting adjusted at Georgia was a long process. I remember scoring a touchdown against Georgia Tech. I was quoted in the paper saying, "All I was doing was my job to help them out." When I saw that I cried, because I wanted to know who "them" was. What that told me was that I had yet to make myself a home there.

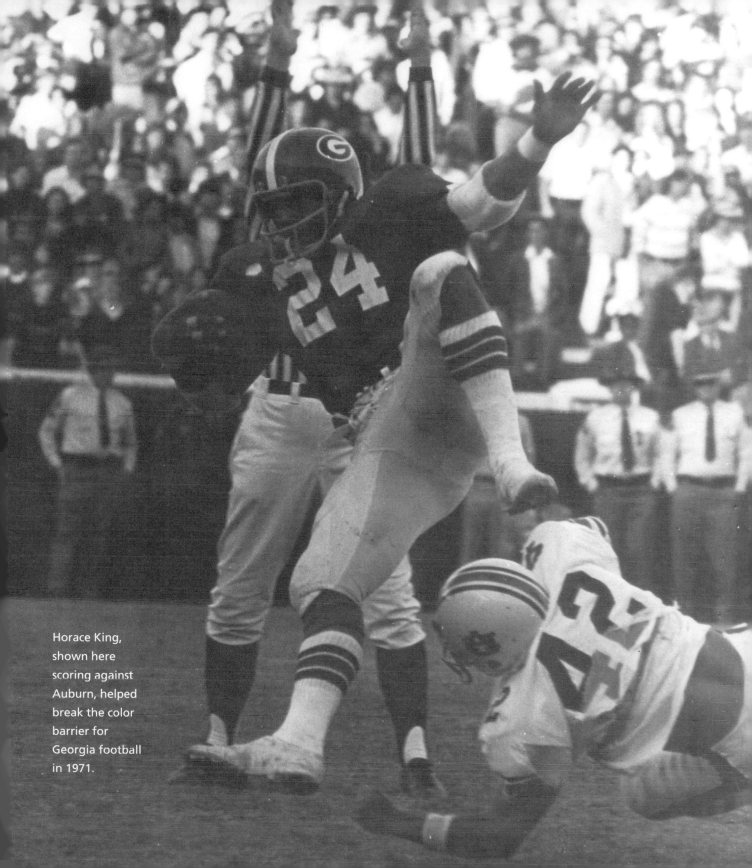

Horace King, shown here scoring against Auburn, helped break the color barrier for Georgia football in 1971.

After that I became a little bit more of a Bulldog each day. Being a Bulldog started oozing into my spirit. That moment was really an awakening for me.

I remember I had a teammate, Dave Christianson, who was a wide receiver from Chicago. One evening he wanted to go eat pizza and invited me and a bunch of guys to come along, so we went over to the Pizza Hut on Baxter. You have to understand that this was the first time I had ever been to a place like that, and I just sat around with my teammates eating pizza and drinking beer. This was all so new to me. We stayed there until curfew, and it was so much fun.

Yes, I'll admit that my tentacles were out, and they were sensitive to see if somebody would say something out of line. It may have happened, but I never heard it. The point is, I never had a moment when I felt like I didn't belong at Georgia. And it got better each year.

I remember sitting in a biology class with about three hundred people. There was a guy sitting next to me named Fred Bentley who had gone to some private school. He was really smart. I asked if I could study with him and told him that I could get him paid as a tutor. He said he didn't want any money, he just wanted one of my jerseys! I thought that was really great. It's a wonderful memory.

186

We had a tough three-year stretch [1972–1974] when I was at Georgia. I thought we were going to be so good when we were freshmen, but for whatever reason, we just couldn't turn the corner and do what the 1971 team did [11–1]. It seemed like those teams were always on the verge of taking the next step, but we never did. As soon as we would solve one problem, another one would pop up.

The toughest year of all was my senior year [1974] because it ended so badly. We lost to Georgia Tech [34–14] in our last home game as seniors. We came out of the locker room that day walking on air. When we went back to the locker room, our feet were buried in the ground. It was the worst football game I ever played in, and I played on some bad teams for the Detroit Lions.

The seniors voted not to go to the bowl game [Tangerine], but we were overruled and went down there anyway. I found out that two or three offensive linemen couldn't play because of grades. I figured that would not be very healthy for the running backs. We played that game [a 21–10 loss to Miami of Ohio] like we did most of that season—half-assed.

Still, I can't imagine having gone to school anywhere but Georgia. Georgia prepared me for pro football, and I was able to live out a dream. It gave me the skills I needed to get a job. Georgia disciplined me and it educated me. It rounded out my life as a young man and prepared me to move into adulthood.

Georgia made it possible for me to be a viable person in any community that I lived in. And it made sure that I wasn't just a resident, I was a participant.

Georgia is a special place and it was a very special part of my life.

Horace King was an All-SEC running back for Georgia in 1974. He was the first African-American to sign a scholarship to play football for Georgia. He went on to play nine years with the Detroit Lions of the NFL. He still lives in the Detroit area, where he is a supervising engineer for General Motors.

BILL KRUG

Defensive Back
1975–1977

Growing up I really didn't know anything about Georgia. I lived in Maryland, and for a while I figured I was going to the University of Maryland to play football. How I ended up at Georgia is a great story, and one of the best things that has happened in my life.

It was early in my senior year, and I remember the game. I played at Bishop McNamara, a private Catholic school, and for the first time we had beaten Georgetown Prep. That was a huge win for us, and I was very happy.

I was walking off the field and met a gentleman named Joe Tereshinski. Mr. Tereshinski had been a great player at Georgia, and I had played against one of his sons, Wally, which is how he knew about me. He said he had been following me for a couple of years and would like for the Georgia people to contact me if I was interested. I sure was. Not long after that I started getting information from Georgia.

Coach [Pat] Hodgson and coach Barry Wilson came up to recruit me together. They came over to the house, as did Mr. Tereshinski, to meet my family. We talked about setting up a visit to Georgia, but I wanted to wait until after the season was over. So in January coach [Vince] Dooley came up to meet my family. They made it very clear that they wanted me, and we set up a visit for late February or early March.

Well, I went to Maryland in late January, and they were pretty heavy-handed in recruiting me. I was getting calls from coaches at all hours of the day and night, and my dad told me when I went there to visit that I could not sign, even if I thought I wanted to go there. My parents did not want to pressure me to stay close to home. Maryland pushed all the right buttons, though. They talked about the fact that I lived only 30 miles from campus, so all of my family could see me play. It really made me think.

I didn't sign, but when I went home I was pretty much thinking I would go to Maryland. Something about Georgia really intrigued me, though. I was supposed to go to Wake Forest that weekend, but I called and canceled. I called coach Hodgson and told him I wanted to come to Georgia right away to visit.

It was a great trip. Dicky Clark took me out on the town in Athens. Coach Hodgson showed me film of the 1965 Alabama game and the flea flicker pass. He mentioned that if I came to Georgia, we would play Alabama twice while I was there. That really caught my attention. He talked about the SEC and how it was a stronger conference than the ACC. I had a great time.

I got home and told my parents that it was going to be either Maryland or Georgia. I told them that Maryland had all the advantages. I said I liked Georgia, but that it was so far away. That's when my mom and dad said something very important. I guess it was Dad who said, "Bill, that's irrelevant. You go where you want to go and we will follow."

189

I canceled the rest of my visits and told the coaches at Maryland and Georgia that I wanted to think about it for one week, and then I would make a decision. I told them both that I didn't want any phone calls. I just wanted to be left alone for a week to think.

Wouldn't you know it? About Wednesday or Thursday a coach from Maryland called. I was leaning toward Georgia, but that sealed the deal. Coach Dooley came up for the signing, and I went to Georgia in the fall of 1974.

Now, when I got to Georgia I saw myself as a running back, but they had switched to the veer offense, and I was about a half-step slower than the other guys. I think the coaches kind of got on me about being a little slow, because they really wanted me to play defense. So I moved to strong safety.

There are two guys I really have to credit for my early development: Mike Castronis Jr. and Buzy Rosenberg. Even when I was a freshman and not playing, they made me watch videotape every day. I remember that the second game I played as a freshman, I made a play based on something I had seen on the tape. After that I was watching film all the time, and it was something that I did for the rest of my career.

I don't think any of us will forget the spring of 1975. The varsity was not very good in 1974, especially on defense. Coach Dooley began spring drills with this speech. I remember it word for word:

"We are going to learn three things: block and tackle, block and tackle, and block and tackle some more."

And we did. We didn't even have spring practice in Maryland, so this was all new to me. Coach Jim Pyburn had tackling drills that I had never heard of. It was brutal. But that spring practice changed the character of our team, and it was sorely needed.

The 1975 team was special because nobody expected us to do anything. We were still kind of small on defense, and people thought we were going to get killed. But I'll tell you what, we had some really tough guys on that team.

I remember one time Jim Baker and Jeff Sanders got in this big fight. They weren't mad at each other, they just wanted to fight. After a while Jim tried to stop it, but Sanders wouldn't quit. Finally Cowboy [Joel Parrish] and Moonpie [Mike Wilson] had to break it up. Sanders showed up at practice the next day with two black eyes. He told the coaches he fell down the stairs. That was the kind of guys we had on defense.

190

There were so many great moments in 1975. When we played Florida in Jacksonville, I was standing next to coach [Bill] Pace when he called the famous Appleby-to-Washington pass. During Thursday's walk-through before the game we were told that they had a trick play for Richard. I can remember coach Pace saying, "Now is the time," when he sent in the play. Beating Florida was always fun, but that game was especially sweet.

I think our expectations in 1976 were pretty high. We had almost all of the offensive line coming back. We had our quarterbacks, Ray Goff and Matt Robinson, back. We lost Glynn Harrison at running back, but Kevin McLee was ready to be the starter, and we knew he was going to be good. We thought we could be one of the top teams in the country. And we were.

I'm an old guy now, but I still get goose bumps when I think of the Alabama game in 1976. The game was great. The party after the game was even better. They had a couple of shots at our defense early in the game and missed them. And when Matt Robinson scored right before halftime, it was over. Our defense dominated that game.

People remember the great second-half comeback we had on Florida that year [winning 41–27], but what I remember most is that our defense sort of

Bill Krug is considered to be one of the most instinctive defensive players ever to wear the Red and Black.

slept through the first half. I don't know what was wrong, but nothing seemed to work. The only guy who was playing worth a darn was Bobby Thompson, and he was running around screaming, "Wake up! Wake up!" He was screaming so much he was hoarse by halftime.

Well, we finally did wake up in the second half. We were down 27–13, but the offense scored pretty early in the third quarter. Then came the play that everybody remembers.

They had a fourth down deep in their own territory. I couldn't believe that they were going for it.

That year we would sometimes make up plays on defense in special situations. I remember I would tell Dicky Clark, our end, to do something a little different, and at first he was hesitant. But it got to the point where he could trust me, because it always seemed to work.

On that fourth-down play Dicky was supposed to take the quarterback, but I told him to take the dive and that I would take the quarterback. Then I looked over at Johnny Henderson, who was the cornerback, and I said, "Johnny, you're all by yourself." That meant that Johnny had the pitch man and nothing else.

It worked perfectly. The quarterback committed too early and pitched the ball to the running back. Nobody was fooled by it, and Johnny came up and made a great play and stopped him. We got the ball back and the game was over. Florida was still ahead, but at that moment they knew they were beat.

That game obviously upset Florida, because the next week they lost to Kentucky. We were at Auburn in the game that clinched the championship. When we heard that Florida had gotten beat, it was great. Everybody was so happy in the huddle. We were ahead 28–0, and there was no way that Auburn was coming back.

After clinching the SEC championship, we almost messed up against Georgia Tech and made their season. The score was 10–10, and we were driving to win, but we fumbled. It looked like Tech was going to tie us and cost us a shot at the national championship.

The conditions weren't great, so Tech was trying to run the clock out. I kept looking for inside running plays because we knew they weren't going to take any chances. They gave it to the fullback up the middle, and then suddenly the ball popped out and was on the ground in front of me—I fell on it.

Over the years I've gotten credit for stripping the ball loose, but I didn't. It was a linebacker named Brad Cescutti. I just happened to be in the right place at the right time. I'm not sure Brad got the credit he deserved for causing that fumble.

I wish we had played better in the Sugar Bowl against Pittsburgh [a 27–3 loss]. Yes, they were a very good team, but we weren't hitting on all cylinders that day. I didn't think everybody was on the same page when it came to that game. I still don't think they were that much better than us. It was a major disappointment, because it was our one shot at the national championship, and we let it slip away.

All I can say about my final season in 1977 was that at the end it was just brutal. I thought we had the potential to repeat as SEC champions. But we had a ton of injuries, and I think we turned the ball over about 55 times. You can't win doing that. By the end of the year, against Tech, we were on our fifth-string quarterback. We lost four out of our last five games [to finish 5–6]. It was really a frustrating way to finish my career.

People still ask me if I have any regrets leaving home and going to Georgia, and I tell them that going to Georgia was the greatest thing that ever happened to me. I learned so many things there that I used in my future life. I learned to never give up and that perseverance is the thing that will always get you through the tough times. I don't get discouraged easily if things aren't going well in my personal or professional life.

I'm back in Maryland now, but there is something that keeps pulling me back to Georgia. I hope someday to be able to move back. I am very jealous of all the guys who are able to go to the home games every week. I just love that atmosphere.

You can't put a dollar value on the relationships I developed at Georgia. I know that those relationships with my teammates will be there forever. As you get older that kind of thing means more and more to you. That's why Georgia will always be a special, special place.

193

Bill Krug was an All-SEC defensive back in 1976 and 1977. Today he is in the construction supply business and lives in Waldorf, Maryland.

KEVIN McLEE

Running Back
1974–1977

Basically, I went to Georgia because they were offering me an opportunity that not a whole lot of other people would give me.

I was highly recruited as a senior in high school in Uniontown, Pennsylvania, but then I had a bad knee injury. Schools like Ohio State, Michigan State, and Pittsburgh backed off then.

Sam Mrvos and Doc Ayers were still recruiting me for Georgia, and I guess they saw something they liked because they offered me a scholarship. I didn't know one iota about Georgia, but I did know that I wanted to get out of the cold weather in Pennsylvania.

Turns out that I really liked Athens. It was small and a whole lot like my hometown. It was quiet and peaceful.

In 1974 I played on the JV team with a bunch of good guys like Bill Krug and Ben Zambiasi. The varsity kind of struggled that year, but we knew that once we got up there things were going to be different.

Things really started clicking in 1975. I think I led the team with 10 touchdowns [and 806 yards] and was named the Sophomore of the Year in the SEC. [Editor's note: McLee was also named the SEC Rookie of the Year by the *Jacksonville Journal*.]

That was a fun season because we surprised some people. The only bad thing about it for me was the Auburn game where I broke my ankle. I had to sit out the Georgia Tech game and the Cotton Bowl against Arkansas.

Kevin McLee was the SEC Rookie of the Year in 1975 and the leading rusher on Georgia's 1976 SEC championship team.

A lot of great things happened in 1976, when I was a junior. It started back during the summer when all of those guys started shaving their heads. Moonpie Wilson got it started, and then I decided to be one of the first ones to do it, too. Some of the black guys on the team were hesitant at first, but they finally realized that it was fun and that it would bring us closer together as a team.

Not a whole lot has ever been said about this, but at that time there were some racial adjustments that had to be made on the team. Let's face it, when I got to Georgia there still weren't that many black players on the team. Our group in 1974 was basically the second wave of black players after the original four, led by Horace King and Richard Appleby.

There were problems with guys not talking things out . . . with holding resentments and bad feelings inside. I had grown up in the North, in an environment where it was never an issue, and I would try to mediate both sides.

The good news is that things worked out well. Everyone adjusted and everything worked out well. It made us a stronger team. That team in 1976 turned out to be a tight group of guys.

I think what we did that year carried over into future years, and over a period of time the issue dissolved. This was just something that had always been on my mind and something about the Georgia program that I thought needed to be discussed. I'm glad to say that it all had a happy ending.

The game that I will always remember in 1976 is when we went to play Florida in Jacksonville. We were getting beat [27–13] at halftime, and we were hanging our heads in the locker room. Coach Dooley came in and really got after us. He told us that this was our opportunity to *be* something. He said that opportunities like this don't come around very often and that we had to find a way to go out and win that game.

Coach Dooley knew we had a better team than Florida. One thing we did was change our cleats in order to run a little better on that sandy surface. We dominated the second half and won [41–27]. That was the best game we ever played as a team.

That was really a good team, and I thought we were good enough to win the national championship. But Pittsburgh got us in the Sugar Bowl.

I'm afraid there is not a whole lot I can say about 1977, my senior year, because I stayed hurt the whole season. We had lost a lot of good players from the year before, and we were really in a rebuilding stage.

I just remember that we fumbled the ball a lot that year. I think we led the nation in fumbles. There were three or four games we should have won, but we just didn't make the plays.

I really enjoyed my time at Georgia. I got a chance to play with great players and work with some great coaches. Everybody was so good to me, including people like Frank Sinkwich. When I was a senior I broke his rushing record, and he was very kind to me.

I remember coach John Kasay, who was a great guy, and his little boy [John], who would go to practice and hold the ball for our kicker, Allan Leavitt. That little boy is now a kicker for the Carolina Panthers.

I was a pretty lucky guy. I had a mother—Elaine Murray McLee—who was known all over Pennsylvania because of her support of athletics. She was a special lady. Now I have a son who is going to be a linebacker at West Virginia. He's much bigger than his dad.

I had a chance to play football at a great place like Georgia and be a part of a special group of guys at a special time in my life. I'll never forget it.

Kevin McLee was an All-SEC running back in 1975 and 1976. He left Georgia after 1977 as the Bulldogs' all-time rusher (2,581 yards). Today he is No. 5 on the Bulldogs' career rushing list. McLee lives in West Covina, California, where he is in private business.

MAC McWHORTER

Guard

1971–1973

W<small>HEN YOUR NAME IS</small> M<small>C</small>W<small>HORTER</small>, people say you have no choice—
you're going to play for Georgia.

There have been eight McWhorters to play for Georgia, and I was the last. My great-uncle, Bob McWhorter, was the first football All-American in the history of Georgia. The athletic dorm at Georgia is named after him. My dad signed a football scholarship to play at Georgia but was drafted by the Milwaukee Braves and decided to play baseball.

So I guess you'd have to say that when it came time for me to go to college, my path was pretty certain. Oh, I thought about Georgia Tech, but that thought was very fleeting, I can assure you. I chose to be a Bulldog, and I have never regretted it.

There were so many people who helped me at Georgia that I can hardly count them all. I came there as a linebacker. I played freshman ball in 1969 and got redshirted in 1970, and the next thing I knew, they were moving me to offensive guard.

I'll never forget that when I made the move, John Kasay, our strength and conditioning coach, came up to me and said, "If you ever think you're going to play in the SEC at guard then you better live with me."

So I did, and he worked me to death. I cussed that man every day, but he bulked me up to around 230 pounds, and in 1973 I made All-SEC. I would have never played as well as I did or accomplished as much as I did without

John Kasay. That's why I named my oldest daughter after him [Kasey]. I think there are about six players who have named children after him.

Coach Erk Russell was really special to all of us. I was an offensive player, and he coached the defense; still, he really touched me. My parents still have a handwritten letter he wrote them when I graduated. They had it laminated, and it still hangs on a wall in their home. He coached guys hard, and he was very demanding, but he had this way about him that let you know that he really cared.

There are so many memories I hardly know where to start. I was a backup guard in 1971, but in the Auburn game in November, Royce Smith hurt his knee. Now, Royce was an All-American and a great, great player, but I had to take his place for the rest of that game with Auburn and then start on Thanksgiving night against Georgia Tech.

Everybody remembers that game because Jimmy Poulos went over the top to score with just a few seconds left. What they don't know is that, with the game on the line and time running out, the coaches called "44 lead," which was an isolation play right over me, the sophomore guard. To this day I'm convinced they thought Royce was still in there instead of me. Thank God Jimmy got into the end zone and we won the game.

199

Later on that year we played in the Gator Bowl, which matched coach [Vince] Dooley against his brother, Bill, who was the head coach at North Carolina. We were 10–1 and had a pretty good football team. What I remember is that coach Dooley *really* wanted to win that game. He stuck us in a Hilton way out of town and didn't let us have cars or anything.

Well, one night a bunch of us decided to have a party in our own room. So we got a huge suitcase and took a cab down to the package store. We proceeded to fill that suitcase up with the beverage of our choice. Then we decided, what the heck . . . we'll just ice down the beer in the suitcase so it will be cold when we get back to the hotel.

So we snuck back into the hotel and got to the elevator. We almost made it, but when the elevator door opened, who do you suppose was inside? It was coach Dooley and Barbara, Erk and Jean, and Pat Hodgson and his wife, Nancy.

It was one of those huge elevators, so they insisted that we get on board. Nobody was saying anything about the suitcase. I got as far into the corner as I could, and I noticed that Erk was standing next to me. I looked down and water was starting to drip from the corner of the suitcase!

Still, nobody said a word. The coaches' floor came first, so Erk held the door and let everybody off while the players and the suitcase stayed on. As he walked out the door, Erk said, "You boys have fun."

The elevator door was almost shut when suddenly in popped a hand with a cigar in it. It was Erk's, and he said, "One more thing, Mac. Next time you go wash your clothes, make sure to dry them before putting them back into the suitcase!" He smiled again and let the door shut.

That was his way of letting us know that we hadn't gotten away with anything.

I remember that at the first of every season coach Dooley would lay down the law. He would list a bunch of "establishments" in Athens where players could not go because previous players had had trouble there. Then coach Dooley would leave, and Erk would come and tell us to add "Cooper's" to that list of off-limits places. Cooper's, you see, was *his* place, and he didn't want us in there.

Then there was the annual party after spring practice, where freshmen would get "initiated." Well, I guess the statute of limitations has run out on this one. Back then the juniors were in charge of getting the "product" for the party. So we would go around to all the different establishments in Athens, and we would tell them what it was for. They were more than happy to make a donation.

I still have a picture at home from that spring. I was living over in married housing, and we had cases of beer stacked up to the ceiling! I was on top of the stack. It was just unbelievable the fun we had!

We struggled in my last two years—1972 and 1973. I remember in 1973 we were playing at Vanderbilt and not doing very well. We couldn't run the ball because they had the line of scrimmage stacked. I looked up on one play and there was a linebacker in front of me and the safety was right behind him. At halftime coach Dooley was really upset.

"We're not running the ball the way Georgia is supposed to run it, and we're not going to throw until we do," he said.

That same year we beat Tennessee up there, after we got a lucky break. They faked a punt, and we got possession deep in their territory. The ball was on about the 10-yard line, and Andy Johnson was supposed to run a down-the-line option. When you're on the offensive line you don't see a whole lot, and the next thing I knew Andy was in the end zone, and we'd won the game

Mac McWhorter, an All-SEC guard in 1973, is one of eight McWhorters to play football at Georgia.

[35–31]. We looked at film the next day and saw that Andy had actually fumbled the ball, and that it bounced right back up into his arms. We couldn't believe it.

I'm a Georgia boy, but Bill Curry at Georgia Tech gave me my first job in college coaching. I remember my first game with Georgia as a Tech assistant. It was in 1980. Georgia was really good, and we were really bad, but I was all excited about going back to my alma mater and being back in Sanford Stadium.

Well, it never occurred to me that some of the Georgia people might not be happy to see me come back. When we got off the bus at the railroad track end of the stadium, all hell broke loose. These people were throwing things and calling me everything, including a traitor. All of the players scurried down the hill, and we finally got into the locker room. Then they looked at me.

All I could say was, "Hey, guys. I'm on your side now."

I'm lucky in that I eventually got to go back to Georgia as an assistant coach. Part of me thought I would just retire there and coach offensive line. At least that was my hope, because I do love Athens. But it didn't work out that way. That's just the nature of our business.

I am so grateful for the years I did have at Georgia. If I hadn't spent those five years at the University of Georgia, I certainly wouldn't have done the things I've done since then. Everything that I have accomplished, professionally and socially, I can credit to the time I spent at Georgia.

I tell my players today that their college experience is just a blur—it goes by so fast. Still, it will be the foundation of your life.

And like we used to say—there is nothing like being a Bulldog on Saturday night. That is one thing that will never change.

Mac McWhorter was an All-SEC guard in 1973 and the offensive captain of Georgia's 1973 team. McWhorter came back to Georgia as an assistant coach for five seasons (1991–1995). Today McWhorter is an assistant coach at Texas.

TOM NASH

Tackle
1969–1971

BECAUSE MY DAD WAS AN ALL-AMERICAN at Georgia, some people believe that I basically had no choice but to go to Georgia. The truth is I had lots of choices. Daddy told me that it was my decision and that I should make it.

I looked pretty closely at Georgia, Georgia Tech, and Auburn. I did not look at Alabama because Bear Bryant once said that if an offensive lineman had any teeth, then he was probably blocking too high.

Like I said, Daddy didn't try to steer me in any particular direction, but I do remember us going to a Georgia–Georgia Tech game in Atlanta. We were guests of Georgia Tech and sitting up in their press box. And while the game was going on, Daddy was ever-so-quietly singing "Glory, Glory to Old Georgia" under his breath. He couldn't help himself.

Seriously, he would have supported my decision no matter what it was. But everything in my life at that time pointed toward my going to Georgia.

Coach [Vince] Dooley was nice enough to do some of the recruiting himself, and he and I developed a very good relationship. Ultimately I decided that given what I wanted to do—which was practice law in the state of Georgia—going to Georgia would seem like a pretty good choice.

When he thought I might be getting full of myself, my daddy always used to say, "Remember, there is always a bigger cat than Tom."

When I got to Georgia in the fall of 1968, I knew exactly what he was talking about.

When you get to college as a football player, all of a sudden you realize that everybody is just as big as you are, and everybody is just as fast as you are. You really need to step it up a notch if you're going to compete.

My freshman year was especially tough. The varsity was out there winning an SEC championship while the freshman coaches were trying to find out how many of us could really play. The competition was at a whole different level. What I found out was that some of the guys with the biggest names weren't always the best football players.

I was lucky enough to become a starter at tackle in 1969. We basically had a sophomore offensive line, but we had a lot of other really good players. After winning the championship the year before, the expectations were pretty high, but we had lost a lot at the skill positions from 1968. Our youth caught up with us, and we really struggled going down the stretch of that season [and finished 5–5–1].

The 1970 season really wasn't any better [5–5]. The only real highlight was that we went down to Auburn and beat them [31–17] when we really weren't supposed to. It's hard to explain those two years. We just had a bunch of tough losses, and our inexperience really seemed to hurt us.

But it all came together in 1971, except for that one afternoon when we played Auburn in Sanford Stadium. [Editor's note: Georgia was 9–0 and ranked No. 3 when it played No. 5 Auburn, also 9–0, at Sanford Stadium on November 13. Auburn won the game 35–20.]

I often think that if we had played that game in Auburn, we might have won. The excitement level was so high that everybody was way past the point of being mentally prepared. It was the most exciting event I have ever been involved in . . . even though we lost it.

The great thing that year was that we finally beat Tech over there on Thanksgiving night. The thing I remember most is that when we were behind with about two minutes left, Andy Johnson came in the huddle and said, "We're going to score." And everybody believed him.

People still talk a lot about the fourth-down pass from Andy to Mike Greene that kept that last drive alive. Many years later we had a reunion of that team, and coach John Kasay said, "Yeah, we had a quarterback who can't throw and called a pass to a tight end who can't catch. And it worked!" Everybody in the room broke up.

Tom Nash followed in the footsteps of his father, Tom Sr., who was also an All-American at Georgia.

That play worked, and once we got close, I knew we were going to score the touchdown. That was the thing I really appreciated about our offense. When we got close to the goal line we could say, "OK, here we come." I think everybody in the stadium knew where that play was going. We got Jimmy Poulos just enough room to get him over the top to win the game [28–24].

The main thing I remember about that night, however, is that my father had a heart attack during the game. He had to go to the hospital, but he recovered from that one.

After my last game, I played in the Senior Bowl and then got drafted in the last round by Philadelphia. They said they drafted me so late because they knew I wanted to go to law school. Pro ball didn't work out, so I worked for a law firm for one year and then went to law school at Georgia.

I'm really one of the lucky ones. Not only did I get to play football at Georgia and go to law school there, but I have been able to have an almost continuous relationship with the university by serving on the athletic board. And the more you're around Georgia, the more you appreciate what a special place it truly is.

The friendships I made at Georgia have been with me my entire life. My daughter, Jessica, is in law school at Virginia, and she is starting to make professional connections with people who went to law school with me. Those kinds of relationships are a lifetime blessing, and that's what Georgia gave to me.

I'm glad my daddy let me make my own decision to come to Georgia. It turned out to be the best one I've ever made.

Tom Nash was a three-year starter at tackle and was an All-SEC selection in 1970 and 1971. Today, he is an attorney in Savannah.

MATT ROBINSON

Quarterback
1974–1976

GROWING UP I REALLY LOVED BASEBALL MORE than football. In fact, my goal was to go to Arizona State on a baseball scholarship. I was drafted by the Reds out of high school, but what I really wanted to do was go to college and play both sports.

For a while there, I was really thinking about going to Tennessee. Bill Battle was the coach at the time. In fact, I called the coach who was recruiting me to tell him I was leaning in that direction, but the coach never called me back. After I had made up my mind to go to Georgia, coach Battle called and wanted to know what was going on, because they thought I was coming. I told coach Battle what happened, and I think he got pretty upset with that recruiting coach.

It's funny, I came to Georgia with Ray Goff, and both of us were baseball players and both of us were planning to play both sports. What we should have done was agree that we were both going to play baseball in the spring. But because we were competing for the quarterback job, both of us were afraid to go play baseball and miss spring football. We were afraid the other guy was going to get a leg up. So I never played another inning of baseball.

Ray was one of the few freshmen that made it up to the varsity in 1973. Andy Johnson was a senior quarterback, and everybody knew the position would stay his. But we knew that the following spring there would be a competition for that job.

The 1974 season was a strange one. Bill Pace came in as offensive coordinator and installed the veer. The offense turned out to be pretty good, as we were scoring about 30 points a game, but the defense was giving up about 34 points a game. Coach [Vince Dooley] said we were scoring "too fast." I'll never forget him saying that—I thought that was the idea.

There aren't a whole lot of great memories from that season because we were 6–6, but I do remember us having to drive the length of the field at the end of the homecoming game to beat Vanderbilt [38–31]. I was able to score the winning touchdown, and I remember that was a pretty emotional moment. I was just a sophomore. It was a great feeling.

Everybody still talks about playing Georgia Tech in the wind and the rain and the cold. I was so cold my teeth were literally chattering in the huddle. They kicked our butts, and then we played Miami of Ohio in the Tangerine Bowl. They beat us, too. It was not a happy time to be at Georgia, that's for sure.

In 1975 it was pretty obvious that we were really going to commit to the veer and running the football. As it turned out, I broke one of my ribs before camp started, and I was out for a while. During that time Ray got the job and stayed there, because he was really playing well.

When Ray was in high school, his team [Moultrie] threw the ball about 28 or 30 times a game. I thought Ray was a passing quarterback when he got to Georgia, but he turned out to be a great running quarterback in his last two years.

In 1975 I basically came into the game when it was obvious that we were going to pass. That's why I was lucky enough to be on the field for one of the greatest plays ever, when we beat Florida in Jacksonville.

All season we had run a play where Richard Appleby, who was a really good tight end, would take a handoff from me and run a sweep around the end. Most of the time we made good yardage from it.

But the week of the Florida game, coach Pace put in a wrinkle. I would hand the ball to Richard, and instead of running it, he would throw a pass to Gene Washington. We had played around with the idea before, but that week the play became part of the game plan.

We were behind 7–3, and our offense just couldn't get anything going. Florida had a great offense, but every time they threatened, our defense found a way to get them stopped. There wasn't a whole lot of time left when the play came in.

Matt Robinson, the "passing quarterback" on Georgia's 1976 SEC championship team, went on to a successful pro career.

The key to the whole play is to really sell the run. Your guys have to make it look like a run block, and then make sure they protect and give Appleby enough time to throw.

Richard started at the left end and came back to the right to get the hand-off from me. A pulling guard went with him for protection.

It was kind of like a slow-motion moment. It was also like a golf shot where your eyes go from the ball in flight to the hole and back. My eyes went from the ball to Gene and back to the ball. The rotation of it seemed so slow.

Gene was so far behind the secondary that if he caught the ball it was going to be a touchdown. When I saw that he had it, I felt the crowd erupt. It was neat to beat those guys [10–7] when nobody thought we could.

We kind of knew going in that 1976 had a chance to be a special year. Normally in a class of freshmen only about 10 or 12 make it all the way through, but if I'm not mistaken, about 22 guys in my freshman class were still there in 1976, and about 17 or 18 of them were starters.

That team bonded at the beginning of training camp, when Mike Wilson and Ken Helms shaved their heads. We saw them and laughed, and after about 15 minutes it was like a shark feeding frenzy. They would take those electric clippers and run them down the middle of your head, so you couldn't change your mind. The next thing you know they've done 28 guys.

Right after that we went to practice, and we noticed that coach [Erk] Russell was not there. Coach Russell is the original bald man, and we wanted him to see this. After a few minutes, through the gate came a figure wearing a full-blown, shoulder-length blond wig. It was coach Russell.

What was great was that every time we won a game, one of the coaches agreed to have his head shaved. They were really starting to get into it. Finally, coach Dooley said that if we won the SEC championship, he would shave his head. None of us thought he would really do it.

We did win the championship, but honestly a lot of us forgot that coach Dooley had said that. But when we had the team banquet that year, out at Poss's, he showed up and it was obvious he had a wig on. Coach Dooley got up and gave one of the most emotional speeches I've ever heard, and at the end he pulled the wig off to show his bald head. The room almost collapsed from people laughing and yelling so hard. It's an incredible memory.

People ask me about my favorite game at Georgia. That's easy: the Alabama game in Athens in 1976.

I will always remember the sequence of plays right before the end of the first half. There was no score, and we were down near the Alabama goal line. Time was running out, and I was trying to get the play in from coach Pace.

I got up under the center to take the snap, but it wasn't the center. It was Joel Parrish, the guard! He waved me off, and I finally got under the center.

Coach Pace was trying to signal in a rollout pass, but I missed the sign and thought we were supposed to run the option to the right. I called the wrong play and ran out to the right, but the offensive line blocked them so well that I scored. That just shows you how important coaching really is!

After we scored, the defense shut them down. They were so dominant that day. The excitement before the game and the celebration after the game provided the greatest college atmosphere for a football game that I had ever seen.

We went on to win the SEC championship and beat Tech, which always makes it a great year.

It's hard to say what happened in the Sugar Bowl against Pittsburgh. Our plan was to go right at them, because they had so much speed on defense. But nothing we tried worked. It was a tough way to end a college career.

I was fortunate to play professional football for a while, but nothing is quite like those days at Georgia, because they were so much fun. We were young and thought we were invincible, but I learned many lessons, too. One of those was not to waste time in your life, even when you're having fun.

211

I look back at coach Dooley and, at the time I was at Georgia, I didn't agree with a lot of the things he did or a lot of the decisions he made. But the older I got, the smarter he got. I always had a wonderful relationship with my father. He was my best friend, and now I have that same relationship with coach Dooley. I'm proud to say that he remains one of my best friends to this day.

There can never be another relationship like the one you have with the guys you played football with. We experienced things together that other people will never experience. The group of players who spent four years together will always be very special to me.

I look back on my life, and I realize that different decisions could have sent me in some different directions. But I do know this: I never once second-guessed my decision to go to Georgia. And I never will.

> Matt Robinson led the SEC in passing in 1974. He went on to play professionally in the NFL and USFL. Today he lives in Jacksonville, Florida, and is in the construction business.

MIXON ROBINSON

Defensive End
1969–1971

I GUESS IF I SHOULD THANK ANYBODY that I went to Georgia, it would be my buddy, Bob McDavid. When I was a senior at Lanier High in Macon, Bob and I would go on recruiting visits together.

By the time we hit the road, I pretty much had made up my mind that I was going to Alabama, Duke, or Georgia.

Bob and I went to Alabama, and man, it was 100 percent football all the time. I was an OK high school player, but nothing great. I thought that might be a bit too much for me.

Then Bob and I went to Duke, and I kind of liked it. I had a brother at Harvard and a sister at Vanderbilt, so it would be kind of in line with what they were doing academically. The guys were pretty nice.

So Bob and I were flying home—it was my first big jet flight—and I told him I might want to go to school at Duke.

He said I was crazy—that I'd never have any fun because I would be studying all the time. He said, "You need to think real hard about that."

Well, Bob must have told the Georgia coaches, because a couple of days later coach [Erk] Russell called. So did coach John Donaldson, who was recruiting me. Let me tell you what—coach Donaldson was a helluva recruiter.

So I started thinking about it, and I decided to play at Georgia. My daddy was a big Georgia football fan, and I think one of his biggest thrills was being able to drive up on Saturday and watch me play. I already had a brother, Don, playing at Tech, so Dad had some weekends when he could watch two games.

212

Mixon Robinson was an All-SEC defensive end in 1971 and became a successful orthopedic surgeon in Athens.

At that point I didn't know for sure if I wanted to go into medicine, but I knew I could get a good education at Georgia. They were always talking about Tommy Lawhorne, who became the valedictorian of the 1968 senior class. He was going on to medical school at Johns Hopkins. Besides, my future wife was going to school there, so there were many things pulling me toward Georgia.

I will never forget my freshman season in 1968. We had a freshman coach named Dick Wood who was one of the meanest, most ruthless guys I've ever been around. He ran off a ton of players, and he tried to run me off. Back then they could afford to have more injuries because they signed so many players. Once we made it through freshman year, though, everything got easier.

My sophomore year I was a backup tight end, and I played in about half the games. It didn't turn out to be a very good year.

Our 1969 team started 3–0, and we were No. 5 in the country when we went down to Jackson to play Ole Miss and Archie Manning. We knocked Manning out of the game and were sure we were going to win. But they bandaged him back up, and he came out in the middle of the third quarter and beat us 25–17. Let me say this: people talk about Archie's boys, Peyton and Eli, and how good they are. The boys are nice players, but they are not better than their daddy. Archie Manning could throw and run, and he could carry an entire team.

Then in the spring of 1970, I got moved to defensive end. Coach Russell could see something in me that I didn't see. The first thing he did was put me on the goal-line defense. He lined up behind the offensive end and said, "I want you to get here as fast as you can."

That was the one thing I could really do—get to a spot in a hurry—so I started playing goal-line defense. I got to play both ways most of the year.

The 1970 season may have been the most difficult time ever for coach Dooley at Georgia. I think we lost three of our first four games, and going back to the season before, we had a stretch where we were 1–7–1.

I was still playing defense when halfway through the season all the tight ends went down, and I moved back there. John Kasay became my personal coach, and he worked me really hard.

I wasn't a very good tight end, but I did have a moment that almost turned into something special. In 1970 we were leading Florida 17–10 and were driving to their goal. I caught a pass near the goal line and stumbled just short of a touchdown. If I had gotten into the end zone we might have won the game, but on the next play Jack Youngblood forced a fumble and recovered it. Florida beat us 24–17.

The only wonderful memory from 1970 was when we went down to Auburn and beat Pat Sullivan and Terry Beasley. We had no business beating that team, but our locker room was as emotional a place as I've ever been around. Erk gave his usual speech, and then a guy named Ronnie Rogers, who was a senior guard, gave one of the most emotional speeches I've ever heard. Then we went out and beat those guys bad.

Thank God for 1971. I got moved to defense and stayed there. I loved it because we had a really good defense. We had four shutouts, and in five other games we gave up one touchdown or less. The only bad game we had was against Auburn, and they beat us pretty good in Athens [35–20]. Still, that year made my career at Georgia. I will never forget being on that team.

The other reason I'm glad I went to Georgia is that I got to meet Dr. Butch Mulherin, our orthopedic surgeon. Once I met him and watched him work, I knew what I wanted to do with my life. And I knew that I would always want to live in Athens.

So in that sense I'm one of the lucky ones. Not only did I get to play at Georgia, but I now live in Athens and still get to work with the football players of today. I get to be around a university and a town I really love.

If I had gone to Duke, I probably wouldn't have married my wife. I probably wouldn't have gotten into medical school. I might have wound up being a football coach. Now that would have been interesting.

When I got out of medical school, it helped that I had played football at Georgia. People had a connection with me, and I had a connection with them. Those kinds of relationships have been a big part of my life and my career.

Going to Georgia and being a Bulldog has been a very important part of my life. I can never give back to Georgia everything it has given me.

215

Dr. Mixon Robinson was an All-SEC defensive end in 1971. Today, he is an orthopedic surgeon living in Athens.

BUZY ROSENBERG

Defensive Back
1970–1972

COLLEGE FOOTBALL WAS SO DIFFERENT back in 1969 when I was a freshman at Georgia. Today, people follow recruiting so closely that they know basically what every kid can do by the time he arrives on campus. When I was a freshman, I'm not sure anybody knew what I could do—including me.

I wasn't tall [5'9"] and I wasn't all that fast, but I was quick and I could jump. I think I caught the coaches' attention one day when they were asking players to jump up and touch the crossbar of the goal posts. The fact that I could do it at 5'9" sort of made them notice me.

Then one day before my sophomore season, the team was practicing punt returns. Coach Jim Pyburn was leading the drills, so I asked him to let me try running back a punt.

"Do you really think you can run back a punt?" he asked. I just smiled and told him I'd like to try.

While the ball was in the air, I looked over at coach Pyburn and said, "Hey, Coach, this one's for you." I took it back about 70 yards. That's how I became a punt returner.

My sophomore season started out with a bang—the first punt I touched against Tulane I took back 68 yards for a touchdown. It was an important moment for me, because until you get out there, you really don't know if you can play with the big boys or not.

Buzy Rosenberg, seen here returning a punt for a touchdown against Oregon State in 1971, was small in stature, but became one of Georgia's best defensive backs.

Unfortunately, we lost the game [17–14]. That would be the beginning of a very strange year. We finished 5–5 with a team I thought had a chance to be much better. But we did make one great memory when we went over to Auburn and beat one of the best teams in the nation [31–17].

Nobody gave us a chance to beat Auburn, who had the great Pat Sullivan and Terry Beasley. And I would be less than honest if I didn't admit that I had my doubts as well. Usually in my pregame prayer I just asked God not to let anybody get hurt and for my team to be able to compete. On the day of the Auburn game, I asked for the same thing, but I added, "And please, God, don't let us get beat by more than 21 points and don't let me get embarrassed."

I don't know if they were overconfident. I think they had only lost one game and were ranked in the top 10 [Editor's note: Auburn was 7–1 and ranked No. 8 when it played Georgia on November 14, 1970.] But we played the game of our lives and beat those guys.

A year later Auburn got their revenge. In 1971 we were undefeated and had a chance to play for the national championship when Auburn came to Athens and beat us [35–20]. Pat Sullivan had a super day, and because of it he won the Heisman Trophy. That day was one of the greatest college atmospheres I've ever been a part of. I just wish we had played better.

I'll bet if you talk to the guys who played in 1970 and 1971, they'll tell you that one of their greatest thrills at Georgia was beating Auburn in 1970. They'll also tell you that losing to Auburn in 1971 was one of their greatest disappointments.

I'm 53 years old now, but I still get asked about the Oregon State game, which was the first game of the 1971 season. Before the game I told Larry West, who was my designated little brother on the team, that I felt really good. I said, "Larry, when I score today I'm going to throw up my hands, and you'll know that I'm waving to you." [Editor's note: On September 11, 1971, Buzy Rosenberg set a Georgia record when he returned five punts for 202 yards and two touchdowns in a 56–25 win over Oregon State. That record still stands today.]

It was just one of those days that you wish could go on forever, because everything was working.

That 1971 team was really good. We played 12 games, and in 9 of them we gave up seven points or less. If we hadn't lost to Auburn, then we probably would have played Nebraska in the Orange Bowl for the national championship. I'm not saying we would have beaten them, because that was one of the best Nebraska teams ever, but I would have loved to have gotten that chance.

We came back to beat Georgia Tech. Andy Johnson played the game of his life and led us down the field. And Jimmy Poulos who, for my money, was one of the best running backs we've ever had at Georgia, went over the top.

There is not a lot positive I can say about my senior year, in 1972. I had torn ligaments in my right foot in the Gator Bowl in the previous season, and I didn't completely recover. We lost a lot of good players off that 1971 team, and we just couldn't seem to get it together. We were 7–4, which is not a bad year, but I had hoped that we would make one more run at an SEC championship.

After my football career was over, I came back to Georgia and went to graduate school for a year. I also worked with the freshmen on the football team. That's how I got to know guys like Bill Krug, who would go on to become a great player.

The only regret I have is that sometimes I wish I had stayed with coaching, because I love working with young people who want to learn. I apply the lessons I learned as a player at Georgia to my life every day.

I remember the motivation of Erk Russell. Coach Russell was a man's man; an honest man; a trustworthy man. He was willing to give you 100 percent of everything he had, and we were willing to do the same for him.

I knew I wasn't the fastest guy in the world, but coach Russell would look at me and say, "I don't care, Rosenberg. As far as I'm concerned you're the fastest man on the field." And you know what, after that I *believed* I was the fastest man on the field. And because of that I think I outran some people I shouldn't have.

219

I still use a lot of coach [Vince] Dooley's sayings today in my business life. When I face a tough situation that I don't quite know how to handle, I think about how coach Dooley would deal with it.

To play football at Georgia was absolutely an honor for me. Many of the friendships I made in those four years are still with me today. You have a very special relationship with people who fought with you down in the trenches.

I don't consider myself a former Georgia Bulldog. Once you are a Bulldog you remain one the rest of your life. That is something that never changes.

Buzy Rosenberg was an All-SEC defensive back in 1970 and 1971. He still holds the Georgia record for punt return yardage in a single game for returning five punts for 202 yards and two touchdowns in a 1971 game against Oregon State. Today Rosenberg works for a beverage distributor in Jacksonville, Florida.

IN MEMORIAM

ROYCE SMITH

Guard
1949–2004

Eᴅɪᴛᴏʀ's ɴᴏᴛᴇ: Royce Smith became the classic American success story when he arrived at the University of Georgia in 1971. Some details of that story were included in a recent press release by Georgia's Sports Information Department:

His success story actually began as a ninth grader at Groves High School in Garden City, Georgia, on the outskirts of Savannah. On the advice of his high school football coach, Jack Miller, Smith gave up basketball and completely dedicated himself to football.

Smith began lifting weights three hours a day because he wanted to be in the best physical shape possible for football. After his junior year at Groves High, Georgia assistant coach John Donaldson came to visit. Donaldson told Smith that Georgia had some interest in him.

"I couldn't believe it," Smith said at the time. "I couldn't figure out why. I knew I couldn't play college football, and I wondered why they were wasting their time on me."

But Miller told him he could play college football if he worked for it. Smith took him at his word.

Royce Smith was so dedicated to off-season conditioning that coach Vince Dooley once banned him from the weight room. An All-American in 1971, Smith died suddenly in 2004 at the age of 54.

"On Saturday nights my senior year I went down to the weight room and worked out," Smith said. "I didn't have time for anything but football. All I could think about was playing football for Georgia. It seemed like the next place to heaven to me."

Other than the early contact from Georgia, the University of Richmond was the only other school that had showed interest in Smith. But Donaldson and Georgia coach Vince Dooley still liked the way he played football, and Donaldson made the trip to Garden City to sign Smith.

He arrived in Athens weighing 190 pounds, and the Georgia coaches quickly determined the best chance for him to play would be at offensive guard. He recommitted himself to the weight room and rose to 6'3", 250 pounds, but he could still run the 40-yard dash in 4.8 seconds—the fastest for a Georgia lineman. And he could bench press a then-Georgia record of 430 pounds. Smith was so dedicated to weight lifting that at times the Georgia coaches had to force him to leave the weight room.

Royce Smith, who thought he wasn't good enough to play college football, became a three-year starter at guard for Georgia and in 1971 was an All-American. He received the Jacobs Award, which goes to the SEC's best blocker. He was drafted by the New Orleans Saints in the first round of the 1972 NFL draft.

Royce Smith was scheduled for an interview for this book when he died suddenly on January 22, 2004, at the age of 54.

Following are the reflections of Smith's daughter, Kaysie, and his son, Royce Jr., on what being a Georgia Bulldog meant to their father.

KAYSIE SMITH

I grew up with my dad and brother [Royce Jr.]. I guess I was quite a bit of a tomboy, always trying to keep up with my brother. Since my father coached my brother's Little League football team, I was always there. That was the phase in my life when I wanted to be a football player.

Looking back on it now, it was probably because I wanted my father's attention. It was somewhere around that time that I realized my dad had named me after one of his college football coaches, John Kasay. I knew that playing football for Georgia must have been a very important part of his life.

I guess I was maybe five years old when my father took me to my first G-Day game. I can remember him and all of his old teammates actually playing in a game. I remember playing with UGA, the mascot, and watching Dad play while he wore No. 66. After the game my father came to the sidelines and picked me up. He was hot and sweaty in his football pads, but I remember thinking how "cool" Dad was.

When my dad moved us to Claxton, Georgia, he became a football coach there as well. Everyone was impressed to have a Bulldog and NFL player as a football coach. I was 13 years old then, and my dream of being a football player had changed. I was now a cheerleader, so I still got to spend time with my father and my brother, who played on the team.

I think that football taught my father many lessons. He learned that dedication and hard work will take you wherever you want to go. Those fundamental values followed him all of his life. He became a school teacher. He was a father who loved his children and put our best interests close to his heart.

He was an avid cyclist who trained for months and accomplished many challenging bike rides. Not only did he succeed in numerous ways, but he took his knowledge of football and taught it to other young football players so they could fulfill their dreams.

My father was a wonderful man. He had a huge heart and would have done anything for anyone. He was a great father, and I cannot thank him enough for everything he taught me. As I write this, I imagine my father is riding his bike through the streets of heaven watching over my brother and me.

And I know in my heart that he loved Georgia, because Georgia gave him the opportunity to live out his dreams.

ROYCE SMITH JR.

My dad was one of the best to ever play at the University of Georgia. I say this because he did not have the raw talent that other players did. He earned everything he got.

One story that sticks out in my mind is about how committed my dad was to be the best he could be for the Georgia football team. He borrowed a key to the Georgia weight room from an assistant coach. After he finished the workout he went to the store and had a copy made. This way he could work out without "permission."

223

My dad knew he had to work harder than anyone else to compete at that level of football. I really think he underestimated his talent, but it only made him work that much harder.

Coach Dooley caught him one day and told him to stop working out so much, because he did not want all that extra weight on my dad. Coach Dooley thought it would slow him down. That sounds funny today, but the training back in the late sixties did not incorporate much weight training.

But Dad kept working out because somehow he knew that the weights would only make him better. He still ran a 4.77 in the 40. That was pretty good for a lineman back then.

At my dad's funeral I had a chance to talk to a lot of his former teammates. I was shocked at how many of them showed up. He was the captain of the 1971 team, and I knew it was a great tribute to a great man. I could see the respect they had for their fallen leader. My dad was a born leader and people were drawn to him. Dad was an All-American that same year, but he told me that being voted as the 1971 team captain was a greater honor than any personal award.

I know my dad was proud of his accomplishments at Georgia. He was always a Bulldog at heart.

Royce Smith was the captain of Georgia's 1971 team. He was an All-SEC guard in 1970 and 1971 and a consensus All-American in 1971.

MIKE WILSON

Tackle
1974–1976

THE AMAZING THING TO ME about my time at Georgia was that it almost never happened. When I got to Georgia in 1973 I hated football. By the time I left I loved it again. That was one of the many things that Georgia gave me in my four years there.

I think Georgia found out about me by accident. Coach [Vince] Dooley and coach Mike [Castronis] were up in the Gainesville area recruiting Tommy West [who would later go on to Tennessee]. I played at South Hall against Tommy's team at Gainesville. They must have spotted me, because I got a letter from them the following week.

When I was a senior at South Hall we got a new head coach who was a Clemson man. So we made a road trip there, and he showed me everything. Clemson recruited me really, really hard.

But I knew Georgia was the place for me. It was only 45 minutes away, and so many of the people I knew were Georgia fans. I'll never forget the day I made my commitment to Georgia. Clemson immediately sent some coaches down to the school and tried to talk me out of it. I didn't budge despite their pressure. It was the smartest move I've ever made.

But it didn't start out that way. When I was a senior in high school, the coach made us practice three hours a day and just beat up on each other. Even on the day before a game we were hitting. It really took all the fun out of the game.

When I started playing freshman ball at Georgia it was more of the same. It seemed like we went through two-a-days for a month. I was thinking,

"Here is the same old crap again." I just didn't like the game anymore. In fact, I quit five times in my first quarter. Every time I would quit and go home, coach Mike would come get me.

Finally, after the last time I quit, coach Dooley asked me to stay after practice so we could talk. We went over to the grandstand around the track, and we talked for about an hour or so. At that point I still didn't like football, and I was thinking about getting on with my life and being a carpenter or something.

Coach Dooley understood what I was going through. He told me to stick it out through this first quarter, because it would get better. He was right. I stayed, things got better, and everything turned out pretty well for me. So I owe a lot to coach Dooley and his patience. I guess he saw something in me that I really didn't know about. He knew that I could play and contribute to the team.

When I was a sophomore, in 1974, I played mostly on defense. Coach [Erk] Russell asked me to help him out, and I was glad to do it. But our defense was pretty mangled up that year. We really didn't stop people the way a Georgia defense is supposed to.

The 1974 season was just miserable. We got the crap kicked out of us at the end of the year. It was the low point of my time at Georgia, and everybody knew that the following spring we had to get things turned around.

In the following spring they moved me back to offense. I didn't really like the move at the time, because as a player you like to have your name called out, but if you're a lineman you really only get that on defense. It was disappointing until the day my dad came down to practice. There was a scout from the Houston Oilers hanging around that day, and he told my dad that my best chance of playing pro ball was on the offensive line. After practice my dad and I went out to supper, and he told me what the scout had said. I didn't think about the defensive line after that.

We all agreed in the spring of 1975 that it was time to get to work. We were at Georgia to play ball and to get an education. We were doing a lousy job as football players. We had too many people looking at us to keep failing.

There have been some pretty good offensive lines at Georgia, but I will take the two I played on in 1975 and 1976 and stack them up with any others. In 1975 I played with guys like Randy Johnson, who was an All-American, and Steve Wilson, who played a bunch of years in the pros. In 1976 me and Cowboy [Joel Parrish] held down the left side, and George

Mike Wilson was so frustrated with football that he quit several times during his early days at Georgia. He came back and left Georgia as an All-American lineman in 1976.

Collins was on the other. We had a lot of good linemen back then. Jimmy Vickers was our line coach, and if you would bust your butt for him he would do whatever he could for you. He was a very good coach and a special man.

There are a lot of good memories from 1975. Everybody remembers the shoestring play that we ran at Vanderbilt. We all got a big kick out of it when they put the play in during the week, but a bunch of us thought we were going to look like fools if we actually tried it in the game. I was over there laughing, saying, "This ain't never gonna work." And darned if it didn't.

We beat Florida on the Appleby-to-Washington pass play that was set up and executed perfectly. Again, that was a little bit of a trick play, and we didn't know if it would work. But it did, and it was a great day to beat those guys, because they were really good.

But we lost in the Cotton Bowl, which reminds me of my only regret at Georgia. I played three years and never won a bowl game.

We lost a lot of good football players after the 1975 season. Guys like Appleby, Glynn Harrison, Steve Wilson, and Randy Johnson. But early in spring practice it became obvious that we were going to reload with some very good football players. I think we all knew that we had a chance to have a special team in 1976.

People always ask me about the head-shaving episode in 1976, and there are a lot of stories about it. Here is exactly how it happened.

Ken Helms was a center for us, and one day he walked in as we were getting ready for practice. He had just gotten his hair styled and had gotten a brand new dryer to keep it styled. So I decided to give him a hard time about it. Well, one thing led to another, and he finally said, "Let's just shave our heads." It didn't bother me, so I said, "Hey, let's go."

We had a couple of sets of clippers and did each other's hair at the same time. The first thing we did was cut a gap right down the middle so there would be no backing out. Then all these guys started coming by and saying, "Do mine! Do mine!" Next thing you know we've got 20-some guys with bald heads. I think that team bonded over that experience, because we went on to be pretty good.

One of the highlights of my entire career at Georgia was when we beat Alabama in Athens in 1976. You have to understand that my dad is from Alabama—a little town near Birmingham, named Jasper. I've got a bunch of relatives over there, and they are all Alabama people. Back then Bear Bryant was the dominant coach in college football and Alabama was the dominant team, but we knew we were good enough to beat them.

I'll never forget the practice on Friday before the game. We were at the stadium and there were already several hundred people on the railroad tracks. We all had chills just watching those people up there getting ready.

I don't think any of us slept that night. We could hear the noise outside as people were getting ready for the game. And when we took the bus to the stadium the next day, there were about five thousand people on the tracks waiting for us. By the time we got off that bus and got through those people, Alabama never had a chance, and we won 21–0.

The party that night was the greatest one that Athens has ever seen. I know I'll never forget it as long as I live.

We went down to Jacksonville to play Florida, and at halftime we were behind, 27–13. What I remember most is that nobody was yelling and nobody was nervous. We knew we were the better team, and we made up our minds at halftime that we were going to win. Once our offense got rolling, they were not going to stop us. We beat them [41–27], and then we went down to Auburn and clinched the SEC championship.

The best part of winning the SEC title was the team banquet. Coach Dooley had promised us that if we won the championship, he would shave his head. We really didn't think he would do it, but at the banquet he got up and gave a speech and pulled off his wig to show his bald head. The room went nuts. That's one of the things that is special about coach Dooley: he is a man of his word. If he tells you he is going to do something, you can count on it.

229

I think we were ranked No. 4 when we played No. 1 Pittsburgh in the Sugar Bowl. I think *Sports Illustrated* told us they would definitely make us No. 1 if we won. We didn't compete very well, and they outcoached us and outplayed us. Basically, we got our butts spanked.

Still, after a shaky start at Georgia when I wanted to quit, things turned out pretty well. I was lucky enough to play 12 seasons in the NFL, but I often tell people that it was nothing like the four years I spent in college. Your college years are the most impressionable ones of your life. The people you meet and the friendships you make will last for the rest of your life.

And when you play on a championship team, like we did in 1976, you really bond with that group of guys. They become your family forever.

What I will always remember and what I am most grateful for is that at Georgia I got my love for the game of football back. If it hadn't been for coach Dooley and coach Mike, there is no telling how my life would have turned out. How do you possibly repay something like that?

Mike Wilson was a two-time All-SEC tackle in 1975 and 1976. He was an All-American in 1976, after which he played 12 seasons in the NFL. He was inducted into the Georgia Sports Hall of Fame in 2001. Today Wilson lives in Gainesville, Florida, where he is in private business.

CHIP WISDOM
Linebacker
1969–1971

I N A WAY I GUESS I WAS DESTINED to go to Georgia, because things in my life just kept pointing me in that direction.

My sister, Lynne, went to Georgia, where she dated a football player named Pat Hodgson, who was a great receiver for them. She was a true Georgia girl.

My older brother, Buzz, was offered scholarships by Georgia Tech and Duke coming out of high school. He chose Duke—unwisely, I might add. He later wised up and transferred to Georgia.

The thing I liked about Georgia was they played with so much emotion. When I was growing up, I played Pop Warner football for the Buckhead Red Devils, who were coached by a man named Bob Blackwell. He taught a lot of guys how to play the game, and a bunch of them went on to get college scholarships. He taught us to play with great emotion and desire.

That's the way Georgia began to play when Vince Dooley and Erk Russell got to Athens. I remember watching Georgia beat Alabama in 1965. I was only about 15 years old at the time, but I recall thinking that Georgia beat them [18–17] on pure emotion and guts. I thought that Georgia was the kind of team I would like to play for.

As a senior at Westminster a number of schools were looking at me. Georgia wasn't really on me hard, but lucky for me Pat Hodgson was a graduate assistant working with the freshmen. Pat told the other coaches about me, so Erk came to see my team play against Decatur in the fall of 1967.

The next morning I found out that Erk sat with my parents during the game. He told them that I had a scholarship if I wanted it. After that I thought Erk Russell was the greatest thing since Mr. Clean. The fact that he said that I had a scholarship to this up-and-coming program got me really excited.

That Saturday Dennis Chadwick and I were going to Alabama for a visit, but it didn't matter. As soon as I found out that Erk Russell wanted me, I knew I was going to Georgia.

I was a freshman at Georgia in the fall of 1968. That campus—and the whole world for that matter—changed a lot over the next 12 months. Kids went from wearing coats and ties to the games to wearing blue jeans and beads. The dormitory where I would pick up my future wife had all kinds of restrictions in 1968. By 1969 it was coed.

It would be a while before football changed, though. Back then it was so different. They could sign so many players even though there was no way to keep them all on scholarship. So it was the job of the freshman coach to see who the toughest guys were and to run some of the others off. We would start practice by running a mile in full pads, and then we would beat on each other. I came in with about 40 or 45 guys, and when I graduated there might have been 13 of us left. That's just the way things were done.

We won an SEC championship when I was a freshman, in 1968, and in 1969 we were picked to repeat as champs. Me, Tom Nash, and a couple of other guys were going to start as sophomores, but we had a lot of good football players coming back, like Mike Cavan, Bruce Kemp, Steve Greer, Tim Callaway, and Lee Daniel. We also lost a lot of great players, like Kent Lawrence, Brad Johnson, Bill Stanfill, and Jake Scott.

We won our first three games [against Tulane, Clemson, and South Carolina] and got ranked pretty high. We got our picture on the cover of *Sports Illustrated*, or at least Bruce Kemp did. Some people say that team got hit by the *Sports Illustrated* jinx. Actually, we got hit by our schedule, which had a bunch of good teams on it.

I should have known we were in trouble when we went down to Jackson to play Ole Miss. We knocked Archie Manning out of the game and were leading at halftime [17–13], so we thought we were in pretty good shape. Then about midway through the third quarter the defense was on the field. We made a good play to stop them, but I heard the Ole Miss side erupt with

Chip Wisdom was an All-SEC linebacker in 1971 and later was an assistant coach at Georgia for nine seasons.

a bunch of screaming. We looked over and here came Archie out of the dressing room. They had patched him up and he was coming back. The rest of that game he made us look like fools, and we lost [25–17].

We won the next two weeks [against Vanderbilt and Kentucky, to go 5–1], but then things started falling apart. We limped through the end of the season and lost to Tech to finish 5–4–1. For some reason the Sun Bowl offered us an invitation. I guess it was because coach Dooley had taken his first team there [in 1964] and Georgia brought in a lot of people.

What we didn't know was that the players at Nebraska, the team we were going to play, were really mad because they had tied with Missouri for the Big Eight championship and Missouri had gone to the Orange Bowl. They didn't want to be there and they kind of let us know we didn't belong in their league. We had a little pushing contest at one of the barbecues. Of course, we stood up to them and told them how we were going to kick their butts.

They went out there and annihilated us [45–6]. I don't think we had a first down until the second half.

In the 1970 season we just broke even again [5–5]. After that season coach Dooley called us together and said there would be a lot of changes come spring practice. He kind of got after the rising seniors, like me. He called us "break even at best" kind of guys, and that rankled everybody. It should have.

Before we started preseason practice that summer, a bunch of us called a meeting. I can't remember everybody involved, but I know that Tom Nash, Mixon Robinson, Chuck Heard, Royce Smith, and I pulled everybody together and sort of held court. Erk came over to the meeting, and we conveyed to him that the coaches needed to understand that we wanted to win as much as they did. We promised Erk that all of us were going to put it on the line. We were going to do whatever it took to turn things around.

That's exactly what happened. After two sorry years we bonded and had a great year. The only smudge on our record was a loss to Auburn, and it took an incredible performance by Pat Sullivan to do it. I still say that Pat owes us part of his Heisman Trophy. After he beat us [35–20] in Athens, there was no doubt in my mind that he was going to beat out Ed Marinaro [of Cornell] for the Heisman.

Sure, we were disappointed after losing to Auburn, but nothing heals those wounds like beating Georgia Tech, which we did on Thanksgiving night. I didn't play in that game because of a knee injury, but I managed to contribute a little bit to our [28–24] win.

We were behind [24–21] late in the game, but Andy Johnson was taking us down the field. We got down deep in Tech territory with the clock running. Nobody could figure out the right call.

James Ray, our backup quarterback, yelled out, "Let [Jimmy] Shirer run that down-and-out that has been working so well." So that was the call.

But there was one problem: Jimmy Shirer wasn't in the game. He was standing next to me, so I grabbed him. "Jimmy, go in there and run that out route," I yelled at him.

Jimmy ran the route, and Andy threw the ball perfectly. Jimmy went out of bounds around the 1-yard line. On the next play Jimmy Poulos went over the top with just a few seconds left.

The next day I got to be on Vince's television show. That was a special game for everybody.

We finished our careers by beating North Carolina [7–3] in the Gator Bowl, and I give Erk Russell full credit for that win.

Erk's trademark as a coach was the fact that before each game he would head butt with his players—and he didn't wear a helmet. He would cut that old bald head of his, and everybody would get all fired up.

On this day Erk didn't do the head butt. We found out that he had promised his wife, Jean, that he wasn't going to do that silliness anymore.

That just wouldn't do. I think it was Mixon Robinson and me who grabbed Erk and said, "Coach, we're not ready to play. This is the last game a bunch of us will ever play and we're not in the right frame of mind."

"What do you want me to do?" Erk said.

"You know what to do, Coach," one of us said.

Erk said, "OK, get everybody in a circle."

Deep in the bowels of that old Gator Bowl, Erk started pounding heads and the blood began to flow. He got everybody fired up—offense and defense—and we went out and had a great game.

This is probably as good a time as any to say that Erk meant everything to me and to the University of Georgia. Some people looked at Erk and thought he was the meanest man in the world, but nothing could be further from the truth. Erk and Jean lost a son, and if that won't put you in a mental institution, nothing will. But he overcame it. Erk didn't want his players to become successful for his glory. He wanted people to be successful for their own good. He wanted you to do good for *you*.

He gave me my chance as a player, and he gave me my chance as a coach. He is a great, great man and has had a lot of influence on the Wisdom home.

After I finished playing I knew that I wanted to be a coach. I came back to help with the freshmen in 1972, and coach Dooley put me in with the varsity in 1974.

235

There are so many great memories from those years, but I'll always remember the national championship team of 1980. Yeah, we won all the games, but what I remember most is how tight those guys were. They had bonded the spring before, when some of them stole a pig for the annual post–spring practice party—the Seagraves party—which was a tradition at Georgia.

The tradition, I believe, goes all the way back to the fifties. The freshmen always had a tough adjustment period from the upperclassmen, and the Seagraves party marked the end of that freshman orientation.

Well, a number of guys on that 1980 team got caught with the pig, and Vince suspended them and ordered them to pay restitution. The whole team got together and helped those guys.

What I remember is that, in an era when people were worried about racial relations, a guy like Scott Woerner—a white country boy from Jonesboro—and Nat Hudson—a proud young black man—stuck together when all that stuff was going on. It was a special time at Georgia, and I was proud to be a part of it.

I got to coach in a number of other places, but Georgia will always be where my heart is. That's where I met my wife, Brooke. Georgia always had the prettiest girls—and the smartest.

When I was recruiting, I would always tell the guys that the three biggest decisions of your life are who you marry, what you're going to do for a living, and where you are going to college. And where you go to college often has a lot to do with the other two decisions.

Georgia set the stage for the rest of my life. And there is not one chapter I would rewrite.

Chip Wisdom was a three-year starter at linebacker for Georgia, earning All-SEC honors in 1971. He was an assistant coach at Georgia from 1972 to 1980. Today Wisdom lives in Tuscaloosa, Alabama, where he is in private business.

The
EIGHTIES

PETER ANDERSON

Center
1981–1985

THE TRUTH IS, GROWING UP IN NEW JERSEY, I was lucky to be recruited by Georgia. I wasn't a highly recruited player, and I played at a pretty small school. Georgia just sort of stumbled across me.

I've often heard that after we won the national championship in 1980, Georgia's recruiting philosophy changed a little bit. We thought that if we were going to keep competing for national championships, then we had to recruit nationally. My sense is that we didn't completely lay the groundwork for that and signed some guys we really didn't know much about. It worked out well for me, but I know Georgia didn't know anything about me.

Georgia didn't really start recruiting me until January of my senior year. I was going through a difficult time. My girlfriend had broken up with me during the holidays, and in January Georgia came walking through my door saying, "Do you want to look at our school?" My attitude was "what the heck," so I went down to visit Georgia.

At that time Rutgers was the only other school recruiting me, and it really was no contest. Rutgers was excited about spending $250,000 to improve their facilities. Georgia had just spent over $2 million to enclose one end of the stadium. Rutgers had about fifteen thousand fans and Georgia was going to have eighty-five thousand. It just wasn't a fair comparison.

To be honest, I really wasn't that big of a college football fan. One of my teammates had to explain to me who Herschel Walker was and the signifi-

Peter Anderson became a team captain in the middle of the 1985
season, the first player ever to be so honored by coach Vince Dooley.

cance of being recruited by a place like Georgia. But emotionally it was the
right time for me to move on, so off I went to Georgia.

When it came to offensive linemen, my position, we were pretty stacked
in 1981, my first year at Georgia. When I didn't dress out for the first game
against Tennessee, I packed my bags and decided to head back home to Jersey. I knew there was a possibility that I might not come back.

The problem was, I left Athens in this big Oldsmobile Delta 88, and I had no idea where I was going. I had to pull into a gas station at 2:00 in the morning and talk this guy into taking my check to fill up the tank. At that point I had no idea where I was. I don't think I was out of the state of Georgia yet. I realized I wasn't going to make it to Jersey that night, so I turned around and went back to Athens. It's a good thing I did.

I ended up playing on some special teams in 1981, but in 1982 I was red-shirted because we were still loaded with great linemen. By 1983 I started to work my way into the lineup, playing as many as four different positions.

I need to say something about Alex Gibbs, our offensive line coach—one of four different ones I played for at Georgia. Coach Gibbs liked to play a lot of guys, and I think that really helped me. When Keith Johnson, our center, got hurt, I settled into that position.

One of my fondest memories of 1983 was beating Florida 10–9 with a 99-yard drive for a touchdown. We fully expected to beat Florida every time we played them because we had had so much success. So when we got the ball back, we knew we were going to find a way to get the job done. I remember there being a third-and-3 play on that drive. We knew that the team that wanted it the most was going to win. Our line just fired off the ball and got the job done. It was one of the proudest moments of my life.

Losing to Auburn [13–7] that year was a big disappointment because we really thought we were going to win that game. Nobody expected us to be in a position to win another SEC championship, because we had lost Herschel [Walker], but that Georgia team was tough and we almost found a way to do it again.

I've heard coach Dooley say that beating Texas in the Cotton Bowl that year was one of his favorite wins. It was one of mine, too, because Texas had one of the best defenses I'd ever seen.

But what I remember most about that game is the speech coach Dooley gave in the tunnel before we took the field. He started talking about the Texas defense and how good people said they were. He would name one of their players and say, "But I'd rather have Freddie Gilbert," and he'd say why. Then he'd name another Texas player and say, "I'd take Tommy Thurson over him because . . ." That was how strongly he felt about the seniors on that team.

Texas led for most of the game, but there at the end we got a fumbled punt and turned it into a touchdown to win, 10–9. Again, like we had so many times before, we found a way to win. We expected it because we had done it so often.

In 1984, however, some things started catching up with us. We lost a lot of good football players from the year before but still started 7–1. We beat Clemson on Kevin Butler's 60-yard field goal, and people thought we were good enough to win another championship.

But against Florida we got exposed and lost [27–0]. We ended up losing our last three and then tied the Citrus Bowl against Florida State. They had told us all week to watch out, because those guys were really good at blocking punts. We were ahead by eight points with about four minutes left, and doggone if they didn't block one and run it back for a touchdown. They got the two-point conversion to tie us, 17–17. Boy, was coach Dooley mad after that one!

My fondest memory of 1985 was at a senior leaders meeting at the Coliseum. Coach Dooley came in and asked me to leave the room. I figured I was in deep trouble and that coach Dooley was announcing that he was kicking me off the team. Instead, when I walked back in, he told me that I was being named captain. I didn't know it at the time, but I was the first person under coach Dooley to be named a captain in the middle of a season. Usually it happens at the end of the season. It was an incredible honor!

It's hard to say what all went wrong in 1985. We moved the Alabama game to Labor Day night for television. [Keith] Henderson and [Tim] Worley didn't play, but we still had a chance when we blocked a punt to take the lead late in the game. But Mike Shula led Alabama the length of the field and beat us [20–16]. That was a tough way to start.

Something was just missing on that team. I remember we went to play Ole Miss in Jackson and sort of slopped around for a half until we put the game away [49–21]. The next week we continued our sloppy play and got tied by Vanderbilt [13–13]. I still can't explain that one.

But that 1985 team will always be able to say that we went to Jacksonville and beat Florida when they were No. 1. We dominated them in every phase of the game, and it showed the potential our team had.

We finished poorly, losing to Auburn and Tech. We tied Arizona in the Sun Bowl, the second of two ties that year. It was a very strange way to go out.

I wish I could express just how much I miss Georgia and being around all the people in Athens. When I was a young man, that kind of opportunity was never on my radar screen, and the fact that Georgia came my way changed my entire life. I learned about hard work, discipline, and how you can never give up no matter how bad things get.

I know the lessons I learned at Georgia made me a better man, and you can't measure the importance of the friendships I made during my time there. Georgia is a special place, and I am lucky to have been a part of it.

Peter Anderson was the captain of Georgia's 1985 team and was an All-American center the same season. He was the first Vince Dooley–coached player to be named captain at midseason. Today Anderson lives in Jacksonville, Florida, where he is in private business.

KEVIN BUTLER

Kicker
1981–1984

I'VE ALWAYS BEEN ONE OF THOSE PEOPLE who believe things happen for a reason, even if we don't understand it at the time. And looking back at it now, it seems like I was destined to go to Georgia.

As I started my senior year [1980], Georgia and Auburn were right there hand in hand. Then on the last play of the first game of my senior year I hurt my knee. I was playing quarterback [for Redan High School in Stone Mountain] and Harris Barton of Dunwoody [who would go on to play for the San Francisco 49ers] landed on my knee and screwed up my kicking leg.

I was in a hip cast for about six weeks, and let me tell you, that was depressing. Here I had worked all these years to put myself into a position to get a college scholarship, and now this. It was a tough situation to deal with, to be honest.

Georgia and Auburn both stuck with me and made it clear that the scholarships were still on the table, no matter what. Duke came in and made an offer that would allow me to keep playing soccer, which was something I loved. But, needless to say, their football was light-years behind the other two.

I was always leaning toward Georgia for a couple of reasons. One, Rex Robinson was finishing up and was the latest in a string of four-year kickers at Georgia. I could see myself taking over that job and holding it for the next four years. The other thing was the way coach [Vince] Dooley used his kickers. He had made Rex a big part of that national championship run. He believed in playing great defense and making his kickers an important part of the game plan.

So that's why I signed at Georgia. Ironically, getting hurt helped me in a way. Because I couldn't play the rest of the year as a senior at Redan, I doubled up on my work and was able to graduate early. So I enrolled at Georgia and was there for spring practice in 1981. It really gave me a leg up on the competition, because there were already five or six kickers there. We competed every day, but I was able to win the job.

My first big memories came early in the 1982 season. In the opener against Clemson I got a chance to kick a couple of field goals, and we won 13–7. Later on I heard that Strom Thurmond, the senator from South Carolina, had written a letter calling me "the most dangerous Butler since Rhett."

That game was on a Monday night, and we had to turn right around and play BYU on Saturday. Steve Young was their quarterback, and they moved the ball up and down the field, but our defense kept making big plays to stop them. It was a misty day, and I remember turning to Herschel Walker and saying, "It's going to come down to one of us." I told Herschel that if he would just get me in position I'd kick a field goal and win this thing.

And that's what happened. [Editor's note: Butler kicked a 44-yard field goal with 1:11 left in the game to give Georgia a 17–14 victory over BYU.] It was the first time I had ever kicked a field goal to win a game.

I didn't make a lot of big kicks in 1983, but every field goal mattered because of the way that team had to play. We had lost Herschel, so it came down to defense, field position, and kicking. We turned every game into a chess match and waited for the other team to make a mistake. Then we would pounce on it. That was never more true than when we beat Texas [10–9] in the Cotton Bowl. I was very proud to be a part of that team.

People like to talk about the field goal to beat Clemson [26–23] in 1984, but what they don't remember is what led up to that. Clemson was ranked No. 2 or something like that, and nobody expected us to win. And at halftime we were getting beat pretty badly [20–6].

I have never seen coach Dooley as crazy or as emotional as he was in that locker room. He really jumped on us because we were playing so lethargically. He wasn't mad because we were losing. He was mad because we weren't conducting ourselves the way a Georgia team should in a big game.

Well, in the second half we took it to them and tied the game. We got the ball back late, put on a little drive, and got it to around midfield. It was fourth

Kevin Butler, who beat Clemson with a 60-yard field goal in 1984, became the first place kicker ever to be inducted into the College Football Hall of Fame.

down. I remember being right next to Vince. He just looked at me and said, "Field goal."

It was going to be a little over 60 yards.

At that point there wasn't a whole lot to say. Coach Dooley had confidence in me, and I had confidence in myself. Coach [Bill] Hartman, my kicking coach, knew I had the leg. So did my teammates. But it freaked out the people in the stands that we were trying it.

Jimmy Harrell was the holder, so I never worried about that. When it left my foot I knew I had hit it solid. I watched it for about a second to make sure that it was going to keep its course. Then I raced down toward the student section and dropped to my knees. I knew it was going to be good and that we were going to win. You never forget kicks like that.

The disappointing thing was the way that season ended. We went down to Jacksonville and got exposed [27–0] by Florida. I had never been on a team that had been beaten that badly. Then we just sort of fell apart, losing to Auburn [21–12] and Georgia Tech [35–18]. At Georgia, those are the three games that define your season. We dropped the ball and laid a big egg, and that still doesn't sit well with me because I was a senior on that team.

We went down to the Citrus Bowl and played Florida State. All week the coaches had been telling us about their ability to block kicks, and darned if we didn't let it happen—they tied us up late [17–17].

It came down to the last play of the game, and we had the ball. I don't know exactly where it was. I just knew that we were looking at a 72-yard field goal!

I remember going out there and hearing the Florida State players chuckle over in their huddle. They were making comments about our mothers and how ridiculous the kick was going to be.

We got to the spot and Jimmy Harrell looked at one goal post and then the other.

"Shoot, we can make this one left-footed," he said.

I said, "Yeah, but we've got to kick it *that way*," and pointed to the goal that seemed like a mile away.

Jimmy said that when he put the ball down, he was going to lean it back a little bit, to give it a little better trajectory. I told him that was a pretty good idea.

I went out fully expecting to make it, but it came up a yard short. I was mad because I thought I should have made it. My last kick at Georgia was a miss, but it could have been one of my most famous kicks.

I've often said that I'm one of the luckiest guys in the world. I got to play for a college coach who appreciated how to use a kicker, and I benefited greatly from that. I got to play on a Super Bowl champion team as a rookie. I'll never forget that Cathy and I were supposed to get married on January 25, the day before the Super Bowl. After I went to my first team meeting in Chicago, I called home and told her that we had to change the date. I knew that team was going to the Super Bowl.

And then, after all the great things that had happened to me, one day coach Dooley called and said that I had been selected as the first kicker to be inducted into the College Football Hall of Fame. That was a very emotional day for me.

But it all started at Georgia. That's where I really learned how to play and to be an important part of the team, even though I was the kicker. I gained a lot of pride in what I did at Georgia, and those lessons carried me through the rest of my career.

Like I said in the beginning, I think I was destined to go to Georgia. Now I'm really glad I did.

Kevin Butler was a two-time All-American kicker in 1983 and 1984. He was a member of the Chicago Bears Super Bowl champion team in 1985. In 2001, Butler became the first kicker to be inducted into the College Football Hall of Fame. Today Butler lives in Atlanta, Georgia, where he is in private business.

KNOX CULPEPPER

Linebacker
1981–1984

As far back as I can remember, one of my main goals throughout my childhood and teenage years was to follow in my father's footsteps and play football at UGA. My dad had played for Wally Butts in the fifties [1954–1956] and was the captain of Georgia's 1956 team.

But when I got to be a senior in high school, the decision became amazingly tough. I don't know if it was because Georgia took me for granted and just assumed I was coming because my dad played there. I don't know if other schools were just outrecruiting Georgia at that time. But when it came down to the end, I was strongly considering Clemson and Florida State.

My final recruiting trip to Georgia made the difference. I distinctly remember sitting across the desk from coach [Vince] Dooley when he looked me in the eye and asked me if I wanted to be a Georgia Bulldog.

As I look back, he was the only coach I visited who put me on the spot and asked "for the sale." He knew what he was doing, and I knew where my heart was. Of course I wanted to be a Georgia Bulldog.

There are so many great memories it is hard to know where to start.

- As a freshman in 1981 I was told by a specific coach I would never play a down that season . . . and I proved him wrong. [Editor's note: Culpepper was a backup linebacker to Tommy Thurson that season and made 15 tackles.]

Knox Culpepper's father, Knox Sr., was also a great player at Georgia.

- The camaraderie with the players, especially when we celebrated the last day of spring practice and the last day of two-a-days.

- The Georgia-Florida game, specifically the smell of liquor coming from the stands as we ran onto the field. There was no atmosphere quite like it.

- If we won a game, there was "nothing like being a Bulldog on Saturday night."

- The sound of the fans when we ran into Sanford Stadium, which is something that will always be with me.

- All of the SEC championships and bowl games, especially my favorite bowl, the Citrus Bowl in 1984. That's where I met my wife, Mandy Glass.

You don't make it through a college career without a lot of people helping you along the way. Coach Dooley, defensive coordinator Bill Lewis, and Dale Strahm, my position coach, helped me more than I can ever say.

After my senior year I took two years off to play football in Canada. But I came back to Georgia and finally walked away with a diploma in business. Dr. E. G. Leveret was responsible for that.

There were others outside the university who helped me so much at that time, too. My mother, of course, was always a source of strength, and Jimmy Fluker, a Georgia alum, is still my mentor today.

As I take this opportunity to look back, I have to say that it means more to me now to have had the opportunity to play ball at UGA than it meant to me at the time. The relationships, contacts, and foundation that I received at Georgia paved the path that I am following today.

I will never forget the immortal words of Lewis Grizzard, one of the greatest Bulldogs of all: "The game of life is a lot like football. You have to tackle your problems, block your fears, and score your points when you get the opportunity."

Georgia gave me that opportunity, and for that I will always be grateful.

250

Knox Culpepper, a two-time All-SEC linebacker (1983–1984), was the captain of Georgia's 1984 team. Today Culpepper lives in Atlanta, Georgia, where he is in private business.

FREDDIE GILBERT

Defensive End
1980–1983

Ι REALLY DON'T KNOW WHAT I EXPECTED to happen when I came to Georgia in 1980. Georgia was coming off a really tough season [6–5] in 1979, so I thought there might be an opportunity to play pretty early. At least that's what I was hoping for. I had no idea that our freshman class would leave Georgia in 1983 with the best four-year record [43–4–1] in school history.

To tell the truth, I thought I was headed to Auburn after high school. I really liked it, and I felt that I would fit in pretty well there. I was also looking hard at Tennessee, Florida, and Florida State. But I really thought I was leaning toward Auburn.

Then I visited Georgia. It was such a great campus, and my mom fell in love with it. It was pretty close to home because we lived in Griffin, and I knew my parents could get there easily.

Then coach [Vince] Dooley got personally involved in my recruiting, and that was impressive. Plus, there were a lot of guys on my visit, like Eddie Weaver, who looked out for me and made me feel welcome. Later on, when coach Dooley came to my home, it kind of closed the deal. I was going to be a Bulldog.

Now, we had won a state championship in high school, so I knew what winning was about. But it's kind of hard to go from a state championship game, where there were about three thousand people, to your first college game, which was at Tennessee with ninety thousand people.

I knew from my recruiting visit that Tennessee had a big stadium, but once you see all those people, it's kind of overwhelming.

It's hard to describe what it feels like to be a freshman and to win a national championship in your first college season. That was a truly special team. We had a bunch of really solid seniors and some talented young guys, like Herschel Walker. All season long the coaches told us to work hard and prepare, and then the game time would be fun. They were right. That team was always prepared, and every week we found a way to win. I had never been a part of something like that.

Some guys said they were surprised by what Herschel did that season. I wasn't. I had run track against him, and I knew how fast he was for a man his size. He was an amazing athlete and made the things he could do look effortless.

What I wondered about was whether or not he could be just as fast when he put on pads. He was.

I was lucky because I got to play a pretty good bit in the Sugar Bowl against Notre Dame as the backup to Pat McShea. I remember that when that game got tight at the end, coach [Erk] Russell kept telling us, "Just do it one more time." What he meant was that we were going to have to keep Notre Dame from scoring for the rest of the game if we wanted to win. I remember turning to Jimmy Payne and saying, "How many times is coach Russell going to say that?" But coach Russell was right. We kept stopping them one more time until we had won the game 17–10.

I want to give a lot of the credit for that win to coach John Kasay, our strength and conditioning coach. One thing we knew going into the game was that we would be ready to play for 60 minutes. We knew that we could run with anybody in the country because of the work coach Kasay did.

Some people disagree with me, but I thought the 1981 team was better than the team in 1980. We could do a lot more things, but we didn't get as many breaks. A bunch of those young players—Herschel, Terry Hoage, Clarence Kay—really started coming into their own.

That team was good enough to go undefeated, but we had a bad day at Clemson [13–3], and we ran into an offense we just couldn't stop against Pittsburgh in the Sugar Bowl. I was really impressed with Pittsburgh's offensive line. I don't think we touched Dan Marino the entire day. We had them beat but gave up a big play at the end and lost [24–20].

We should have won the national championship in 1982, but Penn State made one more big play than we did in the Sugar Bowl [a 27–23 loss by Georgia].

Despite all those wins the first three years, I am most proud of our 1983 season, when I was captain. We lost Herschel, who turned pro early, and

Freddie Gilbert was one of the greatest pass rushers ever to play at Georgia.

people were talking about what a disaster it was going to be. I couldn't believe that attitude. Sure, Herschel was a great player, but we still had a lot of really good football players.

So we all got together and decided we were going to shock the world. We challenged everybody on that team to step up to the plate and take up the slack. And that's exactly what that team did.

We almost won another SEC championship, but Auburn had Bo [Jackson] and they were a little bit too good for us. Auburn won the championship, but I'll tell you what, those guys knew they had been in a game.

And when we decided to go to the Cotton Bowl, nobody gave us a shot. Texas was No. 2, and their fans wanted to know why they weren't playing a higher-ranked team. They thought they had us from the get-go.

But now everybody knows what happened. Our defense kept it close and then the offense finally got a break. Old [John] Lastinger used to get all kinds of grief at quarterback, but he got the ball in the end zone that day, and we won, 10–9.

Man, was that sweet. We knocked Texas out of the national championship and they couldn't believe it. For the next few days I loved it when people would ask, "What time is it in Texas?"

Ten to nine, baby. That was the perfect way for that group of seniors to go out.

My group has a lot to be proud of. To lose only four games in four years is something that has never been done at Georgia. With coach [Mark] Richt running things right now, they may do it in the future.

For now, when the Georgia fans are asked about the glory days, they always say 1980–1983. You gotta like that no matter how old you get.

There is not a thing I would change about my four years at Georgia. There were so many people who helped me. Eddie Weaver took me under his wing and taught me the attitude you had to have to play at this level. I got to play for coach Russell for a year, and I'll never forget that. Coach [Steve] Greer and coach [Bill] Lewis knew how to get the very best out of us. As I got older I realized that's what coaches and teachers are supposed to do.

Georgia was where I learned to be a football player, but it is also where I finally grew up. I learned that in life everybody is going to have ups and downs and when the downs come you have to fight through them. You can't quit. Yeah, I had to learn some hard lessons, because I can be stubborn. But I did learn, and those things made me a better person.

All I know is that it's been 20 years since I played, and I can still walk into a crowded room and somebody will say, "Hey, there's Freddie Gilbert. He played football for Georgia." That's still pretty neat.

Freddie Gilbert was an All-American defensive end in 1983 and a two-time All-SEC performer. He was captain of the Bulldogs' 1983 team, which went 10–1–1. He played for the Denver Broncos before returning to Athens, Georgia, and entering private business.

TERRY HOAGE

Defensive Back
1980–1983

NOT TOO LONG AGO I ASKED coach [Vince] Dooley why he gave me a scholarship. Georgia didn't sign me in 1980 until well after the signing period was over. He said that they wanted somebody who was going to go to class and make good grades. I appreciated that answer because, in retrospect, I'm glad that coach Dooley understood me enough to allow me to enjoy life on campus outside of football.

Still, I had no idea that the journey that I started at Georgia in 1980 would someday take me to the [College Football] Hall of Fame.

I looked at football a little differently than guys I played with in high school. It was something that was fun to play because I really loved competing in just about anything. But football was not something I was going to chase after in my life.

I didn't know anything about Georgia when they came to my hometown [Huntsville, Texas] and started recruiting me. My plan was to enroll at the University of Texas and probably go on to medical school. I would not have walked on as a football player at Texas. I didn't have the desire to play football so badly that I was going to go out of my way.

Steve Greer and Mike Cavan recruited me early, and then they went away, and I didn't hear from Georgia for a while. Then Georgia offered me a scholarship, so it was an easy decision. Bill Lewis came out and signed me, and before too long I packed up my pickup truck and started driving to Athens.

My role in 1980 was to basically be a live tackling dummy. I was on the scout team, and it was our job to give the varsity the best possible look at what the opponent for that week was going to do. I was really too stupid to know what was going on. Coaches would just show us a picture of what we were supposed to do, and I went out there and did it.

I vividly remember one day playing linebacker on a goal line defense. I got the crap knocked out of me and was lying flat on my back in the end zone. Cavan came over and stood over me and said, "Welcome to the SEC."

The truth is, I was enjoying myself, because I was winning just as many battles as I lost against the varsity. There were no expectations of me, so I was free to take chances on the football field and have fun. If I messed up I knew I wouldn't get yelled at, because I wasn't supposed to be doing anything. That freedom to take chances is what eventually led to my blocking kicks in practice.

The whole practice for the Sugar Bowl game against Notre Dame was dedicated to special teams. It was a live scrimmage against the placekicking team, and I was told to sort of stand in the back of the defense and not do anything. This went on for a while, and then I started thinking to myself, "Why am I just standing here when I could run and jump over the line and block the kick?"

So I didn't tell anybody, I just did it. And I blocked the kick. A little bit later I blocked another one. I figured I had nothing to lose. What were they going to say? Don't do that anymore?

Finally, coach Dooley came up to me and said, "Can you do that again?" I said, "Well, I've already done it twice." And that's how my whole kickblocking thing was born.

Now coaches, you know, can really screw up a good thing. After I blocked a couple of kicks in practice they started tinkering with ways to make it better. They got Frank Ros going down on his hands and knees, and they told me to step on his back and jump. All I did was kick him in the butt three or four times and really bruise his hamstrings.

Of course I was cocky and told them I didn't need a platform. All I needed the line to do was to take out the knees of the offensive line and lower the wall a little bit. They finally conceded that it was probably not a great idea to keep kicking Frank in the butt.

So I went on the Sugar Bowl trip, and that was my job. I didn't get the first kick, but the next time it worked, and we blocked it. But to tell the truth, I

Terry Hoage, the last player to sign a scholarship at Georgia in 1980, was called "the greatest defensive player I have ever seen" by coach Vince Dooley.

expected it to work. I didn't see any reason why it wouldn't work. I think I was able to block four or five kicks in my career.

In 1981 I was a sophomore and moved into the rover position, which really suited my talents. I was able to grow into the position. I felt comfortable doing the things they asked me to do because it was all within my physical capabilities. I didn't have to stretch myself. The defense was such that it put me into a position to be around the ball and make plays. That season was a lot of fun.

But the following spring [of 1982] I actually went to coach Lewis during practice and had a conversation with him about not playing anymore. When I signed up to play football I thought it would be confined to the fall. I had no idea that it lasted 365 days a year—right after football was off-season training. Then there was spring ball. That year, about halfway through spring practice, I was sick and tired of playing football and thinking football and everything in my life being about football. It was too much.

I basically tried to quit, but coach Lewis wouldn't let me. He did take it easy on me. He didn't ask a whole lot of me for the rest of spring practice. He told me to just relax and not worry about things.

Still, after spring practice, I told him that I had no intention of coming back in the fall. I didn't have the desire to keep doing it at that level and at that pace. He was very nice and told me to think about it and to give him a call at the end of the summer. So I went to Colorado and basically backpacked all summer. I didn't think about football or anything. I didn't train, but I did carry a 60-pound backpack at a high altitude all summer.

August rolled around and I was back in Texas seeing my folks. Now I had to make a decision. I really hadn't made any alternative plans if I decided not to go back to Georgia. So I just went back and looked up coach Lewis. I asked him if I could come back and hang out with the football team. I wouldn't be first team anymore, but that was fine.

In many ways it was like being a freshman again. Because I wasn't a starter I could just go out and play for the joy of playing. Consequently, I took a lot of risks and reaped a lot of rewards. [Editor's note: In 1982 Hoage led the nation in interceptions with 12 in 10 games.]

It was probably the best year I ever had playing football, because I was able to let go of all the superfluous stuff that people attach to competitive football at the highest level. I was just able to play like a little kid and not worry because I didn't fill the "C" gap. I just had fun.

Because I had so much fun in 1982, I was in a much better frame of mind to come back in 1983. It was not as hard to go through the off-season weight training and, as it turned out, the upper-level genetics classes I was taking had labs only in the afternoon, which conflicted with spring practice. I think that saved my sanity. I was able to come back refreshed.

At the time a lot of noise was made about the fact that Herschel Walker left school early to turn pro. But we had a lot of other good football players on that team. So when Herschel was gone, I think a lot of us felt we could make up the difference. Not that I didn't miss him in our backfield, because he was a great player. But it was our team, and we were happy with it.

My favorite memory of the 1983 season was being so happy for John Lastinger in the Cotton Bowl. He had taken so much criticism throughout his career. I'm sure that Georgia has a special place in his heart, because he rode such an emotional roller coaster while there. It was really nice to see him go out that way. [Editor's note: Lastinger scored a touchdown on a 17-yard run late in the game as Georgia beat No. 2 Texas, 10–9, in the Cotton Bowl.]

It was never my ambition to play professional football. When I showed up in the NFL I don't think I even knew how teams made the playoffs. I just thought I would play a couple of years, bank a little money, and then go to medical school. I was as surprised as anybody when it turned into a 13-year career.

I have to be honest that when the call came about the Hall of Fame, I didn't know anything about it. I didn't understand how big a deal it really is. It is an unbelievably huge honor, and now that I understand it, I am really humbled by it. I'm still not sure I necessarily belong there.

I just remember my family being at the dinner in New York, and there I was standing next to all of these other football players who had accomplished so much more than I had. When I think about how many people play collegiate football and how few get this honor, it is still amazing to me.

Like I said before, the thing that I am most grateful for with regard to my time at Georgia is that coach Dooley didn't handcuff me and keep me under his watchful eye every second. He allowed me to grow up and become responsible for myself. I know a lot of guys don't have that experience.

At Georgia I was able to have the best of both worlds. I was able to live in the world of football and reap those benefits, but I also lived as a college student in the academic setting, which is just as important to me. That was what

I needed and wanted. I don't think I would have survived if it had been any different.

I remember missing curfew one night because I was across campus watching a play and it had gotten out late. I was hurrying back to McWhorter Hall and walked right into coach Dooley. I thought I was in big trouble.

He asked me where I had been, and I told him I had been to see *A Midsummer Night's Dream.*

He said, "OK, just get on to bed."

That was nice. Coach Dooley got it. He understood. I have always appreciated that.

Terry Hoage was an All-American defensive back in 1982 and 1983. Hoage was also a two-time Academic All-American. He played 13 years in the NFL. In 2000 Hoage was inducted into the College Football Hall of Fame. Today he lives in Paso Robles, California, where he owns a vineyard.

JOHN LASTINGER

Quarterback
1979–1983

ONE OF THE GREAT THINGS about football is that no matter how bad things get, if you just keep trying and you just keep working, things have a way of turning out OK. That's what happened to me in my five years at Georgia.

At one point in my career it looked like I was going to be a guy who came to college and never did very much. Before it was over I had played in a national championship game and got a chance to score the winning touchdown in the Cotton Bowl. That was over 20 years ago, and in many ways I still can't believe it happened to me.

I was never really a big Georgia fan growing up. I was a college football fan who liked a lot of teams. I remember Johnny Musso at Alabama and Sullivan and Beasley at Auburn. I loved Archie Manning and went down to the Gator Bowl [in 1971] and saw him play Auburn with a cast on his arm.

I was an OK high school player. I think people noticed me because they came to Valdosta to recruit Buck Belue, our quarterback, who was a year older than me. I played wide receiver as a junior, and after Buck went to Georgia, I played quarterback as a senior.

I really wasn't crazy about playing quarterback, but I wanted to help the team. And we had a very good team in 1978. We lost to Clarke Central, coached by Billy Henderson, for the state championship. Jim Bob Harris was the quarterback for Clarke Central, and he went on to play at Alabama.

262

John Lastinger's up-and-down career ended in glory when he scored the winning touchdown to beat Texas 10–9 in the Cotton Bowl.

It came down to Auburn, Alabama, and Georgia. The difference was coach [Vince] Dooley and Wayne McDuffie, who were recruiting me.

People were telling me not to go to Georgia because I would play behind Buck my whole career. But coach Dooley assured me I could play another position if I wanted to. Besides, I trusted Buck, and he kept telling me about all the great players Georgia was bringing in. That was good enough for me.

I got to Georgia in the fall of 1979 and was quickly moved to defensive back. I just loved playing for coach Erk Russell, the most incredible motivator I have ever met. We opened the season with Wake Forest, and we heard that they were terrible. Well, they embarrassed us [22–21]. We couldn't stop them. The next Monday we started two-a-days again, and I was moved to backup quarterback. My days as a defensive back were over.

What was weird about that year was that at the end of the season we were 5–4, but all of our losses were nonconference—they were all to ACC schools! If we beat Auburn, then we would win the SEC championship. I remember the week before the Auburn game Erk kept saying, "Let's piss 'em off in New Orleans," which was where we would play in the Sugar Bowl if we won. It didn't matter. Auburn beat us good [33–13].

After that season we went through a brutal off-season workout with coach [John] Kasay. My body had never been through such a shock. My legs were so sore that I had to pick them up to get them over the curb as I was walking to class. But it helped me, because I got bigger and stronger and was able to compete.

That spring I moved solidly into the backup quarterback spot behind Buck. Coach George Haffner came in as offensive coordinator, and I was very excited. I showed up at spring practice ready to go. But during a workout I partially tore my anterior cruciate ligament. I had to redshirt the entire 1980 season when we won the national championship. All I did was hold a clipboard and chart plays.

Before we got to the spring of 1981, I hurt my knee again playing basketball. I had to wear a heavy brace in spring practice. That was the low point for me. I was thinking that I would be another one of those athletes who goes off to college, hurts his knee, and is never heard from again. At that point I was motivated by fear. I did not want to be another statistic.

I got to play pretty often as Buck's backup in 1981, and we had a good year. Then came the spring of 1982 and Buck was leaving. I figured it was my time, but all I read in the newspapers was that we had signed this all-world freshman named Jamie Harris. All the stories said, "Look for Lastinger to play early, but look for Jamie Harris to take over by midseason."

I was thinking, "Damn, boys, I've been through a lot. I'm not going to just give up." But it was a struggle to stay positive.

We started the 1982 season with a couple of close wins against Clemson [13–7] and BYU [17–14]. The defense scored the only touchdown against Clemson, and Kevin Butler bailed us out with a late field goal against BYU, who were quarterbacked by Steve Young. We were winning, but it was bittersweet because I had definitely hit a slump.

The low point for me was a game against Vanderbilt. Terry Hoage was the star of the Georgia highlight tape for that game. I was the star of the Vanderbilt tape. I was that bad.

That was the point at which coach Haffner started losing patience with me. They weren't asking me to do a whole lot, but I wasn't even getting that done.

I kind of hung on and played a little bit better against Kentucky [a 27–14 win] the following week. We came back and won, and I started to get back in their good graces.

264

Two weeks later we went to Jacksonville and kicked Florida pretty good [44–0]. All of a sudden we were undefeated and going to Auburn as the No. 1 team in the nation.

Auburn was ready to play. I thought we might put them out of it early, but then Lionel James ran for a touchdown and it was like somebody hit a switch. It was going to be a war. But we won there [19–14] and walloped Tech [38–18], and then we were going to the Sugar Bowl to play Penn State for the national championship.

Back then it was pretty unusual to have a No. 1 versus No. 2 matchup in a bowl game, so that was something special. To tell you the truth, the outcome of that game [Penn State won 27–23] still bugs me. Every Christmas somebody calls me and tells me they are watching it on ESPN Classic.

We fell behind early because they were determined that Herschel was not going to beat them. I was pleading with the coaches to start throwing the ball more, because that was our best chance. We finally cut it to 20–17, but we never got the break we wanted. I remember that I missed Clarence Kay wide open in the end zone early in the game, and we had to kick a field goal. Those four points were the difference.

Still, it was a great season [11–1], and we had a bunch of guys coming back, including Herschel. Or so we thought.

I remember coming back from class and going to lunch when one of the guys told me that Herschel was gone, that he had signed a pro contract. Man, everywhere you looked there were reporters. We had a news helicopter land on the practice field. It was unbelievable! A bunch of us tried to get to him to let him know we weren't mad. After everything Herschel had done for us, how could we be mad at him?

Not long after that we got together and decided that we were not going to let this hurt our team. As great as Herschel was, we still had a lot of good players. I was excited as spring practice began—and then I promptly blew out my other knee. It was supposed to be a simple arthroscopic surgery, but I woke up with a cast on my leg.

Then I really got down. I just didn't know if I had the motivation to come back again.

I ended up going back to Valdosta for the summer, which was one of the best decisions I ever made. There I met Jim Madaleno, the trainer at Valdosta State, and he challenged me to get better. He told me he was going to work with me seven days a week, two times a day. He promised that when I went back to Athens in August I would be ready to play.

I was in great physical shape for preseason practice, but I didn't throw a lot during my rehab, and it showed. In our first two games against UCLA and Clemson I didn't play very well. Todd Williams came in for me against Clemson and played great.

After that game coach Dooley brought me into his office to talk. He asked me if I wanted to start the next game against South Carolina. I told him, "Coach, I'd love to start, but I'm going to have to be perfect or these people will want my head on a platter. And Todd played very well in the second half against Clemson."

Coach Dooley went with Todd. I was a senior, and I had lost my job.

Todd played well against South Carolina, but he hurt his leg. I ended up taking the field and the crowd booed me. I was thinking that wasn't very nice. When I took the field for the second half they booed me again. A year before, something like that might have made me crumble, but this really didn't bother me. I played pretty well that day [a 31–13 win] and basically started from that point on.

There are a lot of great memories from the rest of that season. We drove it 99 yards to beat Florida [10–9]. All we were hoping for when that drive started was just to get the huddle out of our own end zone, but we had a bunch of mature, experienced guys who could handle that situation.

We lost to Auburn [13–7] or we could have won our fourth straight SEC championship. We had a chance to win when we got an onside kick late, but Auburn was very, very good.

Then we had to get a late interception from Tony Flack to beat Georgia Tech [27–24]. John Dewberry was their quarterback, and I couldn't have stood it if they had beaten us.

Not long after that game coach Dooley brought some of the seniors in and told us we had a couple of choices for bowl games. We could go to the Fiesta Bowl and basically just have a good time. Or we could go to the Cotton Bowl to play No. 2 Texas and maybe have an impact on the national championship. There was no question in anybody's mind. We were going to Dallas.

The coaches didn't show us a whole lot of film on the Texas defense. When we got there we saw why. Texas had one of the biggest, fastest defenses I had ever seen. I think 8 of their 11 guys ended up playing in the NFL. They could put eight guys in the box because their defensive backs were so good they could cover anybody.

266

We didn't do anything on offense all day, but late in the fourth quarter we were still within striking distance at 9–3.

I remember that we had to give up the ball with about five minutes left because we couldn't get a first down. I was mad because I was afraid that we wouldn't get the ball back. I always had the utmost respect for coach Dooley and his decisions, but I was mad.

Well, we got the ball back when their guy fumbled the punt and we recovered down deep in their territory. All day long we had been waiting for a break and it had finally come. Somehow, some way, we knew we had to get that ball into the end zone.

The first play we put a guy in motion and ran a fullback dive, which didn't get much. I carried out the fake and noticed that when I got to the corner, there was really only one support guy, because their cornerback had gone all the way across the field with our guy in motion.

I was thinking that we might have something there.

The second down went to Tron Jackson and left us about four yards short of a first down. I figured that we would have to throw the ball downfield to get the first down.

But coach [Charlie] Whittemore signaled in the play, and the coaches had obviously seen what I saw on first down. They called an option to the right.

We put a man in motion to the left, and the Texas cornerback went with him. That left one corner on that side with the safety, Jerry Gray, in the middle of the field. My job was to read the corner. If he came to me, I was to pitch the ball. If he leaned to the pitch man, I was to keep it. Gray was supposed to come over and run support if I kept it.

The key to the play is getting a good block on the linebacker, and we did. When I got to the outside, the corner went with our defensive back and, for a split second, I saw an opening to the goal line. I could see Gray coming over.

The first thing I thought about was that I had the first down. Then I realized I might be able to get to the goal. I saw the orange pylon, I saw Jerry Gray, and I thought, "Lord, please let me get there first."

Jerry got there, but it was a moment too late. We went into a heap in the corner of the end zone, and when I looked up the official had his arms raised in the air. The pylon actually stuck to my pants. My buddy Perry McIntyre took a great picture of it.

I just remember my teammates grabbing me. I was thinking that so many players have had their Georgia moments and maybe now I had mine.

267

We won the game [10–9], which was a fitting way for that group of seniors to go out. It was just hard to believe that after all the bad stuff that had happened in my career, this was the way it was going to end. This was how I was going to be remembered.

That was 20 years ago, and today it is still fun to go back to Athens. When they say my name at the stadium now, people cheer and I smile. I remember there was a time when they didn't do that.

When it's all said and done, that's what being a Georgia Bulldog is all about. It's about never quitting. It's about a bunch of guys pulling together toward a common goal. During my time at Georgia I formed relationships that will be with me for the rest of my life. Georgia is where I grew up and learned to be a man.

That's why Georgia is such a special place.

John Lastinger had a record of 20–2–1 in games he started during the 1982 and 1983 seasons. Today Lastinger lives in his native Valdosta, Georgia, where he works for an investment comany.

REX ROBINSON

Kicker
1977–1980

ONE OF THE REASONS I DECIDED to go to Georgia was that under coach [Vince] Dooley the kicker wasn't just "the kicker." He was considered to be a very important part of the team. The way coach Dooley managed a game, the kicker had a chance to become a star if he produced. I was fortunate in that I was put into some very important situations, and I feel like I did produce.

And today it's been over 23 years since I kicked my last field goal for Georgia, but people will still walk up to me and say, "Are you *the* Rex Robinson?" A bunch of my coworkers think it's so funny that they have nicknamed me "The." That people still remember me after all those years still blows me away.

It's funny, but I was playing on the junior varsity team in high school when somebody first noticed that I could kick. I kicked a 51-yard field goal in a junior varsity game. The word sort of got around, and the next thing I knew Don McCellan of Channel 2 was out at practice with a camera crew. He came out there to verify that I could do it. It took me four tries, but I did it for him.

That next summer, before my junior year at Marietta High School, I met Peter Rajecki, who was a former Georgia kicker. He went to Sprayberry High School to do his off-season training. He was playing in the World League at the time. He showed me a lot of things that helped me improve—like taking three steps back from the ball and then two across to set up for the kick. I will never forget that.

Rex Robinson, one in a long line of All-American kickers at Georgia, was a member of the Bulldogs' 1980 national championship team.

Now, when I was a senior in high school, a lot of colleges wanted you to walk on, because they didn't want to use a full scholarship on a kicker. But I got offers from three—Memphis State, Georgia Tech, and Georgia. Georgia Tech seemed too close, and Memphis was too far away. Georgia seemed just right. They had just won an SEC championship in 1976, and coach Dooley had a reputation for having four-year kickers. Allan Leavitt was finishing up his four years as a starting kicker, so the situation seemed perfect for me.

What does the book say? "It was the best of times. It was the worst of times." Well, my freshman year in 1977 was the worst of times for me.

Expectations were pretty high on that team after winning the championship the year before. Instead, we gave coach Dooley his only losing season [5–6] in his entire time at Georgia. I certainly didn't do my part, making only 10 of 20 field goals. I would watch the game film and could see the entire team sag when we drove the ball down into position and I missed the field goal. They were so let down.

But that was also the turning point for me. I set some very high goals for the next season and came to camp in the best shape of my life. The coaches were really surprised to see this old tubby guy actually show up in shape. A lot of the guys on the team that year had the same resolve.

In 1978 people called us the "Wonderdawgs" because we won so many close games. I just think it was a group of guys who really hated losing the year before and who were going to do whatever it took to win. And after we won a few close games, we felt confident we were going to find a way to get it done.

When you're a kicker, you sort of remember things a little differently. I remember the first game against Baylor and their great linebacker, Mike Singletary. He made a tackle on our sideline, and for the first time, I saw the eyes that everybody would later talk about when he was with the Bears. That was scary.

I remember Lindsay [Scott] running the second-half kickoff back against LSU, which got us going for another close win [24–17], at Baton Rouge.

Of course, people still like to talk about the last-second field goal to beat Kentucky [17–16]. It's amazing. Hardly a day goes by where I don't meet somebody who was either there or listened to Larry Munson call it on the radio.

It's funny, the things you remember about certain games. I remember that I had missed a couple of field goals early in the game that could have made things easy on us. And I remember that when the score was 16–14 Kentucky missed a field goal that would have given them a five-point lead and made the last few minutes of that game totally different.

We got the ball back with 4:03 left, and immediately I realized that the game was going to come down to a field goal. We were getting big chunks of yardage, but I knew that when we got close coach Dooley was not going to take any chances. That's exactly what happened. We got down around their 10-yard line and called timeout with just a few seconds left.

Now, I tell young kickers today that they can't control all the noise and stuff going on around them, but they can control their own routine. It's like a preshot routine in golf. So I was going through my set routine when Kentucky called timeout to "ice" me.

It's a good thing they did, because Tim Morrison, who was supposed to be in the game, was kneeling on the sidelines praying. Coach Dooley always likes to tell the story of leaning down to tell Tim, "Your prayers have just been answered. Kentucky called timeout."

Charlie Fales was the snapper, and Mike Garrett was the holder. I had complete confidence in them. It wasn't the greatest kick in the world, but it was good, and the whole field was just pandemonium. They would deny this today, but some of the guys told me they loved me. Guys who had never spoken 10 words to me in two years were suddenly jumping up and down on top of me.

It was the first time in my career that I had ever kicked a field goal to win a game. And it felt great.

The only other great memory I have of that year is the Georgia Tech game, where we came back from 20–0 to beat them 29–28. Drew Hill ran back a kickoff about 100 yards against us to give them the lead. I dove and got a hand on his thigh pad, but I just didn't get there quick enough. The only good part of that play was that I took out a couple of Tech coaches when I dove at their sideline.

I never have been able to figure out what happened to us in 1979. I think we all felt pretty good about that team, but then we lost the opener to Wake Forest [22–21] and things just went downhill after that.

Everything seemed different going into the summer workouts of 1980. I started keeping a diary of what I heard and saw during those workouts. I just remember that it all started to click, even the little things like how we did our warm-up exercises. I remember writing that everything just seemed to be on point.

I believe we would all agree that the main thing missing from the 1979 team was a marquee running back. We had had Willie McClendon in 1978. We thought Herschel Walker might be it, but we had no idea how that was going to turn out.

Everybody says they knew Herschel was great after the first game against Tennessee [a 16–15 Georgia win]. For me it was the first home game against Texas A&M when I saw him break off his first long run. I had never seen anybody that size who could run that fast. I knew we had something pretty special.

271

When that year started I just wanted us to win the SEC championship. After all, I had never won any kind of athletic championship before, and I figured it was a realistic goal. But we just kept winning, and around the time of the Vanderbilt game I started thinking that we could win them all. In fact, we had a pep rally before that Vanderbilt game, and I said something about it then.

I guess the game that I'm most proud of that year was when we beat South Carolina 13–10. The two teams seemed evenly matched. They had George Rogers. We had Herschel. I thought it might come down to kicking.

I missed an easy 22-yard field goal early in the game, and I was pretty upset by that. By my senior year I didn't expect to make a mistake like that. All I did was miss my alignment on the kick.

One thing I had learned how to do was forget about bad kicks, so when we had a chance to kick a 57-yarder later in the game, I was confident I could do it. Coach Dooley could tell I was confident, and he let me kick it. I made that one and then made a 51-yarder in the second half. I think that year I made four field goals that were over 50 yards. That was a great day and a great win for us.

People ask me all the time what I was doing when Lindsay Scott scored the miracle touchdown against Florida. The truth is, I really didn't see him score, because when Lindsay got to midfield I started running to the end of the bench to get my tee, thinking he'd get tackled and I'd have to kick a field goal to win the game. By the time I got my tee he was in the end zone and being mobbed. We didn't kick the extra point because we went for two.

That was a great plane ride home from Jacksonville to Atlanta. We had learned earlier that Georgia Tech had tied Notre Dame and that we'd be No. 1 in the next polls. We would get a shot at the national championship if we could just beat Auburn and Georgia Tech, which we did.

The play I get asked about from the Sugar Bowl is the kickoff that the Notre Dame guys forgot to field. We knew going into the game that one of their kickoff guys, Jim Stone, was considerably better than the other one. So my job was just to kick high and away from Stone.

The two guys just didn't communicate, and they both ran away from the ball. Bob Kelly got down there and got on the ball, and we got an easy touchdown. After the game some of the sportswriters actually asked me if we did it on purpose. Erk [Russell] called it "the longest onside kick in history." But it was one of those plays that showed that it was our day.

What happened on the field right after the game was just incredible. It only took a few seconds before that field was covered in red. What was so weird was that I saw a lot of people I knew, and we were having a great time. It took me quite a while to get to the locker room because the celebration was still going strong.

It's been over 20 years since I played my last game at Georgia, but today little kids come up to me and know who I am. Their dads introduce them to me, and they know what jersey number I wore. It's kind of mind-blowing to me that after all this time a kid would even *care* to know about something like that.

My wife is from Michigan, and when we met I didn't make a big deal about the fact that I played at Georgia. Now she is working in Atlanta and teaching with people who make a big deal about it when they find out we're married. She thinks it's really funny.

But that's one of the many things that makes Georgia special. When you're 18 years old you have no idea that the decision of where you are going to school will shape the rest of your life. The Georgia people become your family, and once you wear that uniform they never forget you. And the friendships I made at Georgia are the ones I'll have the rest of my life. I know a lot of other guys have probably said this, but it was the most important four years of my life.

Rex Robinson was an All-American place kicker in 1979 and 1980. Today Robinson lives in Atlanta, Georgia, where he works for a sporting goods manufacturer.

FRANK ROS

Linebacker
1977–1980

I CAME TO COLLEGE FOOTBALL in a little different way from my teammates at Georgia.

I was born in Spain, where my father eventually became a political prisoner of Franco. He was a textile engineer, but when he was released there was no way that he could get a decent job, so we decided to come to the United States.

I was six years old when our ship pulled into New York Harbor in 1964. We were on the ship for two and a half weeks crossing the Atlantic, and then suddenly, there was the Statue of Liberty, so big that you feel you can almost reach out and touch it. That was my first impression of America.

We settled in Greenville, South Carolina, which at the time was considered to be the textile capital of the world. I didn't speak a word of English. Actually, I had learned to say "Good morning" on the ship, but that was it. It's funny the things you remember. On that ship an American businessman befriended me. When he left, he gave me his scarf. I still have it.

We were totally immersed in the American culture. I had to learn English as fast as I could. My daddy worked hard to realize the American dream. He began by cleaning machines at a textile factory. I'm proud to say that he eventually became that company's CEO.

The first American football I ever saw was on our little black-and-white television set. I didn't understand it. But in the summer between my sixth and

Frank Ros, who came to the United States from Spain when he was six years old, was the captain of Georgia's 1980 national championship team.

seventh grades I met Ben Cornett. Ben asked me to come out and play midget football. Ironically, Ben and I would play against each other in college, because he went to South Carolina while I went to Georgia.

It's hard to explain why, but the first time I ever put on a football uniform I knew I had found the thing that would bring out the passion in me. It gave me self-esteem, and I decided to be totally committed to it. I wasn't all that talented, but I did try to build myself up by spending a lot of time in the weight room. I never thought that much about getting a college scholarship until the recruiters started showing up my senior year.

The recruiting process was really funny for our family because nobody understood it. I remember when the first recruiter came to my house and started making his pitch to me and my dad. About five minutes into it Daddy stopped the coach and said he wanted to speak to me alone.

He said, "Son, I do not understand what is going on."

I explained to him that this coach was asking me to play football at his school and that they were willing to pay for my education.

Then his eyes got real wide and he said, "What's wrong with you? Take it now!"

I explained to him that all of the other coaches coming by were going to be offering the same thing. Dad thought I should take the first offer because it was a sure thing.

By all rights I probably should have ended up at South Carolina. My brothers and sisters went to school there. My buddy Ben signed there, and, knowing my personality back then, I would have blindly gone there, too. But sometimes the grace of God just comes into your life.

South Carolina recruited me early in the year, but then halfway through the season they seemed to back off. I looked hard at East Carolina because Pat Dye was the head coach, and let me tell you what, that man can recruit. But I knew coach Dye wouldn't be at East Carolina much longer.

That's when I looked hard at Georgia. I had seen Georgia play on TV and when I had worked concessions for games at Clemson. Something about Georgia just caught my eye. So in my hotel room after the Shrine Bowl in Charlotte, coach Frank Inman signed me to go to Georgia.

I've always thought it ironic that I was a freshman in 1977—the only losing season that coach [Vince] Dooley ever had. When we were seniors in 1980, that same group of guys would help him win a national championship.

As a freshman I was a gung-ho kind of guy, always going all out. That team didn't win many games, but it had some great players, like Ben Zambiasi, who was sort of my role model when it came to playing linebacker. He went 100 percent at all times and that was the kind of player I wanted to be.

Coach Dooley let me dress out for the South Carolina game and put me on the kickoff team. Now, you can imagine how fired up I was for this game because of all the people I knew at South Carolina. All I wanted to do was run down there and really crank somebody.

Well, of course, I ran down there as fast as I could, and when I got to the guy with the ball, the kid just made a little juke move and went by me. Coach Dooley was so mad. He taught me that you can play the game all out, but you still have to be under control.

The thing I remember most about that year is that I think we led the nation in fumbles, and before the season was over we went through five quarterbacks because of injuries.

In 1978 I thought I was ready to be a starting linebacker. I made sure that I was the best-conditioned player on the team and the position was open. But in the spring coach Dooley decided to move Steve Dennis, who was a senior, ahead of me. That didn't make me very happy, but as I look back I understand the decision. When it comes to football, there is nothing like experience, which is something we would all understand in 1980.

It was 1978 when coach [Erk] Russell called us "From Underdawgs to Wonderdawgs," and the name just stuck. When we started winning all those close games, the name really caught on with the public. Coach Russell just had a knack for saying the right thing at the right time for a team or an individual. He was simply amazing in that respect.

What I will always remember from 1978 was Scott Woerner in the Georgia Tech game. Early in the game a Tech guy hit him when he was trying to make a fair catch. It cut him under the chin and he was so ticked off. The next time we received a punt he said, "Guys, just block somebody. I'm taking this thing in." He had stitches in his chin, but he took that punt all the way back for a touchdown. That was the kind of character we had on that team.

I was sure that 1979 would be the year when I would become a starter. But on a Wednesday scrimmage three days before the first game with Wake Forest, I tore a ligament in my knee. I didn't have surgery, but I missed three games. I played a little bit on special teams in the fourth game, against Ole Miss. The following week we were practicing and getting ready for LSU.

Somebody messed up at linebacker and coach Dooley yelled, "Put Ros in there and see what he can do!"

I started that game and then every game for the rest of the year. We only won six games that year, but we all felt that with a little luck we could be pretty good in 1980.

We felt that way because we had a good group of seniors and some kids with really good character. But we also knew that we were missing a piece. We needed a big-time, go-to guy at running back. We had Willie McClendon in 1978, but in 1979 we just didn't have a guy who could carry it 25 or 30 times a game if we needed it. We didn't know it that spring, but help was on the way.

There were a lot of things that bonded that team together even before we had played a game. A bunch of us got into trouble when we stole a pig for our annual party celebrating the end of spring practice. Now, everybody was involved in the party, but only four of us got caught with the pig and got suspended. But the other players rallied behind us and helped us pay back what we owed for the pig. Later on coach Russell would say that the incident really brought us close as a team.

I also remember that in the spring of 1980, coach Dooley brought in a motivational speaker. He began talking about the elements that make up a winner. He pulled out an index card and asked, "What is your team goal for 1980?"

At that moment, for the first time, a bunch of us seniors thought about the national championship.

He asked us when the national championship would be decided. We said January 1, 1981. So he told us to write that date down on an index card and attach it to our bathroom mirrors so that we would look at it every single day. I still have that card.

Like I said earlier, we knew that the missing piece on our team was a big-time running back. But when we started practice that summer, we really didn't know what Herschel Walker was going to become. I remember one of our very first hitting drills involving the freshmen. Herschel had to run over "Meat Cleaver" Weaver, and Eddie just cranked him, and there was a bunch of whooping and hollering. But Herschel never said a word, and he never took it personally. He just put the ball back and jogged to the huddle.

We beat Tennessee [16–15] after Herschel had those two big runs, but people forget that we had to make a defensive stand at the end of that game to win. Nate Taylor and I hit the Tennessee ball carrier and caused a fumble to save that game.

At the end of the Clemson game we were winning [20–16], but they were driving late. A pass went right through my hands, but it fortunately fell into the arms of Jeff Hipp, our safety. I never would have forgiven myself if they had scored.

People talk about the great win over Florida [26–21] that put us in position to win the national championship. In my opinion, the game should have never been that close. But when Lindsay Scott was running down the sideline for the winning score, I was running down the sideline with him. I remember jumping on the pile of players in the end zone. Then here came crazy Jeff Harper, and he tried to head butt me—but I didn't have my helmet on. Then it dawned on me that the defense had to go back on the field to protect the lead.

The Notre Dame team that we played for the national championship was the biggest football team I had ever seen. A lot of stuff happened in that game, and there were a lot of big plays made that day. But what I remember most is being on the sideline in the fourth quarter. I've seen pictures of coach Russell talking to Eddie Weaver, Nate, and myself during the final stages of that game.

Every time we would come off the field he would say to us, "Guys, I need you to go back out there and do it just *one more time*! Guys, can you do it just *one more time*?" That man was a helluva motivator.

Of course we *did* do it enough times to win the game. I remember standing on the sidelines next to coach Dooley in the final minute when we had the ball. When Buck [Belue] completed a pass to Amp [Arnold], it gave us a first down, and Notre Dame was out of timeouts.

I looked at coach Dooley and said, "We won it."

He gave me that glare, as only he can. "The damn game ain't over until it's over."

I told coach that they didn't have any timeouts left. That's when he gave me a little grin. Then he went right back to his incredible concentration.

It was an incredible thing when our fans stormed the field and turned it into a sea of red. It seemed like the field was completely covered in just a few seconds. Dee Matthews has sent me pictures of that scene taken from up above. All of us who were there will remember that day for the rest of our lives.

I'm 45 years old now, and it's hard to completely explain what those years would mean to the rest of my life. But I do know this: take away those four years at Georgia and the course of my life would have been totally different.

Just think about all the traditions of being a football player at Georgia: playing Between the Hedges, the fans on the track, which I still miss, the overall thrill on a game day in Athens. And what it means to be a Bulldog on Saturday night after a win. Knowing that you played for the best, most respected football program and coach in the country.

I also had a chance to play with the man who I think was the greatest football player of all time: Herschel Walker.

The lessons that I learned from the people in that program combined with the pride that was instilled in us—that is what it means to be a Georgia Bulldog. I played with a group of guys who could say that for one moment in time, we were the very best at what we did.

Frank Ros was the captain of Georgia's 1980 national championship team. Today Ros lives in Atlanta, Georgia, where he works for the Coca-Cola Company.

TROY SADOWSKI

Tight End
1985–1988

W HEN I THINK OF MY TIME AT GEORGIA, my first memories aren't about the games, even though I played in some pretty big wins and some very disappointing losses. The first thing I think about is what the people at Georgia did for me—people like Hornsby Howell. Not a lot of people know this, but in the fall of 1985 my mom was suffering from breast cancer. By then the cancer had gotten into my mom's hip, and she was starting to lose her mobility.

Coach Howell got a parking pass for my mom so she could park right outside the stadium. Before every single home game, he would meet her at the gate with a wheelchair and take her to her spot in the stadium so she could see the game. At halftime he would go get her and take her to the recruiting lounge so she wouldn't get too hot. Then after the game he would make sure she got back to her car OK. I lost her in the summer of 1986, but thanks to coach Howell and the other people at Georgia, she got to see me play every single home game in 1985. How do you possibly repay people for something like that?

Coach John Kasay, our strength and conditioning coach, either felt sorry for me or he saw something in me that I didn't see in myself. When I got to Georgia I was so skinny that he let me borrow his personal weight set. He did everything with us—he was really one of us.

I remember running the mile-plus-mile. You would have to run a mile, and then when your heart rate dropped back down to a certain level, you had to run another mile. You had to do both miles in a certain time in order to pass. I can't remember what that time was, but I can tell you that it wasn't easy for anybody.

Once I was really struggling on my second mile, and I looked up and saw coach Kasay. He started screaming, "You're not going to fail this thing. I've brought you too far!!!" And I made it. I know he did that with a lot of guys, not just me, but coach Kasay poured his heart into getting us ready to play. To me, that is what Georgia football is all about.

I remember the day that coach [Vince] Dooley called to tell me that I had been named a Walter Camp All-American. I could hear the pride in his voice because it was such a big moment for me. It was a special award because it wasn't just about stats, it was about your value to your team.

I remember a teammate, Mike Brown, who had lost his mother to cancer as well. We had to learn to lean on each other for a long time to get through some of those days. My roommate, Scott Adams, was a great guy then, and he's an even better friend today.

I know it is a cliché to say that the people who play football together are like a family, but when it comes to Georgia and the people I played ball with, it is absolutely true.

Now, our freshman class in 1984 was really in a tough position. Georgia was coming off the best four-year period in our history. The pressure was really on to keep it going.

We didn't win as many games in my four years as those guys did, but we made a lot of memories that will stay with us forever.

My first game as a Georgia player was in 1985 against Alabama. I was just a kid, and my job was to block Cornelius Bennett, their two-time All-American. Needless to say, that was a learning experience. They came back and beat us at the end, which was a real heartbreaker.

Later that year we beat Florida when they were No. 1 and it killed them. We had the mind-set against Florida that we were going to win that game. They knew it and we knew it. Gosh, I loved that old Gator Bowl. You could feel the vibrations in the locker room from people stomping in the stadium.

In 1986 we went to Auburn and beat them, and they turned the hoses on us. I remember catching a touchdown pass and somebody taking a picture of me celebrating with Kirk Warner. I still have that picture.

Really my only regret about my time at Georgia is that we never won an SEC championship. I thought we might be good enough in 1988 when I was

Troy Sadowski was an All-American tight end on coach Vince Dooley's last team at Georgia in 1988.

a senior, but we stumbled at Kentucky [16–10], which was one of the toughest losses I was ever a part of.

What I am most proud of is that my senior class gave coach Dooley his 200th win, against Georgia Tech [24–3]. Then, after he announced his retirement, we were able to send him off as a winner by beating Michigan State in the Gator Bowl [34–27].

It was an honor to be a part of coach Dooley's last senior class at Georgia. Frankly, we were shocked that he was retiring. He had been so good for so long. He was still on top of his game when he stepped down. But I always trusted coach Dooley's decisions, and I knew he had a good reason. I'm just glad I was there when he was carried off the field for the final time down there in Jacksonville.

They say college is supposed to be some of the best years of your life, and that was really true for me. I didn't have very many chances to get back to Athens right after I left, because I was playing pro football and it was hard to remain in touch. But now I'm starting a new chapter in my life, and I'm looking forward to Saturdays in Athens and being a part of something that has meant so much to my life.

Whenever anybody mentions Georgia it always puts a smile on my face. There really is no experience to compare with being a Georgia Bulldog.

Troy Sadowski was an All-American tight end for Georgia in 1988. After 10 years in the NFL, Sadowski returned to Atlanta, Georgia, and entered private business. He currently lives outside of Atlanta in Woodstock, Georgia.

LINDSAY SCOTT

Wide Receiver
1978–1981

I T'S FUNNY, BUT WHEN YOU'RE YOUNG you have no idea how a few seconds on a football field in Jacksonville, Florida, will change your life. You have to grow older and get a little perspective to realize the real impact of something like the touchdown play that beat Florida in 1980.

It's not something I talk about every day, but I don't mind if other people want to ask me about it. I'm flattered that they still remember because it was over 20 years ago.

When I look back on my time at Georgia, I like to remember just hanging out with my teammates in the locker room. I like to remember getting ready for the games and the celebration after a game when we won. I like to remember the friendships that I made then that are so important to me today. For me, that was the real joy of my four years at Georgia. That's what being a Bulldog is all about.

When I was a senior at Wayne County High School in Jesup, I was looking around outside the state. I wanted to go somewhere where I could get the opportunity to get the ball on a regular basis. My high school coach, John Donaldson, was a Georgia man, and I think he figured out that I would score a touchdown every four times I touched the ball. So he put together all kinds of ways for me to get the ball. That was the only drawback when I thought about Georgia, because they had a great history of running the ball—three yards and a cloud of dust, you know.

My dad really liked the Tennessee offense. Coach Johnny Majors had come to Tennessee, and they were known for sending a lot of great receivers to the NFL. But my mom really wanted me to go to Georgia because she wanted to come see me play. I had an older brother, Dennis, who went to Virginia Tech, and there was just no way that we could get up to Blacksburg to see him play very often.

The other thing was that I had developed a bond with coach Mike Cavan. That made all the difference in the world. When Georgia signed Buck Belue at quarterback, I was convinced they would open up the offense because Buck was a great passer. So I decided to stay at home and go to Georgia.

I'll never forget my freshman year, in 1978. I expected to play early, and by the LSU game I was a starter. I was able to run the second-half kickoff back for a touchdown, and we went on to win that game [24–17] over there in Baton Rouge. I wish I could explain what it felt like to do that in front of those ninety thousand people. It was really something, and I believe that's when people started to notice what I could do. You always wonder as a young player if you can compete at this level. That's when I was sure that I could.

286

Later on that year we beat Georgia Tech [29–28] in the wildest game I've ever been a part of. Buck came off the bench and brought us from behind to win that game. I know that was a big moment for him.

That was a good team for a lot of reasons, but the guy I looked up to was Willie McClendon, our running back. We played against a lot of good running backs, but nobody ran harder than Willie. I really looked to him for my inspiration.

I wish I knew what happened in 1979 [when Georgia went 6–5]. We lost a lot of good players, like Willie, and that was a team that really needed to grow up. We were talented but still very young. That was such a weird year; we started by losing to Wake Forest [22–21]. We lost all of our nonconference games but kept winning the conference games until we got to Auburn, who beat us pretty good. But if we had beaten Auburn, we could have gone to the Sugar Bowl with a 6–5 record. That was really strange.

I'll never forget something that coach Wayne McDuffie said during that time. Coach McDuffie once told us that we were happy winning on a regional level when we should be thinking on a national level. He believed that Georgia had everything it needed to compete for the national championship. Now, nothing was broke at Georgia, but he thought that we should

Lindsay Scott's 93-yard catch and run for a touchdown against Florida in 1980 launched the Bulldogs into a national championship season.

be thinking bigger. I think our class listened to him. We thought we could do something big.

[Editor's note: In the spring of 1980, Lindsay Scott lost his football scholarship for one year after an altercation with an athletic department official, but was allowed to stay with the team and pay his own way to school. In late summer, he was involved in an automobile accident that left him with a concussion and several dislocated bones in his foot. One of the doctors told Scott's mother that he would never play football again.]

After the accident I did sit around for a while and wonder "why me?" But the honest answer was that I had never had to face any real adversity in my life. Things had always rocked along pretty well for me.

The fact is, I had to grow up a little bit. I'm sure that at some point every college kid goes through what I went through. It's just not all over the papers the next day. But that's part of being a college football player at a place like Georgia. I had forgotten who I was supposed to represent. I wasn't just representing myself. I was representing my family and my school. I had to learn that.

Yes, a doctor told my mother I would never play again, but that was a joke because I knew I was coming back. I didn't care how hard I had to work. I know my mother was afraid for me, but she never questioned me when I said I was going back and that I was going to play. She never asked me not to play. She knew deep down inside that I was going to be all right.

It took a while before I felt right again. The foot healed up fine, but it took me a while to get my equilibrium completely back. I don't think I ever felt completely right until we got to Jacksonville to play Florida.

We weren't throwing the ball very much, but I understood why. Herschel Walker had come on as a freshman and had been an incredible running back. And with a player like that, you knew coach Dooley was going to keep giving him the ball.

But you know how it is when you're a receiver—you want to catch the ball. It's funny now, but back then an article came out where a reporter asked some of us receivers if we wished we were throwing the ball more. Well, what would you expect us to say? Of course! What receiver doesn't want to catch the ball more?

But the article made it sound like we were unhappy with the way the offense was being run. Well, if you know coach Dooley, you know that wasn't going to work. He pulled us aside the next day and politely told us what he thought. That was the last time we talked about that issue.

When we got to Jacksonville I had not caught a touchdown pass all season. We had played nine games and I was shut out. We were winning and I was happy about that, but catching a touchdown pass does wonders for your confidence. You feel like you're an important part of the offense.

And to be perfectly honest about it, I needed something good to happen to me. With everything that had gone wrong in my life—losing my scholarship and the accident—I just needed something to go my way for a change.

I really thought we were going to put Florida away. We jumped on top of them early, but all of a sudden they jumped ahead of us, 21–20. After all we had been through together, I just didn't see how we were going to let this thing slip away. And when they kicked the ball out of bounds at the 8-yard line things didn't look good.

I remember that in the huddle Nat Hudson wouldn't let anybody get down. We knew what we had to do. We had an All-American kicker in Rex Robinson. We just had to get it close enough to give Rex a shot.

The first two plays were really frustrating. Buck lost a yard scrambling on the first play, and on the second play they took me out of the game. I was thinking, "What the hell are you doing! You brought me here to make plays. We talked about it! And with the game on the line I'm on the sideline!" I just didn't understand.

289

But I was put back in the game on third down, and coach [George] Haffner called Left 76. All we wanted to do was get a first down and keep the drive alive.

My job was to go down and do a little curl pattern. I didn't know what was going on behind the line of scrimmage. All I knew was that Buck got me the ball, and when I caught it I knew I had the first down.

But at that moment my mind went back to something that John Donaldson had taught me in high school. He always said, "Don't fall; keep on running after you catch the ball." So when I caught the ball and felt myself going down, I put my hand on the ground to steady myself and kept running. Once I caught my balance I saw a guy go down, and then I saw an opening.

When I started running my first thought was that I could get us into field goal range. After about 10 more yards it dawned on me, "Hell, I can take this thing to the house."

I have no idea who was behind me or how close they were, but I knew I was fast enough to outrun them if I just didn't fall down. And the second I got to the end zone it seemed like the whole world came down on top of me.

Everybody called it a miracle. To me it was the greatest feeling in the world. It was the shot in the arm that I really needed.

Like I said before, I didn't understand the magnitude of that play for a long, long time. It began to sink in a little after we won the national championship. If we hadn't beaten Florida [26–21] that day then we probably never would have gotten the chance to play Notre Dame in the Sugar Bowl.

That team was really special. We had that big play against Florida, but guys had been making big plays like that all year. Every week it was somebody different. I can't begin to tell you how many plays Scott Woerner made during the course of that season. It was incredible.

The fact that we're still talking about that play over 20 years later tells me that it is something special. But it was just one great moment in the four years that I spent at Georgia—the best four years of my life.

At Georgia I had the opportunity to play ball, travel, and meet friends who would stick with me the rest of my life. I had a chance to be with a group of guys who could say that we were the best team in college football. Not a lot of people get to say that.

The entire Georgia experience affected the way I think about life. Sure, I've had to regroup a couple of times in my life. And when I did, I would go back to the lessons I learned at Georgia from coach Dooley. When things get tough, you always go back and pull those lessons out of the closet. That's because they work.

For me, going to Georgia was a once-in-a-lifetime experience. There has never been anything else like it.

Lindsay Scott was an All-SEC receiver in 1981. He was later drafted by the New Orleans Saints. Today Scott lives in Valdosta, Georgia, where he works for a trucking firm.

HERSCHEL WALKER

Tailback
1980–1982

I remember when the call came telling me that I had just been named to the College Football Hall of Fame. My first reaction was that I thought they were kidding. I really didn't think I had done anything yet because I still felt so young. That's because I felt that my freshman year at Georgia wasn't really all that long ago. I laughed when I got the news because I thought that you were supposed to be old to get those kinds of honors.

I'm so humbled by all the things that have come my way in life because I feel I still have so much to learn. Time goes by so fast. You just have to remember to stop and count your blessings along the way, and God has really given me more than my fair share.

When it comes to the memories, it's hard to know where to start. There are so many wonderful football memories because we were able to have some success while I was at Georgia. But what sticks with me today, and what I am most grateful for in my life, are the people I met at Georgia and how good they were—and still are—to me. Georgia was the best place in the world for me because I always knew that the people there cared about me as a person first. I never had any doubt about that.

The list of people is too long, but I always have to give thanks to coach [Vince] Dooley and coach Mike Cavan, and teammates like Frank Ros, who have remained close to me. Ros is like a brother to me, and he has always been there for support.

People ask me all the time, if I were 18 years old, would I want to go back to Georgia and do it all over again? I don't think we're meant to live our lives over. One shot is all we get and we have to make the most of it. If I did go back, though, I wouldn't want to change a thing.

I really, really enjoyed my time at Georgia. As everybody knows, I wasn't sure if I was going to go to Georgia. But once I got there I knew that Georgia was the only place for me. It was an experience that will always be with me and I will always be grateful for it.

I look at Georgia as a huge family. My sister was there. I met my wife, Cindy, there. And once you are part of the Georgia family, you remain in that family for the rest of your life. No matter what happens, they will always be with you.

And it was at Georgia where I learned to grow up and be a man. We had some good times at Georgia, but we also had some trials and tribulations. Those made me a much better person and built me into the kind of man I am today.

People ask me if I miss football and if it was hard to give up playing. It really wasn't. I don't miss the game, but I really miss being with the guys in the locker room. I miss seeing their faces after we have won a big game. I miss the crazy stories they would tell. I miss being with a group of guys that has a common goal. When talented people work together and care about each other, it's amazing what they can accomplish. That is what I miss.

And that is exactly what happened at Georgia in 1980, my freshman year. Georgia had had a tough season the year before [6–5], so nobody thought our team could be special in 1980. But that group of guys was really close. We stayed together as a team. No matter how tough things got, we always believed that if we just kept playing as hard as we could, we would find a way to win. That's what we did for every single game that year. That is why my freshman year at Georgia is still my number one moment in sports.

Because I went to Georgia and because I played for coach Dooley, I received some opportunities in life that other young people don't get. So I guess that's why I have always felt it was up to me to make a difference in this world. There are so many young people out there who need support—who just need a chance like the chance I got at Georgia.

Herschel Walker led Georgia to the national championship in 1980 and became the Bulldogs' second Heisman Trophy winner in 1982.

After all, when I get to heaven, God is not going to ask me how many Heisman Trophies I won or how many yards I gained. He's going to ask me what I did for my fellow man. I would like to have a good answer for Him.

Herschel Walker was the 1982 Heisman Trophy winner and is still Georgia's all-time leading rusher with 5,259 yards. When he left Georgia after the 1982 season, Walker held 11 NCAA records, 16 Southeastern Conference records, and 41 Georgia records. In his three seasons at Georgia, the Bulldogs posted a 33–3 record and won three SEC championships and the 1980 national championship. In 1999, Walker was inducted into the College Football Hall of Fame. Today Walker lives in Dallas, Texas, where he is involved with several charitable causes.

EDDIE WEAVER

Defensive Guard
1978–1981

GROWING UP I THINK MY ATTITUDE was about the same as any teenage athlete's. I had an ego and I believed in my ability. I had lettered in four different sports in high school and was a state champion in all four. The thing that was most important to me was going to a school where I could play right away.

I remember very well my recruiting visit to Georgia in 1977. Georgia was playing Kentucky that day and was in the middle of the first [and only] losing season coach [Vince] Dooley would ever have.

I just remember that Georgia was having a really bad day. [Editor's note: Georgia lost the game 33–0.] After the game Kentucky's quarterback said that he had so much time setting up to pass that he could have had a soft drink. From the point of view of an 18-year old, that was all I needed to hear. I knew the Georgia coaches were not going to be satisfied with the team, and there would be an immediate opportunity to play next fall.

Wayne McDuffie recruited me for Georgia, and since he was the offensive line coach I figured that was the position that I would be playing. That was certainly the position I wanted to play. In fact, I had really enjoyed my visit to Kentucky, but they told me up front that they wanted to move me to defense. So I scratched them off my list and picked Georgia.

At our very first practice I walked onto the field sure that I was going to be an offensive guard. So when the rest of the offensive linemen walked onto the field, I started sizing them up as an egotistical young person would do. But when the defense came out of the locker room, one of the coaches told me to go with them. I didn't know what was going on, and I was pretty confused.

I guess coach Dooley knew I wasn't completely happy with the situation because one day he came and asked if I wanted to play offense or defense. I told coach Dooley that it didn't matter to me because I came to Georgia to participate—not to spectate. I told him I wanted to play the position that would get me on the field the fastest. He said that would be on defense and from that day on I was happy to be a defensive lineman.

I still have a lot of memories of those first days at Georgia. I remember thinking that I was never going to finish the two-mile run. But Sam Mrvos, our strength and conditioning coach, jumped out there with me and wouldn't let me stop. He said he would run with me the rest of the way. That meant something to me.

Coach Erk Russell, our defensive coordinator, was an extraordinary man. He had a unique ability to know how to motivate each person as an individual. I've never met anyone else who knew how to read people the way coach Russell did. When things got tight, he always knew how to break the tension by telling some old corny joke. He was always a good human being, so guys would always go the distance for him.

I remember my first season, in 1978, because I was a backup to Paul Petrisko at one of the defensive guards. I wasn't thrilled about playing behind Paul, but I trusted coach Russell. He knew what he was doing. I knew I would eventually get my chance.

We won a lot of close games that year and went to the Bluebonnet Bowl. But the thing I remember most about 1978 was Willie McClendon, our running back. Willie was one of the toughest, most physical running backs I had ever seen. You could count on him hurting one of the other guys at least once a game. I always knew I would get one prolonged break per game. That's how tough Willie was.

I really don't know what happened to us in 1979 [a 6–5 record]. It seems to me that a lot of people got hurt before the season started. We started out awful and just couldn't get it turned around.

I've been asked many times what I thought of Herschel Walker when he arrived at our practice before the 1980 season. I would have to say that early on I was not impressed. Herschel just didn't do anything in practice to make him stand out. I had played with Willie McClendon and to me he set the standard for what a running back should be. I had also played against [Joe] Cribbs and [James] Brooks at Auburn, and I thought both of them were better.

Eddie "Meat Cleaver" Weaver was a defensive stalwart on Georgia's 1980 national championship team.

But then came that day against South Carolina when he ran a lead draw or something. I watched Herschel run up the sideline toward the bridge. I saw the safety man pick his angle to make the tackle, but when the safety got there Herschel was gone! At that point I remember saying to myself, "Our buddy here might be serious." From then on it was obvious to me and everybody else that he was something special.

My favorite memory of 1980 was beating Florida [26–21]. Being from the state of Florida, that game felt the same way to me as the Georgia–Georgia Tech game felt to our guys from Georgia. My brother, Curtis, went to undergrad and medical school at Florida, so I guess they assumed I was coming, too, and they didn't recruit me very hard.

In fact, when my little brother Michael came along, Florida recruited him hard from the very beginning. They brought him into a film room and pointed out that their offensive guard had only graded out about 30–35 percent against me. They told him that they needed guys like him to block guys like me.

Well, this idea of them trying to pit us against each other did not go over well with my mother. She told Mike that either he could go to Georgia, or he could go somewhere where we wouldn't compete against each other. He came to Georgia.

The 1980 season just sort of fell into place for us all the way through the Sugar Bowl against Notre Dame. I remember that in that game, it seemed like coach Russell knew everything they were going to do before they did it. He was a nervy old man and the tougher the situation was the better he seemed to be.

298

Except for a bad performance against Clemson [in a 13–3 loss] we could have been playing for another national championship in 1981. Erk had left, but the nucleus of a great defense was still there with guys like Tim Crowe and Jimmy Payne.

The main memory I have of that season is one that will stick with me the rest of my life. We were in the Sugar Bowl against Pittsburgh, and we thought we had them stopped at the end of the game. I could see the pass going in the direction of their player [John Brown] in the end zone. The second he touched the ball, our guy popped him good. Ninety times out of one hundred, the receiver drops the ball when he gets that kind of lick. But he held on, and they beat us.

People ask me all the time what I enjoyed most about playing football at Georgia. I always go back to a little phrase that coach Dooley always used. He always said it was the little things that set you apart and make you special. Everybody can do the big things well, but it's the little things that matter most.

Coach Dooley was talking about football at the time, but I've found that you can apply that to everything in life.

I remember one day a motivational speaker came to see our team. He talked about the importance of "holding on to the rope." In other words, if you were dangling off a cliff by a rope, who could you trust to hold on to the other end? Would you trust your teammates to hold the rope and, more importantly, could they trust you?

At Georgia I learned that there is nothing like being with a group of guys that you trust to hold on to the rope when things get tough. I also learned that no matter how tough things get, you never quit. You just keep playing. You just keep working. Those are the kinds of lessons you never forget.

Eddie "Meat Cleaver" Weaver was an All-SEC nose guard in 1980 and 1981. Today he lives in Atlanta, Georgia, where he is an electrician.

The
NINETIES

CHAMP BAILEY

Defensive Back
1996–1998

W HEN I LOOK BACK ON IT, I guess there were all kinds of reasons for me to go somewhere other than Georgia.

Coach Ray Goff started recruiting me early, but during my senior year he was let go. Coach Glen Mason came in for a week and recruited me, but then on Christmas Day of 1995 he decided he was going to stay at Kansas. I really didn't know what to think.

But coach [Jim] Donnan came and really made me feel like he wanted me at Georgia. I know some coaches will tell you anything to get you to come to their school, but that wasn't coach Donnan. He stood by his word. I was really blessed to have him as a coach because he pretty much let me do what I wanted to do on the football field.

That first season [1996] was pretty tough. [Editor's note: Georgia was 5–6 in the 1996 season.] We really had some growing pains as everybody got adjusted to the new staff. But it helped me to have my older brother, Ronald, already there. He was a starter and he just kind of showed me what to do. I just followed in his footsteps and tried to get a feel for things.

We had some good wins when I was a freshman, like the game at Auburn where we beat them [56–49] in four overtimes. Nobody expected us to do that. But I think after that game we knew that if we did what coach Donnan and the staff asked us to do, we'd eventually be a good football team.

I will always remember my sophomore season in 1997. By then I felt I had pretty much mastered what they wanted me to do at cornerback. That's

Champ Bailey may have been the best cornerback ever to play at Georgia.

when coach Donnan started to use me some on offense and special teams. I really loved it.

In high school I had played a lot of offense, and once coach Donnan gave me a taste of it, I didn't want to go back. I really liked making plays and getting the ball in the open field.

The two greatest memories of that year were the Florida game and the Georgia Tech game. I know a lot of people didn't expect us to beat Florida because we hadn't been able to win against the Gators for a long, long time. But, growing up in south Georgia, you pretty much learn to hate Florida, and I was really looking forward to that game.

We knew we were good enough to beat Florida. We had a lot of guys on that team—guys like Robert Edwards, Matt Stinchcomb, Hines Ward, Chris Terry, and myself—who went on to do well in the NFL. When we got up on them 14–3 at halftime, we knew we had a great chance to beat them, and we did [37–17].

After that game there was such a great celebration. Out in the parking lot of the stadium in Jacksonville, people just stayed around and had another great party. Most of the players on my team were going back to Athens, but I got in my dad's car and rode home with him. I remember walking out to the car and the people were just so happy. I had never seen anything like it.

If you're a Bulldog, beating Georgia Tech is always great. But it's even better when you win the way we won down there in 1997. Tech thought they had us beat when they scored late to take the lead. [Editor's note: On November 29, 1997, Georgia Tech's Charles Wiley scored a touchdown with 48 seconds left to give Georgia Tech a 24–21 lead at Bobby Dodd Stadium in Atlanta.] But we got the ball back in good field position when their guy kicked the kickoff out of bounds.

Coach Donnan put me into the game and we ran what we called a "tunnel screen." I lined up at receiver on the right side and just came across the middle of the field and caught a pass from Mike Bobo. Now you never know what kind of opening you're going to get on that tunnel screen, but I was lucky to get a big one. I just wanted to get as many yards as I could so that we could at least get a field goal to tie the game. [Editor's note: Bailey took that pass 28 yards to give Georgia a first down at the Georgia Tech 37-yard line. Bailey then caught another pass from Bobo for seven yards and Georgia was at the Georgia Tech 30-yard line with 29 seconds left.]

After I caught those two passes it was pretty clear to me that we weren't going for the tie. We were going for the *win*! And that's what we did. We got it down there close after Tech was called for pass interference, and then Bobo hit Corey Allen for the winning score. The Tech people couldn't believe we had snatched that thing away from them. That was a sweet, sweet win.

We were so close to being a great football team in 1997, so a lot of us thought that 1998 would be our year. And when we started 4–0 and beat LSU [28–27] down in Baton Rouge, we were convinced that we were going to win the SEC. But Tennessee came to our place the next week and they just beat us [22–3]. At the time we didn't know how good Tennessee really was, but they went undefeated and won the national championship.

We had a bad game against Florida [a 38–7 loss]. But the game that will always hurt was the loss to Georgia Tech [21–19]. We were so much better than they were. It didn't make sense for us to lose to them. I just couldn't believe we lost that one.

I knew pretty much at the end of my junior year that turning pro was going to be the right thing to do. There were reasons to stay. Boss, my little brother, was a freshman and I wanted to sort of look after him. But it was the right thing to do. Coach Donnan was with me every step of the way and really helped me. I will always be grateful to him for that.

305

I've been lucky in my life. I come from a great family and they have always been there to support me. And my brothers and I were lucky that we all played at Georgia. I'm still taking some classes at Georgia, and the people there still treat me and all the members of my family well. When you come to Georgia, it is like being a part of a family and that family is always with you.

I love Georgia. I grew up a Bulldog fan, and I always knew I wanted to be a Bulldog. But the experience was everything I hoped it would be. Georgia was the perfect fit for me, and I felt like I had a great career there. I wouldn't change it for anything in the world.

Champ Bailey was perhaps the most versatile player at Georgia since the inception of two-platoon football. Bailey participated in more than one thousand plays in 1998 as a cornerback, wide receiver, and special-teams player. He was a first-round draft choice of the Washington Redskins in 1999 and was traded to the Denver Broncos in 2004. His brothers, Ronald and Boss, also played for Georgia.

MIKE BOBO

Quarterback
1994–1997

WHEN YOUR DAD IS ALSO YOUR HIGH SCHOOL COACH, you look at the recruiting process a lot differently. [Editor's note: Bobo's father, George, was a longtime head football coach at Thomasville High School. When Bobo signed with Georgia in 1993, his dad left his head coaching job to become an assistant in the Athens area so that he could see his son play on a regular basis.]

He wanted me to never lead another coach on. So if I wasn't interested in a school, I had to tell that coach up front. It made for a much simpler process for me.

To tell the truth, I was never really a big Georgia fan growing up in Thomasville. Both my parents went to Georgia, but I was a big Auburn fan. Dad never pushed me toward Georgia, even though he went there.

But when it came time to make a decision, I had to look at what was the best situation for me. It was 1993 and I liked what Georgia was doing in their passing game with Eric Zeier. I knew that if I went to Georgia I could learn under Eric for a couple of years and then get my chance to play. I thought it was the perfect fit for me.

The plan in the fall of 1993 was that I would redshirt because Eric was a junior, but I quickly found out that that plan was not set in stone. Just prior to the first game with South Carolina [quarterbacks coach] Steve Ensminger brought me in and said, "We were going to try and redshirt you, but you're the backup quarterback. If Zeier goes down then you're the guy. If it's just mop-up duty, we'll send the other guy in."

Well, there were no problems with that for the first three games, but then we went down to Ole Miss. Those guys just beat poor Eric to death. They hit him something like 38 times in the game. Over on the sidelines under my breath I was telling him, "Get up, get up." I was thinking, "Oh my Lord, I'm going to go into this game and get drilled." I don't know how Eric survived that night but he did, and I did get to use a redshirt that year.

In 1994 I was the clear backup to Eric. Now, the job of a backup quarterback is to prepare like he is the number one guy, because he's only a snap away from being in there. That is easy to say, but sometimes it is hard to do because Eric would get most of the reps in practice. Here I have to give Eric a lot of credit, because he was competitive in everything he did. In every drill, every day, he competed, because he wanted to be the best, and that made me compete, too. That helped me stay sharp and stay perfect. I was really fortunate to play behind a guy like him and that really helped me.

My most meaningful playing time that year came in the last regular-season game, against Georgia Tech. Eric got hurt in the second quarter, and I had to play the rest of the day. I can't tell you how nervous I was, because the first time that you go out to play some meaningful minutes, you're not completely sure if you belong out there. I remember watching the game on tape, and when I came off the field for the first time the TV camera cut to me. I was trying to drink some Gatorade, but my hand was shaking so badly the drink was splashing out of the cup.

But I had some success that night. [Editor's note: Bobo came off the bench to complete 13 of 16 passes for 206 yards and a touchdown in a 48–10 win over Georgia Tech. Bobo had a 30-yard touchdown pass and another completion for 50 yards.]

From that game on I felt like I could play at Georgia.

Ironically, when I had my first big success at Georgia my dad wasn't there to see it. We moved the Tech game to the Friday after Thanksgiving for television, and his high school team was in the state playoffs that night.

In 1995 I became the starter, but my season didn't last very long. We went down to Ole Miss and I got hurt in the first quarter. I checked off to a pass, and we missed a block. I got hammered and suffered a fractured knee that knocked me out for the rest of the season.

That was a tough year all the way for injuries. Robert Edwards got hurt in the game with Tennessee. I got hurt and was out for the year. It also turned out to be coach [Ray] Goff's last year. In many ways I just didn't think it was fair for that group of coaches to get fired because of all those injuries.

The 1996 season was one of the toughest of my life. Coach Jim Donnan had come in with a brand-new system. I came off the knee injury, but I never really got back into shape. I was catching a lot of heat because I really wasn't playing very well.

The only bright point we had in that entire season was when we came back to tie Auburn and finally beat them in four overtimes [56–49]. The good thing about that game was that we finally started to believe in one another and started playing hard. After that the players bought in to what coach Donnan was doing. We knew we had a chance to be good down the road.

In the off-season coach Donnan brought me in and laid it on the line. He told me I was not going to be guaranteed the starting job for next season. He was going to throw it open for competition in spring practice.

At that point I thought about moving on. I was going to graduate that spring anyway, and I knew I wanted to get into coaching. I thought that maybe I should just get on with my life.

But then I realized how lucky I was to be playing football at Georgia and that when my playing days were over that was going to be it. So I decided I would do everything I could to make my senior year special. I worked my tail off and got in shape, and when the season rolled around I was ready to go.

We knew going into the Florida game that season that we could win. It didn't matter how many times Florida had won in a row [seven]. That game really epitomized what that Georgia team was all about. I threw three picks early, but we never got down. We just kept playing and beat those guys pretty good [37–17].

As great as that win was, there has never been a sweeter win than the one at Georgia Tech in 1997. To drive the ball the length of the field to win [27–24] in the final seconds at their place—man, it doesn't get any better than that. I get chills right now just talking about it.

The seniors on that team made up their minds before the season. We didn't talk SEC championship. We talked about getting Georgia back to being competitive with the best teams around, and I think we did that in 1997. We won 10 games. We beat Florida and we beat Tech. In my mind that's a pretty good year.

Mike Bobo led Georgia to a 10–2 season in 1997. The Bulldogs beat Florida in Jacksonville that season, 37–17. Today he is an assistant coach at Georgia.

As much as I enjoyed my playing days at Georgia, the real honor has been the opportunity to come back as an assistant coach and to work for coach Mark Richt. Under coach Richt Georgia is winning again, and we're competing for championships again. When I was a student at Georgia I knew it was one of the greatest places in the country to go to school. Now every day I get up in the morning and go to work for a university I love that is located in one of the best college towns in all the world.

It just doesn't get any better than this.

As a senior, Mike Bobo threw for 2,751 yards and 19 touchdowns and led Georgia to a 10–2 record. He directed Georgia's offense in a 37–17 victory over Florida, its only win over the Gators in the past 14 meetings. Today, he is an assistant coach for the Bulldogs.

GARRISON HEARST

Running Back
1990–1992

THERE WERE A NUMBER OF REASONS I chose to go to Georgia. I grew up in Lincolnton, which is only 60 miles away from Athens. When I was growing up I used to go to games at Georgia all the time. It was a place where I felt comfortable.

Just looking at the football side of it, I knew there was going to be an early opportunity to play, and that was important to me. Rodney Hampton was leaving at running back, so I knew I'd get an early chance to prove myself, and that's all I wanted.

The running backs coach was Willie McClendon, and I liked him a lot. My relationship with him was one of the big reasons I said to myself, "Forget this other stuff and go to Georgia." I wanted to play for coach McClendon.

I looked at some other schools. I had a really good visit to South Carolina. I also went to Florida State and Tennessee. I was scheduled to visit Clemson, but on the day I was supposed to go Danny Ford resigned as head coach. I canceled that trip.

Besides, Lincolnton was a big Georgia town, and two of my former teammates—Dwayne Simmons and Curt Douglas—were already there, so really there was no way I could go anywhere else. I would never hear the last of it.

I loved being in college and being a part of the atmosphere of the games at Georgia. It was really exciting. What I didn't love was losing, and we lost seven games when I was a freshman. This was something I was not used to.

At Lincolnton we only lost two games in my four years of high school football. College life was great, but I wanted to win and win soon.

In 1991 everything changed. Wayne McDuffie came in as offensive coordinator and changed everything we were going to do offensively. He made it clear to me that we were going to throw the ball because we had great receivers and Eric Zeier was coming in at quarterback.

I have to admit that initially I was a little upset with the new offense. I trusted coach McDuffie because he recruited me for Florida State. He promised me that even though we were going to throw, it would help the running game. But at first I thought he was stressing the pass so much that he was going to forget about the run.

Well, he was right, because after a while things began to balance out. Because we were throwing the ball so much, teams couldn't put eight or nine men in the box to stop the run.

The perfect example of this was the game we played against Clemson. Man, I had a ball that night. Clemson was ranked pretty high, and people didn't know if we could do anything. We beat them [27–12], and I don't ever think they figured out what we were doing.

But at times we played like we were still trying to learn the offense. Somehow we got beat at Vanderbilt [27–25]. We got up on them early, but we didn't put them away. I still can't believe that happened!

All of us knew that we were going to have a really good team in 1992. It would be the second year for everybody in this new offense, and we wouldn't have to play and learn at the same time. We went into the winter quarter workouts saying that we just needed to get faster and stronger and we'd be ready.

Let me tell you, that team could play with anybody. Offensively, that team could do everything, but we were five points from playing for the national championship.

It's hard to talk about the games we lost to Tennessee and Florida that year. Against Tennessee [a 34–31 loss] we were moving the ball up and down the field on those guys. That game really ate me up when we lost it.

I still haven't gotten over the Florida game [a 26–24] loss. I only had 12 carries in that game, and I was standing over on the sidelines begging them to please use me. I hated losing that game because I thought I could have contributed more.

In 1992 Garrison Hearst won the Doak Walker Award, which goes to college football's best running back.

We did finish off that season with a good win over Ohio State [21–14] in the Citrus Bowl. Man, did they talk a lot of junk. They thought they were the team of the century because they were from the Big Ten. They thought they shouldn't have to play a team like Georgia. But we showed them why the SEC is the best conference in the country.

People are going to be surprised to hear me say this, but there are times now that I wished I had stayed for my senior year instead of turning pro. If I had it to do all over again I probably would stay, because I really missed my friends. I know that I missed out on a lot by not being a senior in college.

I loved being a college student, and I loved being at Georgia. Going to Georgia was really the turning point in my life because it taught me so much. It taught me a lot about football, but it also helped me learn about what it is like to be around people from all over the country. Georgia gave me the chance to make some lifelong friends who are still close to me today.

When you're playing pro ball, it is really hard to get back to Athens, but I hope to do that some day down the road. It's a special place, and I loved every minute I stayed there.

Garrison Hearst was an All-SEC and All-American running back in 1992. Hearst also received the Doak Walker award, which goes annually to college football's best running back.

Hearst played for the Arizona Cardinals, the Cincinnati Bengals, and the San Francisco 49ers before being traded to the Denver Broncos in 2004.

MATT STINCHCOMB

Offensive Tackle
1995–1998

I GUESS YOU COULD SAY THAT I went through one of the strangest times in the history of Georgia football. When I was a freshman in 1995 we ended up having three different head football coaches in about three weeks.

I was recruited by Mac McWhorter and head coach Ray Goff to come to Georgia. The truth is, they really didn't have to work that hard.

I started going over to Athens for games with my coaches pretty early in my high school career. I didn't have a family connection with Georgia, but for some reason I always felt comfortable when I was there. By the time I got to be a senior it was pretty much a foregone conclusion for me: I was going to be a Bulldog. Nobody ever noticed, but when I would take my unofficial visits to other schools, I would always do it on the Saturday they were playing Georgia.

As a freshman in 1995, I was a backup to Paul Taylor at the tight-side guard. I don't know if Paul was a first-team All-SEC player that year, but he should have been. He was a great player.

That was really a tough year, and things really worked against our team. We started out great when Robert Edwards scored five touchdowns against South Carolina. And the next week against Tennessee we were running up and down the field when Robert got hurt. Then things just began to fall apart because of injuries. Before the season was over we had Hines Ward, a wide receiver, at quarterback.

We finished the season 6–5 [6–6 after losing the Peach Bowl] and things began to get very strange and very surreal. In December Glen Mason was named the head coach. A week later, on Christmas Day, we heard that he was going to stay at Kansas.

I can say this now: I really and truly think that situation worked out for the better. The players liked and respected coach Goff, and a lot of them told me that they weren't sure that coach Mason would have been a good fit. We only had a very short time with coach Mason, I know, but it just didn't seem like it was going to work.

A lot of stuff changed when coach [Jim] Donnan came in. First of all, no one was retained from the previous staff, and that is always difficult. It would have been different if there had been a lack of respect for the previous staff, but this was a wholesale change. It was a tough transition, particularly for the older guys.

The first season was tough because we went 5–6, but we did have a couple glimmers of hope, as I recall.

We lost our first two games to Southern Miss and South Carolina and were behind at home late in the game to Texas Tech, 12–7. We were looking right at 0-3, but Mike Bobo drove us 97 yards in the last two minutes, and we beat them 15–12. From an internal standpoint that was huge. We really needed that win—it gave the players a little confidence in the new coaching staff.

Then came the game at Auburn where we were behind 28–7 and just getting killed. Everybody thought we would probably fold up, because the week before we had been destroyed by Florida [47–7].

Mike Bobo didn't start the game, but he came on and somehow threw a touchdown pass on the last play of regulation to tie the game and send it into overtime. That ended up being the first four-overtime game in SEC history and we won [56–49]. If I had to pick a game that was the most important one of my time at Georgia, it would probably be that one. At that point we were a beleaguered football team that really needed something good to happen. The win was a glimmer of hope that one day we were going to be good.

In 1997 good things finally started to happen. The biggest moment was when we went to Jacksonville and beat Florida for the first time in a really long time. I'm sure a lot of people didn't see it coming. I was rooming with Steve Herndon at the time. We were sitting in the hotel room the night before the game, and we just kind of looked at each other. I think I said, "Does it kind of feel different this time?" He agreed. It's hard to explain

Matt Stinchcomb, an All-American tackle in 1997 and 1998, also won the Draddy Award, which goes to college football's top scholar.

because you always feel you have a chance to win, but for some reason my gut felt really different.

Beating Florida [37–17] was a very pleasant surprise. It had been so long, and the Georgia people wanted it so badly.

After that game against Florida we thought we might be in a position to do something pretty big, but the next week we lost to Auburn [45–34], and that kept us out of a big bowl.

When I was a senior, in 1998, we thought we really had it going after we won at LSU [28–27] to go 4–0. We went home to play Tennessee, and everybody was really excited. *College Game Day* was in Athens. But then we went out and didn't play very well at all and got beat [22–3]. It was a huge letdown for everybody.

What we have to remember is that Tennessee had a great team that year. They went on to win the national championship. In fact, Tennessee was the biggest hurdle we faced during my entire career at Georgia. They had some very good teams, and you have to give them credit.

Of course, we went back to our old ways and lost to Florida again [38–7]. For some reason the guys wanted to wear black pants, as we had done in the Outback Bowl against Wisconsin. I wasn't for it. Maybe if we had worn the silver britches we would have won. I'm sure those black pants made a 31-point difference.

What I remember about that game is that Bill Goldberg came in and gave us his best pump-them-up speech. To his credit he stayed the whole game, because it was a bloodbath. They just jumped all over us.

I really don't want to talk about the Georgia Tech game in my senior year [a 21–19 loss]. Our senior class had made it a big deal that we weren't going to be the class that finally lost to those guys. I know this will come off as bitter, but there were a lot of strange things that happened in that game—and they all went against us. You can't go back and argue about it now, but that game and the loss the year before to Auburn were the two toughest losses I had at Georgia.

Still, I wouldn't trade anything for my four years at Georgia because it sort of set the stage for the rest of my life. I knew that I ultimately wanted to live in Georgia and that I would make a group of friends and contacts there that I would always have. Today my closest friends are the guys that I played with.

Georgia is a great institution with great traditions, and I feel I was lucky to be a part of it and remain a part of it. Playing at Georgia really has become the centerpiece to everything else I've done in my life.

Matt Stinchcomb was an All-American offensive tackle in 1997 and 1998. He was a two-time academic All-American who graduated with a 3.96 grade point average. In 1999 Stinchcomb was a first-round draft choice of the Oakland Raiders, where he still plays.

ERIC ZEIER

Quarterback
1991–1994

Because my dad was in the service, I spent my entire childhood moving all over the world. There is no question that it affected my personality and shaped me into the kind of person that I would become.

When you move that much, it presents a situation where you always have to prove yourself. You can't rest on anything that you've done in the past because the new people you meet don't know anything about it. As a result, you are always looking forward in your life and not back. That's a good thing.

When I was a sophomore in high school we moved from Heidelberg, Germany, back to Marietta, Georgia, where I got a chance to finish up high school. So when it came time to pick a college, I knew I wanted to stay close to home. My family is very important to me, and I wanted to make it easy for them to see me play.

Georgia was where I really wanted to go, but I also had Florida State and Alabama in my final three. But right before my Georgia visit, coach [Ray] Goff hired Wayne McDuffie and Steve Ensminger to run the offense. When those two coaches came on board—with what they could bring from an offensive perspective—that really sealed the deal.

I was able to graduate from high school early and enter Georgia in the winter quarter of 1991. Now, I was no different than most guys coming out of high school. I had confidence in my ability and felt that if I worked hard at it, I could compete at this level. But I'll never forget my first visit to the weight room at 6:00 in the morning. It was the day after I arrived at

Georgia. I was surrounded by a bunch of guys I didn't know, and it was an atmosphere that was a lot more intense than I was used to. I knew right away that I was in a different ball game. For a minute there I thought, "What in the world have I gotten myself into?"

So all I did that winter and spring was put my head down and try to work as hard as I could to learn the offense.

Going into the season Greg Talley was the number one quarterback, but I knew I would get a chance to come into the game and play some. Things began to come around for me on an October night against Clemson in 1991.

That was such a tremendous day, and I don't think anyone there will ever forget it. Earlier in the day the Atlanta Braves had clinched the first Division championship that began their great run. Clemson was ranked in the top 10, so the crowd was really jacked up. You could feel the excitement in the air when we went out on the field. Then we went out and won the game [27–12].

If I didn't understand it before then, that night I completely understood what it meant to be a Georgia Bulldog.

320

I got my first start the next week against Ole Miss and played pretty well, but the following week against Vanderbilt I got benched. I didn't have a good game at all, and we lost [27–25]. The next week against Kentucky I was again the starter, and to me that was very important. If I hadn't been put back in the lineup at that point my whole career could have been different. But from that point on I felt like the number one guy, and it really helped my confidence.

Our 1992 team at Georgia had as much talent as anybody in the country. The only problem we had was that we had not been in tough positions before and hadn't learned how to win close games. We were certainly good enough to beat Tennessee [a 34–31 loss], but we helped them with a bunch of turnovers. Then there was a tough loss to Florida [26–24] when we were basically just as good as they were, but we didn't make enough plays in the fourth quarter.

I wish that nucleus of guys could have stayed together for another year. We had great receivers, and we had Garrison Hearst at running back, who could do so many things.

My last two years at Georgia we just came up short. I get asked a lot about the 1993 game against Florida in that driving rain in Jacksonville. I have always been a team guy, but on a personal note I have to say that it was one of the greatest games I had as a player at Georgia. [Editor's note: Eric Zeier

Eric Zeier, a two-time captain at Georgia, is the Bulldogs' all-time leading passer.

completed 36 of 65 passes for 386 yards and two touchdowns in a 33–26 loss to Florida in the rain in Jacksonville on October 30, 1993. Georgia had seemingly tied the game when Zeier hit Jerry Jerman with a 12-yard touchdown pass with five seconds left. But officials ruled that a Florida player, Anthone Lott, had called timeout before the play was run. Zeier's 65th and final pass attempt, an SEC record, fell incomplete on the final play of the game.]

Both teams fought so hard. I wish they could all be like that, but I wish we could have come up on the right side of the scoreboard.

We had another heartbreaking game like that in 1994 when we lost at Alabama [29–28]. We were basically one completion away from putting that game away, but then they marched down the field to win the game. [Editor's note: Georgia led Alabama 21–10 at halftime on October 1, 1994, in Tuscaloosa. Alabama rallied and Michael Proctor kicked a 32-yard field goal with 1:12 left to win the game.]

That game really took the air out of our season. I have always believed that if we had won that game, the year would have been entirely different [Georgia finished 6–4–1 in 1994].

Later on that year we lost to Vanderbilt [43–30] on homecoming, which is a game I have put out of my memory. Then we tied Auburn [23–23] over there, when they had won their last 20 football games. Like I said, I thought we had a good football team that year, but things didn't always work together like we had hoped.

But the bottom line for me has always been this: we didn't win as many football games as we would have liked at Georgia, and we didn't reach all of our goals, but even if I had never played football, Georgia is where I would have gone to college. I made friendships there and established relationships that will be with me for the rest of my life. You can't put a price on that.

Georgia gave me the foundation I needed as a young man. Watching how coach Goff and coach [Vince] Dooley would handle situations taught me lessons that I still use in my daily life.

And let me take this opportunity to say something about coach Goff. There are a lot of things that go on sometimes that are beyond the control of the head coach. But the real measure of a head coach, I think, goes beyond wins and losses. The legacy that a head coach leaves, I believe, is in the lives of the young people he touched and the kind of people they become.

If you look at that, then coach Goff was a great success at Georgia. If you talk to any of his former players, they will say the same thing. If I had to go to war tomorrow, I would want Ray Goff by my side. When it comes to being a true Bulldog, he is the best. And he taught a lot of us to how be Bulldogs, too.

When Eric Zeier left Georgia after the 1994 season, he owned 18 SEC and 67 Georgia passing records. He is still the SEC's second all-time leading passer (behind Peyton Manning) with 11,155 yards. He was the captain of both the 1993 and 1994 Georgia teams. Zeier lives in Athens, Georgia, where he works in banking.

The
NEW MILLENNIUM

BOSS BAILEY

Linebacker
1998–2002

BECAUSE I HAD OLDER BROTHERS WHO PLAYED FOR GEORGIA, people have always asked me if I had a choice to go anywhere else. Sure, I had a choice, but the honest answer is that after Ronald and Champ played at Georgia, it just seemed like a second home to me.

Ronald and Champ never put any pressure on me. In fact, Champ wanted me to go to these other places and have some fun. But when I hurt my knee in high school I decided to go ahead and tell the Georgia coaches I was coming.

I really enjoyed my freshman season, in 1998. Champ was still on the team, and it was nice having my brother around. I was basically a special-teams player and a backup linebacker to Dustin Luckie. I got on the field a pretty good bit, and it was great to put on the uniform and be a football player at Georgia.

About the only real memory I have of 1998 is when we went down to LSU and beat them [28–27]. That put us at 4–0, and we came home to play a big game with Tennessee. That was an incredible day. ESPN brought *College Game Day* to Georgia, and people were really fired up.

Tennessee was undefeated, too, and we really didn't know how good they were until we got on the field. Our defense was concerned with stopping Tee Martin and Peerless Price, but Tennessee lined up and ran the ball against us with Travis Henry and Travis Stephens. They beat us pretty good [22–3]. Tennessee went on to go undefeated and win the national championship, so we can't feel too bad about that loss.

In 1999 I got my first chance to start, and I was really excited about that. That was the year, though, that coach [Kevin] Ramsey came in as the new defensive coordinator. He brought in a brand-new system, and at first it was tough for us to learn. It took longer to adjust to what coach Ramsey was doing than we thought it would. That's why our defense struggled. We had a lot of problems defensively, but I still think I had a chance to show the coaches what I could do.

After a so-so season in 1999 [8–4] I think we were all excited about what could happen in 2000. We knew that a little heat was on coach [Jim] Donnan, but we really thought we were going to have a big year and that everything would be fine.

Unfortunately, my season ended during the first game, with Georgia Southern. That year coach Donnan decided that some of the starters needed to play on special teams. I was on the kickoff team. On the opening kickoff I was running down the field and planted my foot to avoid the blocker. I felt my knee give way. Nobody ever even touched me.

As soon as it happened, I knew the knee was gone because I had hurt the other knee like that in high school. I knew that I was done for the season.

At first I was down about it, but it turned out to be a blessing in disguise. My young son was about to have heart surgery, and this gave me more time to spend with him. As soon as I got home after the game and saw him, I was through feeling sorry for myself. [Editor's note: Bailey's son, Kahlil, was born with a heart defect and underwent four hours of surgery in 2000 to correct the problem. Today, Kahlil is fine.]

It really surprised me when they fired coach Donnan after the 2000 season. We didn't have a great season, but we were 8–4. That's not awful, either. We did have talent, and I guess they thought we should be winning more than that with the players we had.

I remember meeting coach [Mark] Richt for the first time. I had heard a lot of things about him when he was at Florida State. We knew he was coming from a great winning tradition. I went up to his office and chatted with him. I was immediately impressed with how calm he was about life and how he went about his job. I knew there was something special about him.

Another reason I liked coach Richt was that he never sugarcoated anything. He made it clear that he believed in hard work. The first thing he talked about was winning the SEC championship. He said we couldn't think

327

about the national championship until we were good enough to win the SEC. I really respected that about coach Richt.

The worst day of my college career was not when I hurt my knee. It was the day that I was introduced to mat drills in the off-season. [Editor's note: Mat drills are a series of strenuous exercises that are run on a conditioning mat. They are designed to push the player past the point of exhaustion and to test his ability to push through fatigue. Like basic training in the armed services, it also serves as a bonding experience for the players.] It was funny: they showed us videotape of the guys at Florida State running them, and I remember looking at Peter Warrick—he seemed to be enjoying it. So we're thinking, "Hey, this is going to be a lot of fun. This is something we can do together to get in shape."

Well, I think they just showed us the good parts of the tape, because when we started running them ourselves it was no fun at all. I was wondering what kind of mess we had gotten ourselves into. Some of the guys were thinking, "Man, we should have played harder for coach Donnan, and we wouldn't be doing this right now."

328

I thought that day was never going to end, but it did and we survived. And the mat drills, as bad as they were, brought us together as a team. And that's where our motto was born: "Finish the Drill." It means that no matter how tired you are, you have to find the energy to finish the drill. Those mat drills made us mentally tough.

I think that toughness really paid off for the first time when we won at Tennessee that fall [of 2001]. Tennessee thought they had us beat when they scored late. Another team would have been tired and would have given up, but we had something left and found a way to win that game [26–24].

That game was the turning point for this team and this program. After that everybody had the greatest confidence in the world in each other and in coach Richt and the staff.

We didn't talk a lot about it publicly, but I really believed we had a chance to be pretty good in 2002. We had some great leaders on that team, guys like Tony Gilbert and Jon Stinchcomb and myself. And we had some younger guys who wanted to be good and would follow.

I think the turning point in our season was when we went to Alabama. I think that may have been the toughest place I've ever played. That was SEC football at its finest. We fell behind late, and Alabama was sure they were going to win. Then our offense really got rolling and just marched the ball

Boss Bailey, Champ's brother, overcame a serious knee injury to lead Georgia to the 2002 SEC championship.

down the field. Billy [Bennett] kicked the field goal and we won [27–25]. It's hard to explain, but we really knew we were going to win that game.

That win was especially sweet because before the game coach Pat Dye, who used to be the coach at Auburn, said that we weren't "man enough" to beat Alabama.

I had the exact same feeling when we played Auburn. We played a lousy first half, and late in the game we were still behind. But I just knew that somebody was going to step up and make a play. Then David Greene and Michael Johnson made the play [a 19-yard touchdown pass with 1:25 left] to give us the win and put us in the SEC championship game.

The night of the SEC championship game at the Georgia Dome was really, really special. I remember seeing the look on the face of Jon Stinchcomb. His brother [Matt] had played at Georgia with Champ, but they had never won an SEC championship. I remember looking at Jon and we both thought, "This is for all those guys." [Editor's note: On December 7, 2002, Georgia beat Arkansas 30–3 in the SEC championship game in Atlanta. It was Georgia's first SEC championship since 1982.]

I remember talking to my brothers after the game, and I think they were more excited than I was. It had been so long for Georgia, and to be a part of the team that finally brought the championship back to Athens was really special. I still have a picture of me, Stinchcomb, Tony Gilbert, and Burt Jones. We were the captains of that team and the captains for that game. That is something that I will always have with me.

I began to visit the University of Georgia when my brother, Ronald, went there in 1993. Ronald had his time. Champ had his time. And now I've had my time.

I just know that my brothers and I wouldn't give anything for our time at Georgia.

I guess you could say that Georgia has been pretty good to the Bailey family. I hope that we have been good for Georgia, too.

Boss Bailey was an All-American linebacker in 2002 and the captain of Georgia's SEC championship team. Two of his brothers, Ronald and Champ, played for Georgia. Today Bailey plays for the Detroit Lions in the NFL.

DAVID GREENE

Quarterback
2001–2004

I'VE ALWAYS BEEN ONE OF THOSE PEOPLE who believe that things happen for a reason. And now that I'm a senior I'm convinced that I was meant to be at Georgia.

If you look at my family you would figure I should have played at Auburn. My granddad went to Auburn and my dad went to Auburn. My sister graduated from Auburn. When I was a kid I dreamed of playing there. As a family, when we went to college football games, we went to Auburn—not Georgia.

But when it came time for my decision, I knew I had to look at the bigger picture. I wanted to play in the state I grew up in, and I wanted to be close to home so it would be easy for my parents to come see me play.

Once I went to camp at Georgia I knew that's where I wanted to be. I knew I wanted to be a Bulldog and be a part of those great traditions and the atmosphere at Sanford Stadium.

I really wasn't all that highly recruited, but coach [Jim] Donnan seemed to see something in me that I really didn't see in myself. In my dealings with him he gave me the confidence that I could be a good player if I worked at it.

I pretty much knew I was going to get redshirted as a freshman in 2000. Coach Donnan's offense is really complex, and you had to know your stuff if you were going to run it. I wasn't ready to step into the huddle and have a presence with older players. I understood that. Besides, Quincy [Carter] was already here at quarterback; I was willing to wait my turn.

Because coach Donnan had shown so much confidence in me, it was a really tough and weird time when he got fired that December [of 2000]. But when that happened I looked back on the best advice I ever got, which was from my high school coach, T. McFerrin. He said don't go somewhere because of a coach. Go where your heart is because coaches can always change. Still, we were all disappointed when coach Donnan left, because we didn't know what was going to happen.

The early days under coach [Mark] Richt were tough. Anytime you get a new coaching staff it is tough because it's about first impressions. They wanted to make us understand at the very beginning that they were in charge and what was going to be expected of us. The first day we ran mat drills we almost died, but it was just their way of getting us acclimated to a new way of doing things.

We listened to coach Richt because we knew that he knew what he was talking about. Because of his time at Florida State, he knew what a national championship football team was supposed to look like. We knew he had won big games and had coached Heisman Trophy winners. We always had our ears open when he talked.

332

The good thing for me in that spring was that all the quarterbacks were having to learn a new system at the same time. I never approached it as if I were fighting for the number one job. I figured Cory Phillips was going to be number one because he had played. I just wanted to be good enough so that if I did get in the game, we would have a chance to win. [Editor's note: Greene was listed as co–number one quarterback with Phillips going into preseason practice for the 2001 season. He was eventually named the starting quarterback for the first game with Arkansas State.]

People point to our win at Tennessee in 2001 as a big game and they are right. The one thing that had hurt Georgia for so long was that we won the games we were supposed to win, but we didn't win anything else. And that Tennessee team we beat up in Knoxville was one of the most talented teams we've ever played. It was a huge win for our program.

Jon Stinchcomb would kill me for saying this, but I remember standing in the huddle during a TV timeout during that game with Tennessee. Stinch came over and pointed in Tennessee's direction and said, "Can you believe how big those guys are over there?"

They were huge, but our team was not intimidated, even when we fell behind late and things didn't look very good. What I remember is that a

David Greene's touchdown pass to Michael Johnson in the final moments against Auburn put Georgia into the 2002 SEC championship game.

bunch of guys stepped up and made plays. Damien Gary caught a little dump pass and made two guys miss, and then all of a sudden we were at midfield. Then Randy McMichael went off and started making one huge catch after another. That guy made himself a lot of money in the draft on that day.

The touchdown pass to Verron Haynes was really an easy play. Either it was going to be wide open or it wasn't. When you're a freshman you need that kind of play. All I had to do was dump the ball to him. I knew it was going to work before we snapped the ball.

From that point on I think our team always thought it had a chance to win when it took the field.

I thought we had a chance to be pretty good in 2002. Obviously our goal was to win the SEC championship, and after the win at South Carolina [13–7] the tone was kind of set for us.

What people forget about the game with Auburn is that we played an absolutely brutal first half. Auburn's a tough place to play as it is, but there we were with everything on the line and we were just getting it handed to us in the first half.

I really believe that's where having great seniors comes in—Stinch, Boss, Tony Gilbert. They knew our whole season was on the line. They weren't going to let us lose.

When you think about the touchdown play to Michael Johnson, you have to think that it was meant for us to win that night. We were down to our last play, and I had been taught to get the ball there and give the receiver a chance to make the play. Michael fought for the ball, the defender slipped a little bit, and he timed his jump perfectly. There were a million ways that play could have turned out, but we made it, and it put us in position to win the SEC championship.

I've heard that people will be talking about that play 20 or 30 years from now just like they talk about the other great plays in Georgia history. That really blows my mind. Because at this time in our lives, those of us who play don't realize what is taking place. We think we're just out there playing ball, but at the same time we're really making history.

The great thing about winning the SEC championship was that I was born in 1982, and it was hard for me to believe that Georgia had not won a championship for as long as I was alive. I know we can't wipe out all the suffering the Georgia people had to go through in those 20 years, but I am glad I was part of the team that got us back there.

The 2003 season was tough. It really tested our patience and our character. We faced more adversity last year than any year since I've been at Georgia. We had more injuries. We were younger than we had ever been. At times we played with some young guys who really didn't know what was going on. But we went 11–3, and two of the games we lost were against the team [LSU] that won the national championship.

I would never say I was satisfied if we didn't win the SEC championship, but given everything we went through, and the holes we had to fill, that was a pretty good year.

I know that someday I'll look back on my years at Georgia and call them the best of my life. That's what I've heard other people say about their college years. And now that I'm at Georgia I can't imagine having gone to school anywhere else. It has been everything I dreamed about and more.

But right now I don't have a lot of time for reflection. Until you stop playing there is always some unfinished season. And we have to start getting ready for one more season. Being a senior, I'm hoping that 2004 will be a very special year.

335

David Greene was the All-SEC quarterback and the Most Valuable Player of the SEC Championship Game in 2002. Greene entered the 2004 season having started 40 consecutive games at quarterback for the Bulldogs.

FRED GIBSON

Flanker
2001–2004

I HAVE TO BE HONEST AND SAY that when I was growing up in south Georgia, I really didn't know anything about Georgia. I watched Florida because they were the hot team. I liked the way they played and the way they threw the ball all over the place. That just seemed like the place for me.

But when it came down to signing day, I had a difficult decision to make. I had narrowed it down to Georgia and Florida. As I was headed to school that day, I had both scholarships in my hand, and I still didn't know what to do.

The story I like to tell is that I decided to flip a coin. If it's heads I'm going to Florida. If it's tails I'm going to Georgia. Let's just say that it came up for Georgia and that it was the luckiest thing that ever happened to me.

One of the reasons Georgia was a good situation for me was that I knew I would get a chance to play right away. I started out as a freshman behind Reggie Brown, but then Reggie got hurt. I hated that for Reggie, but it was my opportunity to show what I could do. I think I had something like five 100-yard games in a row, and I got the chance to make some plays.

That team had some high moments and some low moments, but I don't think any of us will forget the win at Tennessee [26–24] in 2001. I think that was when we knew that, down the road, we would probably be a good football team.

It was really fun to be a part of that SEC championship team in 2002. When people told me that Georgia had not won an SEC championship in 20 years, it was really hard for me to believe. That was a super night, playing Arkansas in the Georgia Dome. It was something I will never forget.

Fred Gibson was an immediate star as a freshman in 2001 and is considered one of Georgia's greatest receivers.

The 2003 season was the most frustrating thing I've ever been through. I kept getting hurt and that was really hard for me to accept. The team was out there fighting, but I couldn't get out there and help. Nothing like that had ever happened to me. I just felt like I couldn't do anything right.

That's why I'm so excited about my senior season. First of all, I can't believe I'm a senior. It seems like I got here yesterday.

That's one of the funny things about being in college. When you're a freshman you look down the road and think you've got plenty of time to do what you want to do. You don't worry a whole lot because if you miss something today, you will always get a chance to do it tomorrow.

Now this is it. I can't believe it has gone by so fast.

Like I said, I didn't understand Georgia football and what it was all about until I got here. People would mention Herschel Walker and I really didn't know who Herschel Walker was. Everybody would look at me like I was crazy. "How could you *not* know about Herschel Walker?" they would say.

But in three years at Georgia I have to say I have learned a lot. I know so much more now about the school and its history and what it really means to be a Georgia Bulldog. And to me it is the greatest feeling in the world.

Georgia has the greatest atmosphere for football. The fans are great and they really care. I may have wondered about my decision back when I was a senior in high school, but there is no doubt in my mind now that I made the right decision. You can now say that I'm a Bulldog through and through. I couldn't ask for anything more than being at Georgia.

As a freshman in 2001, Fred Gibson set a Georgia receiving record with five 100-yard games in a season. He led the 2001 team in receiving yards with 772.

DAVID POLLACK
Defensive End
2001–2004

I REMEMBER THE EXACT DAY when I knew I wanted to be a Georgia Bulldog.

I was a senior in high school, and I was on an official visit during the 2000 season. It was the night that we beat Tennessee for the first time in a long time and the fans stormed the field. It was an incredible experience and it sealed the deal for me. I wanted to be a part of Georgia and all of its great traditions.

Sure, I looked around at schools like Florida, Georgia Tech, Ohio State, and Clemson. But everything that I wanted in football and in a college was at Georgia, and it was only 45 minutes from my house. It made the decision very easy.

Now, I'll admit that I wavered a little bit when Georgia made the change and let coach [Jim] Donnan and his staff go. They had recruited me all through high school, so I thought that maybe I should look around some more. But coach [Mark] Richt had some good things to say, and he made me feel comfortable that the program was in good hands.

I came to Georgia as a fullback because I thought that would give me the best chance to play early. But we had a bunch of injuries early in preseason camp, and coach [Brian] Van Gorder asked me if I wanted to move to defensive tackle. I was a little hesitant to make such a big move that quickly in my career, but in high school I had loved to play defense because you could get in there and throw your body around and have fun. I was just happy to get on the field.

People remember that we beat Tennessee up there in 2001, but I'm not sure most people understand how big a game that was. We were a young team with a new coaching staff, and when we went up there I really don't believe we thought we could beat Tennessee. We had not won up there in forever. And for us to come back and beat them the way we did was a big hurdle to get over. We left Knoxville that day believing we could win if we played our game, because that was a great Tennessee team.

After my freshman season I got introduced to mat drills. I had never experienced anything like it. If you're young it is meant to break you down, but it also teaches you a lesson, because when you're exhausted you have to find a way to push yourself through it. Those drills teach you that when you're tired and you think you have nothing left, you do. You just have to go find it. It is a big part of our program now.

The day before spring practice started in 2002 coach Van Gorder brought me in again. This time he asked me to move to defensive end, because we had lost a lot of guys at that position. Again, I was hesitant, because I had gotten comfortable at tackle, but I said I'd give it a shot. So I went over with coach [John] Fabris and gave him a chance to coach me up a bit.

340

For the first two weeks I was like a fish out of water. I really didn't know what I was doing. But then we had spring break, and when I came back things started to click a little more. By the end of spring practice I knew I could be pretty good at the position if I kept working at it.

People say they didn't know that 2002 was going to be a special year. But I thought we were good enough to win the national championship if we got a few breaks and stayed healthy.

There's no question that we got some momentum when we went up to South Carolina and beat them [13–7]. People like to talk about the play where I took the ball from the quarterback and scored a touchdown. That was a big play, but it was the kind of thing that the team did all year.

For the record, I've gotten a little tired of seeing that play. My dad told me that I need to make a new play to replace it. He's right.

But after that South Carolina game we seemed to keep rolling. We had to come back to beat Alabama over there, but we had confidence that our offense would put Billy Bennett in a position to win the game with a field goal.

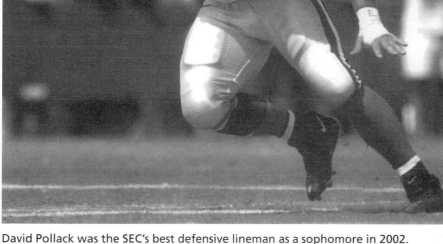

David Pollack was the SEC's best defensive lineman as a sophomore in 2002.

And the play that David Greene threw to Michael Johnson to beat Auburn is one of those moments and was one of the greatest plays that you're ever going to see. There are a bunch of plays in Georgia football history like that. I'm really glad we were able to contribute to that tradition.

The fact is, 2002 was a special season, and you don't have that kind of season without guys making big plays. That group of guys believed in each other, and by the time we got to the SEC championship game against Arkansas, we were a very good football team.

We did everything in 2002 except win them all. We had our chance against Florida but just didn't cash in [losing 20–13]. I don't think I'll ever forget that loss.

With all the people we lost off that team, I'm sure nobody expected us to go 11–3 in 2003. But there is still a part of me that feels like we could have won them all.

Somebody told me that people were always going to talk about the 2002 season, because we won the first SEC championship in 20 years. I'm hoping they will talk more about the 2004 season—my senior season.

I can't believe I'm a senior already, and when I look back I realize that the good Lord was looking over me when he sent me to Georgia. I just know there is a reason why I'm here. Knowing what I know now about college and about football, I can't imagine being anywhere but Georgia.

There is just something special about being a Bulldog. That's why I had to stay for my senior year.

David Pollack was an All-American defensive end and the SEC Player of the Year in 2002.

JON STINCHCOMB

Tackle

1999–2002

M Y BROTHER MATT AND I have lived very similar lives, and to a lot of people it was a foregone conclusion that I would follow in his footsteps to Georgia. But the fact is, we are different people, and I wanted to look around a little bit more to make sure that I was going to get the right fit for me.

So I looked around to make sure a place like Auburn or Clemson wouldn't be better for me. But every place I went I just kept comparing it to Georgia and what Georgia had to offer. I realized that no matter where I looked, there wasn't going to be a better place for me than Georgia.

Matt was really hands-off during the process. He and the rest of my immediate family were comfortable with letting me make the decision. Others were a little more pushy, especially living where we live with all those Bulldogs. Let's just say there were a lot of happy people when I made my decision.

I graduated from high school early so that I could come to Georgia in the spring of 1998. I did that for a couple of reasons. I needed to rehab a torn anterior cruciate ligament, but the main reason was so that I could spend more time with Matt. He was going to be a senior and the coming year would be the last chance to spend any significant time together.

I get asked a lot what having an All-American brother at Georgia meant to me when I got there. It meant a lot. To have a role model who is also someone you love is very special. Watching the way he worked and prepared was obviously a learning experience for me. I watched Matt and Chris Terry,

Georgia's other tackle, and learned from them. There is no doubt in my mind that being around them created a work ethic in me and gave me the good habits that put me on the path to success.

I redshirted my first year in 1998, and today I'm thankful that I did. At the time I was a little bitter. I'm sure ego always comes into play, because when you're young you want to prove yourself. I took that year to get stronger and to get better. If I had played right away, I'm sure the comparisons to Matt would have started way too early, and that's not fair to an incoming freshman.

In 1999 I was the backup right tackle to Kelvin Williams, but then he got hurt. Suddenly I was in the starting lineup as we went to Tennessee. I remember that game because Shaun Ellis was the big dog of their defense that year, and it was going to be my job to block him most of the time. I'll never forget that on the trip Miles Luckie called me up to sit with him.

Miles said that at some point in your career as a football player you have a game that separates you from where you are and where you want to be. He said, "You have a great opportunity, today."

He was right. Shaun Ellis was one of the best players in the country. I'm not saying I played a world-beater of a game, but I played pretty well against him. From that point on I felt I belonged. I knew I could play at this level.

The other game that stands out that year was when we lost to Georgia Tech in overtime [51–48]. That was the Jasper Sanks fumble that I don't think was a fumble. The whole play never made sense. They took the ball away from us, and I still don't get it. I will always be bitter about that game.

I thought expectations might be pretty high in 2000. When coach [Jim] Donnan got up and said publicly that he had been waiting for a team like this all his life, I knew there was going to be pressure. But the truth is, when I looked at that team on paper, I thought we matched up well with anybody that we were going to play.

That team had the talent and it had the system. We just didn't put it all together every Saturday.

South Carolina [21–10] was really the eye-opener. I think all of us had bought into the hype about our team, but five turnovers later we realized that we weren't invincible after all.

I thought we had gotten it back together after we beat Tennessee [21–10] at home for the first time in ages, but we stumbled down the stretch. After

Jon Stinchcomb
proudly followed
in the footsteps
of his brother,
Matt, as an All-
American tackle
for the Bulldogs.

we lost to Georgia Tech [27–15] the players were making a push to keep coach Donnan around. He was a players' coach and the guys really liked him.

But it didn't work. I was headed to the Butts-Mehre building for a meeting, and we were all pretty sure what it was about. A coaching change is never a great thing for the players, but it was going to happen to us.

All we could do was try to send that coaching staff out as winners when we went to Hawaii for the bowl game. That was a strange situation, knowing that none of those coaches would be back. At least we were able to beat Virginia [37–14] in coach Donnan's last game.

You could tell early on that things were going to change under coach [Mark] Richt. Coach Donnan's approach and coach Richt's approach were very different. Coach Richt is a more hands-on coach, and he wants things done his way every time.

It wasn't long after coach Richt got to Georgia that we were introduced to mat drills, which was the off-season conditioning program that coach Richt brought from Florida State. That was an eye-opening experience. The first thing that a new staff wants to do is show that they are completely in charge—that things are going to be done their way. They proved it with those mat drills, and we paid for it.

There were 10 sets of mat drills, and after we had gone through about one and a half, some of us were ready to hang it up. But the good thing was that after we did the 10th one, we looked around and realized we had made it through together as a team. I believe it brought us closer together as a team.

Whenever you have a new coaching staff there comes a moment when everybody finally buys in to what they are selling. For the 2001 team, that moment came in Tennessee.

I mean, that stadium was really rocking, especially after Tennessee scored late on a screen pass to take the lead [24–20]. We got the ball back with less than a minute left, and to be honest with you, nobody in the huddle thought we were going to lose. It was like, "OK, let's go score."

It all started with a quarterback like David Greene. Maybe it was because he was so young, but I don't think David was really aware of how serious a situation we were in. He basically said, "Let's go do it."

You don't make a big drive like that unless guys step up and make plays. And Randy McMichael stepped up big time to put us in position to score with a couple of big catches. The play to Verron Haynes was one that we had run in practice a bunch of times. It was a great call by coach Richt, and we caught them in the right defense to make it work.

I can say that game was the starting point for building the team that would win the SEC championship in 2002.

Early in the season every good team needs to define itself, and I think we did that when we came from behind to win at Alabama [27–25]. Alabama had a very good team, but when we fell behind we didn't panic. We ran our offense and put Billy Bennett into position to win the game.

The Florida game [a 20–13 loss] is still a burr under my saddle. Here was a time when we were confident that we were the better team, but we just let too many opportunities go by the wayside. It was really disheartening, and when we walked off that field in Jacksonville, I was worried that maybe we had just let the SEC championship slip away.

Whenever people ask me about the big play against Auburn, I figure they mean the fumble I recovered in the end zone for a touchdown in the third quarter. I'm kidding, of course.

I mentioned how cool David was in the Tennessee game the year before. It was the same thing that night at Auburn. Everything was on the line in that game. We were behind and facing fourth down at the 19-yard line, and Greene came into the huddle and said something like, "OK, we need to make a play here. Make sure you give me enough time."

347

So he threw that ball up there, Michael Johnson just jumped up and grabbed it away from the guy, and we won. What a great play!

Coach Richt always talks about knocking the lid off the program and achieving big things. That's what we did in the SEC championship game. We knew we were going to win, and when we did it was like a huge weight had been lifted off our shoulders. We were carrying the weight of the past 20 years because it had been that long since Georgia had been able to win an SEC championship. We had a lot of fun that night.

I'm only a year removed from it, but I know what a big deal it was to be a part of the team that finally brought a championship back to Georgia. And I know that the further removed I am from it, the more pride I will feel.

When I came to Georgia it was because of its great tradition. I knew what Georgia represented, and I wanted to be a part of that. Hopefully my senior class left its mark on Georgia, and what better way to do it than with a championship? I know it is something that I am going to be proud of for the rest of my life.

Jon Stinchcomb was an All-American tackle in 2002 and a two-time Academic All-American. He graduated with a 3.75 grade point average in microbiology. He plans to attend medical school. His brother, Matt, was also an All-American at Georgia. Today Stinchcomb plays for the New Orleans Saints.

HONORABLE MENTION

*These men did not play football
for Georgia, but through their words
and deeds, they proved that they know what it
means to be a Bulldog.*

IN MEMORIAM

LEWIS GRIZZARD

1947–1994

Lewis Grizzard, a native of Moreland, Georgia, was an award-winning syndicated columnist for *The Atlanta Journal-Constitution*. He was also the quintessential Bulldog. He wrote many columns about his beloved football team, but this one, reprinted from the *Journal-Constitution* of September 24, 1984, perfectly captured Grizzard's feelings about Georgia and what it means to be a Bulldog.

He died in 1994 at the age of 47 but lives on in the hearts and minds of Bulldogs everywhere.

TO MY SON, IF I EVER HAVE ONE

Kid, I am writing this on September 23, 1984. I have just returned from Athens, where I spent Saturday watching the University of Georgia, your old dad's alma mater, play football against Clemson.

While the events of the day were still fresh on my mind, I wanted to recount them so if you are ever born, you can read this and perhaps be able to share one of the great moments in your father's life.

Saturday was a wonderful day on the Georgia campus.

We are talking blue, cloudless sky, a gentle breeze, and a temperature suggesting summer's end and autumn's approach.

Lewis Grizzard was an honorary coach for the G-Day game in 1978. Here he gets a ride on the shoulders of his players after a victory. Grizzard died in 1994 at the age of 47.

I said the blessing before we had lunch. I thanked the Lord for three things: fried chicken, potato salad, and for the fact he had allowed me the privilege of being a Bulldog.

"And, Dear Lord," I prayed, "bless all those not as fortunate as I."

Imagine my son, 82,000 people, most of whom were garbed in red, gathered together gazing down on a lush valley of hedge and grass where soon historic sporting combat would be launched.

Clemson was ranked No. 2 in the nation, and Georgia, feared too young to compete with the veterans from beyond the river, could only dream, the smart money said, of emerging three hours hence victorious.

They had us 20–6 at the half, son. A man sitting in front of me said, "I just hope we don't get embarrassed."

My boy, I had never seen such a thing as came to pass in the second half. Todd Williams threw one long and high, and Herman Archie caught it in the end zone, and it was now 20–13.

Georgia got the ball again and scored again, and it was now 20–20, and my mouth was dry, and my hands were shaking, and this Clemson fan who had been running his mouth the whole ballgame suddenly shut his fat face.

Son, we got ahead 23–20, and the ground trembled and shook, and many were taken by fainting spells.

Clemson's kicker, Donald Igwebuike, tied it 23–23 and this sacred place became the center of the universe.

Only seconds were left when Georgia's kicker, Kevin Butler, stood poised in concentration. The ball rushed toward him, and it was placed upon the tee a heartbeat before his right foot launched it heavenward.

A lifetime later, the officials threw their arms aloft. From 60 yards away, Kevin Butler had been true, and Georgia led and would win 26–23.

I hugged perfect strangers and kissed a fat lady on the mouth. Grown men wept. Lightning flashed. Thunder rolled. Stars fell, and joy swept through, fetched by a hurricane of unleashed emotions.

When Georgia beat Alabama 18–17 in 1965, it was a staggering victory. When we came back against Georgia Tech and won 29–28 in 1978, the Chapel bell rang all night. When we beat Florida 26–21 in the last seconds in 1980, we called it a miracle. And when we beat Notre Dame 17–10 in the Sugar Bowl that same year for the national championship, a woman pulled up her skirt and showed the world the Bulldog she had sewn on her under britches.

But Saturday may have been even better than any of those.

Saturday in Athens was a religious experience.

I give this to you, son. Read it and re-read it, and keep it next to your heart. And when people want to know how you wound up with the name "Kevin" let them read it, and then they will know.

—Lewis Grizzard

DAN MAGILL

I REMEMBER SITTING ON THE TEAM BUS with coach [Wally] Butts during the fifties and listening while he bemoaned the fact that we didn't have as much money as Georgia Tech.

Tech, of course, was in its heyday under Bobby Dodd, and it seemed like they had everything going for them. Tech could get the best players out of Atlanta, and they were also able to tap the best prep schools in the South, where there was really good talent.

I remember telling coach Butts that at Georgia we needed to start playing to our strengths. Our strengths were that we had more alumni than any other school in the state of Georgia. No matter which of the 159 counties you went to, Georgia was the majority party. We had more alumni in Atlanta than Tech did. So we had to do something to take advantage of that.

So after a disappointing season in 1953 [3–8] we founded Georgia Bulldog Clubs in every county in the state. We had a big rally at the Biltmore Hotel in Atlanta and our slogan was "We're Coming Back!"

It took us a while to get back, because we didn't win another SEC championship until 1959 when the hometown boy, Francis Tarkenton, led us to the 14–13 win over Auburn.

But the point is, whenever it seemed like the Georgia people were down, we have always found a way to come back and establish our birthright. We are, and have always been, the Majority Party of the great Empire State of the South. We have always come back because we have great coaches and great players to represent our great university. And we have always come back because of the Georgia people and the love we all have for a very special place.

Coach Butts took us to four SEC championships, but then things trailed off in the fifties and early sixties. In the fifties we lost eight straight games to Georgia Tech, which was a hard thing to handle. Then coach Vince Dooley came along and took us to six SEC championships and the glorious national championship in 1980.

After coach Dooley retired [in 1988] we hit a dry spell like all schools do, but now we're back in the hunt again with coach Mark Richt. Through all the tough times, the Georgia people were disappointed but never disheartened.

I am 83 years old, and I can't remember a time when I wasn't a part of the university. I was eight years old when Sanford Stadium was dedicated in 1929 against the great team from Yale. I was dressed in the football uniform that I had received the Christmas before, but when I got to the game it had already started. I told my daddy, who was up in the press box, "Daddy, they've already started. They've already chosen up sides."

In the early thirties I used to chase foul balls for the baseball team, which was coached by Bill White. Back then baseball was a big deal and the merchants would close their stores by noon on the day of a game. Coach White didn't have any money to pay me, but he let me clean up under the grandstand and keep any money that I found. One day I found a silver dollar, and I was scared of it because I didn't know what it was. Coach White let me keep it, and my dad made me open a bank account with it.

In high school they used to let me run the Georgia tennis courts and charge 10 cents for anybody who wanted to play there. Times were tough back then so I would keep a ledger for people to pay me at the end of the month. There's no telling how much interest I am owed on that money now.

I joined the Marine Corps on the day after Pearl Harbor, but the government told me I could finish college before I enlisted. And while I was in college I was a correspondent for the *Atlanta Journal* and later went to work for the *Journal* full time.

That's how I got back to Georgia. Back then I was covering high schools for the *Journal* and I would tip off coach Butts about the top prospects in the state. So on September 1, 1949, I went back to Georgia as an assistant to the athletic director. I think coach Butts just wanted some help with recruiting.

But around that same time, we lost our sports information director, and coach Butts asked me if I would fill in. I was qualified, so I filled in—from 1949 to 1976.

Many of those years I was the tennis coach and the head of the Bulldog Clubs, too. Finally, in 1977, I turned sports information over to Claude Felton,

In addition to being the greatest of Georgia historians, Dan Magill is the most successful coach in the history of men's college tennis.

who is the best sports information director in America. Loran Smith took over the Bulldog Clubs, and, of course, he's the best.

There are so many great memories I have that I can't possibly list them here. And I know that Georgia has changed a great deal from 1949 to today. But the thing that has never changed is the love that the Georgia people have for their alma mater. I realize that everybody loves his school, especially in the South. But we at Georgia have the oldest land-grant university in the United States, founded in 1785. We have earned a great reputation for building the leaders of tomorrow. Today, we have one of the top public universities in the country, and we should be very proud of that.

I have loved every minute of being a Bulldog. I wouldn't trade it for anything in the world.

Dan Magill served as Georgia's sports information director from 1949 to 1976. He founded the Georgia Bulldog Club in 1953. In 1988 he retired after 34 seasons as Georgia's men's tennis coach. At the time of his retirement, he was the winningest tennis coach in NCAA history.

A TRIBUTE

LARRY MUNSON

1966–Present

Since 1966 there have been hundreds of Georgia football lettermen. There have been four head coaches and scores of assistant coaches. Each of them gave everything they had to make Georgia successful.

But over the past 38 years, no one has lived and died, laughed and cried, with the Bulldogs each Saturday more than their incomparable radio voice, Larry Munson.

A Minnesota native who began his broadcasting career at the age of 20, Munson came to Georgia after 16 years as the play-by-play voice for Vanderbilt football and basketball.

Before coming to Athens, Munson did it all as a broadcaster. He was a member of the Atlanta Braves' original broadcast team. For 23 years he hosted his own fishing show in Nashville.

But once Munson called Georgia's 1966 SEC championship season, he knew he was home.

"I didn't know how it was going to turn out, but I knew Georgia was one of those jobs that guys could hang on to for a long time," he said. "One year just sort of followed after another and here I am."

Munson replaced the highly respected Ed Thilenius for the 1966 season and at first, the Georgia people did not warm to him. But that all changed on a Saturday afternoon in 1973.

356

After Georgia rallied to win at Tennessee 35–31, Munson shouted over the airwaves, "My God! Georgia has just beaten Tennessee in Knoxville!"

For the first time, Munson's passion for the Bulldogs caught the attention of the Georgia people.

Two years later Munson forever solidified his place in the heart of the Bulldog Nation with his call of the miracle 80-yard pass play from tight end Richard Appleby to wide receiver Gene Washington against Florida in Jacksonville.

Appleby, the end around, just stopped, planted his feet and threw it. And Washington caught it, thinking of Montreal and the Olympics, and ran out of his shoes down the middle—80 yards! Gator Bowl! Rocking! Stunned! The girders are bending now!

Look at the score!

The touchdown call, which gave Georgia a 10–7 upset victory, was replayed over and over on radio stations throughout the state for the rest of the season. The legend of Larry Munson was born.

Since then Georgia football has been defined by "Munson Moments," where Larry's call not only captured the excitement of the play but also froze the moment in time for future generations of Bulldogs. Here are but a few of those moments:

- 1978: After trailing 16–0, Georgia rallied and Rex Robinson kicked a field goal with three seconds to beat Kentucky 17–16. Munson never said the field goal was good, he just yelled, "Yeah! Yeah! Yeah! Yeah!"

- 1980: Herschel Walker's first touchdown run against Tennessee as a freshman got Larry excited and in turn, he got the entire Bulldog Nation excited, too:

My God Almighty he ran right through two men! Herschel ran right over two men! They had him dead away inside the 9. Herschel Walker went 16 yards. He drove right over those orange shirts and is just driving and running with those big thighs. My God, a freshman!

357

- Later in 1980, Munson became immortal with the call of what many people consider the biggest play in Georgia football history. Down 21–20 to Florida with time running out, quarterback Buck Belue hit Lindsay Scott on a short pass, and Scott turned it into a 93-yard touchdown to give Georgia a 26–21 victory.

  It would serve as the springboard to Georgia's national championship
  In the middle of Scott's run, Munson screamed "Run, Lindsay!"
  At the end of the run Munson never said, "Touchdown!" He just screamed, "Lindsay Scott! Lindsay Scott! Lindsay Scott!"

  Then he remembered that Georgia's fans, who annually turn that game into what has become known as "The World's Largest Outdoor Cocktail Party," would be celebrating well into the wee hours of the morning and said, "Man, is there going to be some property destroyed tonight!"

- 1982: Georgia was clinging to a 19–14 lead at Auburn, where a win would give the Bulldogs their third straight SEC championship. Auburn drove the ball deep into Georgia territory, but Munson would not let the Bulldogs lose. On every play he would implore the defense, "Hunker down one more time!"

  Munson's pleading worked. Georgia stopped the drive with 42 seconds left in the game and preserved the victory, which gave the Bulldogs a berth in the Sugar Bowl, where they would play Penn State for the national championship. As the final seconds ticked off the clock, Munson uttered the words that will forever live in the hearts and minds of Bulldogs everywhere: "Oh, look at the Sugar falling out of the sky! Look at the Sugar falling out of the sky!"

  It remains one of Munson's signature moments.

- 1984: Kevin Butler kicks a 60-yard field goal with 11 seconds left to upset No. 2 Clemson, 26–23.

So we'll try to kick one 100,000 miles. We're holding it on our own 49 and a half! Gonna try to kick it 60 yards plus a foot and a half! And Butler kicked a long one! A long one! Oh my God! Oh my God! . . . The stadium is worse than bonkers! Eleven seconds! I can't believe what he did! This is ungodly!

358

Larry Munson has been the voice of the Georgia Bulldogs since 1966.

359

• 2001: Now 80 years old, Larry showed he had not lost his touch when Georgia went on the road to Tennessee. Georgia fell behind 24–20 on a touchdown by Tennessee with 44 seconds. But Georgia roared back down the field, and with five seconds left, David Greene hit Verron Haynes with a six-yard touchdown pass:

Touchdown! My God, a touchdown! We threw it to Haynes! We just stuffed them with five seconds left! My God Almighty, did you see what he did? David Greene just straightened up, and we snuck the fullback over! . . . We just stepped on their face with a hobnailed boot and broke their nose! We just crushed their face!

Larry Munson has never made a pretense of being objective. He loves Georgia and Georgia loves him. The 2004 season will be his 39th behind the microphone as he pulls for his beloved Bulldogs. May he remain there for at least 39 more.

ERK RUSSELL

To TELL YOU THE TRUTH, I think I'm the luckiest man on the face of the earth. I got to spend 17 years in the prime of my life at the University of Georgia, which is one of the most special places in the world. Then I had a chance to go to a place like Georgia Southern and build something there. I'm just a lucky guy who had one great experience after another.

All those players and all those coaches I worked with at Georgia will always have a special place in my heart.

I was very fortunate to have gotten to Georgia in the first place. After spending a year at Vanderbilt I developed a great sense of humility. I was fortunate enough to know coach [Vince] Dooley, and he was kind enough to give me a job. For that I will always be indebted to him. And from the beginning it was a great experience.

That first year [1964] was one of the finest years of my life. We were a new staff in a new situation, and we felt like we had to do well. And I thought we did pretty well for a new crew. When we had our first practices at Georgia we found guys who were more than willing to play and to listen to what you had to say. They were as hardworking and hard-hitting a group of people as I have ever been around, and we just went from there.

That first year we went to a bowl game with a 6–3–1 record, and the excitement was incredible. The last year [1980], of course, we found a way to win them all. Our motto that year was "Do it one more time," and every week we found a way to do it one more time to win a national championship.

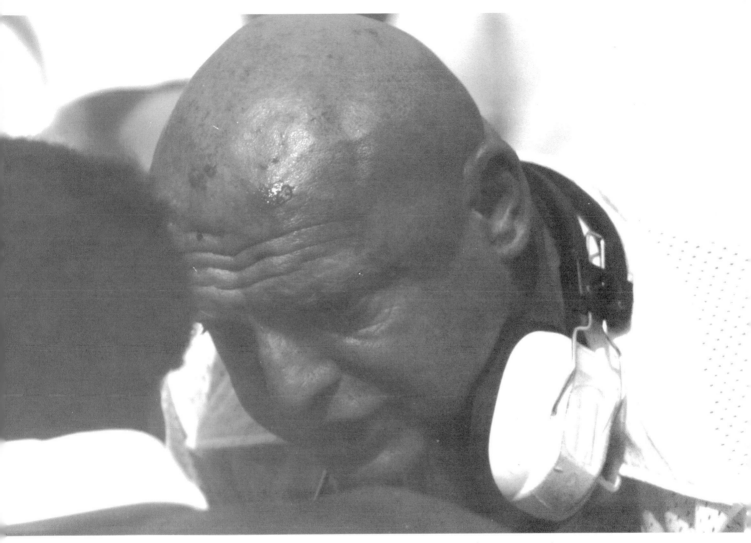

Erk Russell could be fierce during the game, but for 17 years he was Georgia's most beloved assistant coach.

In between the first year and the last year I had a chance to work with some young people who were very, very special. At Georgia we always wanted football players who could run and who could carry out assignments. But we also looked for character. We wanted people who had a strong desire to play football.

So many memories:

- The SEC championships in 1966, 1968, 1976, and 1980.

- The year [1976] all the players shaved their heads and looked like me. I still have the picture of all of us together.

- The first Junkyard Dawgs in 1975, who were a bunch of small, tough guys who really wanted to win.

- Beating Florida down there in 1975 [10–7] when nobody thought we had any business being on the same field with those guys.

- The 1980 team, which was as close a group of guys as I've ever been around. We had come off a mediocre year [6–5] in 1979. Then there was the pig incident, which got some of the players in trouble. That incident brought that team together as much as any one thing I have ever seen. What a year!

- The final seconds of the January 1, 1981, Sugar Bowl against Notre Dame. I had had my son, Jay, bring down a box of cigars in case we won. What I wanted to do was get all the defensive players together and enjoy one last cigar together when the game was over. As it turned out we had to run for our lives just to get off that field. But we got to enjoy those cigars together inside.

I went to school at Auburn, so people sometimes ask me how long it took before I felt like a Bulldog. It didn't take long at all. That's one of the special things about Georgia.

Like I said, I'm a lucky guy. I still hear from people about how I touched their lives during my time at Georgia. I don't really think about having done that, but if it worked out that way, then it's great. I'm complimented that those guys remember that I was there. I'd just like to say that the feeling is mutual.

Erk Russell was Georgia's defensive coordinator from 1964 to 1980. He left Georgia to become head coach at Georgia Southern, where he won three Division I-AA national championships.

IN MEMORIAM

HERSCHEL SCOTT, "MR. BULLDOG"

1921–2003

I N ITS 112 YEARS OF FOOTBALL HISTORY, the University of Georgia has had thousands upon thousands of loyal fans who would go to the ends of the earth to support their beloved Bulldogs.

But there have been very few Georgia fans like Mr. Herschel Scott of Monroe, who passed away on November 7, 2003, at the age of 82. At the time of his death "Mr. Bulldog," as he liked to be called, had attended 471 consecutive Georgia football games—home and away.

Mr. Scott had business cards that declared him Mr. Bulldog, which he handed out to everyone he met. He was listed as Mr. Bulldog in the Monroe telephone directory.

He became a celebrity at all Georgia games.

Mr. Scott began his unprecedented string of games in 1962. His last game was at Tennessee on October 11, 2003. He missed the following week's game at Vanderbilt in order to have surgery. Just three weeks later he was gone.

"We've lost one of the greatest of all the Bulldogs," said Georgia athletics director Vince Dooley. "It just won't seem right not seeing Mr. Bulldog around anymore."

At the time of his death in November 2003, Herschel Scott, also known as "Mr. Bulldog," had attended 471 consecutive Georgia football games.

Photo courtesy of The Atlanta Journal-Constitution/W. A. Bridges.

364

Mr. Scott made sure that his love for Georgia would continue after he was gone. Several years before his death, he had a red and black marble gravestone created. On it reads: "A Bulldog Born, Bulldog Bred, Here I Lie, A Bulldog Dead. How 'Bout Them Dawgs!"

Herschel Scott knew what it meant to be a Bulldog. And for 471 consecutive games, he proved it.

LORAN SMITH

I'VE ALWAYS BELIEVED THAT THERE IS nothing quite as uplifting as living in a college town and being around the campus environment. So I feel very lucky to have spent the majority of my life associated with the University of Georgia.

Growing up in Wrightsville, Georgia, we didn't take the newspaper, but I remember listening to the Georgia games on the radio called by Ed Thilenius. I would play out in the fields with my neighbor, and he would pretend to be Charley Trippi. Those are my earliest memories of Georgia.

And once I got to Georgia I remember reading *A Bulldog's Life*, by Jack Troy, which was a book they encouraged every freshman to read. I read that book with great relish because I wanted to learn about all of Georgia's traditions.

But the most important thing that contributed to my Georgia education was the osmosis that took place when I was a junior and became an ally of the great Dan Magill. When you're young your memory works so well, and when Dan would mention a great Georgia player—like Catfish Smith—I would go to his files and read about him. As our sports information director, Dan had the greatest files—they are still in use today.

I began going to Bulldog Club meetings with Dan and coach Wallace Butts. That was just marvelous fun. Later on we would spend time in a bar around Five Points and listen while coach Butts told his stories. He was a marvelous and creative raconteur.

Coach Butts was one of the most interesting characters I have met. I remember after Fran Tarkenton led us to a win over Auburn for the 1959 SEC championship, I wanted to do a story on him. So one day shortly after that game I went to see coach Butts and told him I wanted to do a story on Tarkenton for the *Red and Black*. And he said, "I don't know why you would want to do a story on him. The son of a bitch hasn't thrown a block in his life."

Coach Butts could be abrupt and tough on the field, but at the same time he would give his players the shirt off his back if they needed it. I'm talking to a lot of his former players for a book I'm working on, and it's heartwarming to hear how the old-timers talk about coach Butts.

I was still too young to know what was really going on, but there is no question that the Georgia people were really divided during the Johnny Griffith years [1961–1963]. The split among the alumni was so great that there was really no way for Johnny to succeed. It was a no-win situation for him and a tough time for Georgia.

And when Vince Dooley was hired in 1963, the attitude ranged from utter disbelief to total contempt. People were prepared to start fresh. They wanted that, sought that, and supported that, but they were dejected. After all, we had a basketball coach [Joel Eaves] as an athletic director. Some people wondered, "How stupid can we be?" Then he goes out and hires a freshman coach from Auburn who had never seen the forward pass. The Georgia people were as downcast as they could be. They wondered, "How did we get in this position?"

But things quickly changed as they began to identify with the spirit of that first Georgia team under Vince [1964]. I remember a game against Kentucky when they drove the length of the field for a touchdown. The Georgia crowd gave the defense a standing ovation because they saw and appreciated the heart in that team.

The 1964 season was one of the most rewarding ones that Georgia has ever had. To win six games and to go to the Sun Bowl after everything we had been through was something very special. Coach Dooley and his staff had put the fight back into Georgia football!

Erk Russell was one of the members of that staff, and he remains one of the most beloved coaches in Georgia history. I always had a great affection for him because of the way he knew how to handle people. And the image people had of him as a tough guy was anything but the truth.

Loran Smith came to Georgia as a track star in the fifties. Today he remains the executive secretary of the Georgia Bulldog Club and the sideline reporter for UGA's radio broadcasts.

I remember riding on a plane with Bud Carson, the old Georgia Tech coach. He told me what he needed was somebody who could do a good, old-fashioned butt kicking like Erk Russell.

That's when I told Bud that he was misreading Erk completely. I said that Erk was not mean at all. He does it by leadership. The kids play their asses off for him because they love him.

I remember that around the South Carolina game I began to think that the 1980 season might be special. Lewis Grizzard was at my house for dinner and we began to talk about doing a book. We had the Herschel angle, and the chance to do something special about a young man from my hometown [Wrightsville] just seemed like something really exciting.

We figured that Georgia needed to win the SEC championship to make the book viable. And that didn't look too good until Belue got it to Scott down in Jacksonville. That whole season was an incredible time that none of us will ever forget.

What was fun was that for a three- or four-year stretch, we were the most dominant team in college football. It's really nice to be the team to beat in the league. And through it all we got to see Herschel, who became the Trippi and Sinkwich of his generation. We were all very fortunate to be around Georgia when Herschel came our way.

When we won our third straight SEC championship in 1982, no one would have believed that it would be 20 years before we won another one. The Georgia people went through some really tough times, particularly after Vince retired in 1988.

But now Mark Richt is in charge of the program, and he has put the fun back into it for everybody in our building. Mark is an unflappable fellow who genuinely feels he has been called to help young people. He feels very strongly about his faith, but at the same time he is a very tough competitor.

The Georgia people feel like he is a really good football coach and that we'll win a bunch of games with him. But they also feel we got something else in the package. We got a good man.

Now things have come full circle at Georgia. We won a championship in 2002 and played for the championship in 2003. We have the right coach at the right time. The Georgia people are more excited than I've seen them in a long time.

That's why I feel so fortunate to still be here at Georgia after all these years. Not only have I had a chance to be a part of a great university, but I have also been given the chance to be around all of the Georgia heroes, like Trippi and Sinkwich and Tarkenton and Walker. Many of them I have gotten to know very well and consider them as friends. And for my money, there is still nothing like being a Bulldog on a fall Saturday afternoon in Athens. I never get tired of it.

Loran Smith, a native of Wrightsville, Georgia, was the MVP on Georgia's 1959 track team. Since 1974 he has been the sideline reporter for the Bulldog Radio Network. In 1977 he became the executive secretary of the Georgia Bulldog Club, a post he still holds today. He is the editor of the Georgia game programs and packages the Bulldogs' radio broadcasts. He has authored more than a dozen books, including four on Georgia football. He was inducted into the State of Georgia Sports Hall of Fame in 1997.

UGA I–VI

1956–Present

Editor's note: Since 1956 Georgia's mascot has been a pure white English Bulldog that goes by the name of UGA (pronounced "UH-gah"). In the past 47 years there have been six UGAs who have roamed the sidelines during Georgia's football games. And in that span, UGA has become one of the most popular and recognizable mascots in all of college football.

All six of the Bulldogs who have served as UGA have been owned by Savannah attorney Frank W. "Sonny" Seiler and his wife, Cecelia. And on almost every football Saturday since 1956, UGA has roamed the sidelines as the living symbol of what it means to be a Bulldog.

UGA has appeared on the cover of *Sports Illustrated* [April 28, 1997] as the best mascot in all of college athletics. He has appeared in two feature films, the latest being *Midnight in the Garden of Good and Evil*, directed by Clint Eastwood. He was even fitted with his own white collar and black tie in order to attend the Heisman Trophy banquet in New York in 1982 when Georgia's own Herschel Walker won the award.

Obviously, nobody knows more about what it means to be a Bulldog than UGA VI, who took the mantle from his father, UGA V, in 1999. Given the language barrier between dog and writer, Sonny Seiler agreed to speak on behalf of all six UGAs.

It's really unfortunate that all the UGAs can't speak for themselves. Because I can assure you, after 47 years of taking UGA all over the country,

UGA V appeared on the cover of *Sports Illustrated* on April 28, 1997. The magazine proclaimed what the entire Bulldog Nation already knew: UGA is college football's greatest mascot.

they are very much like humans. When we lose a game they can sense that their family is down, and they get down. And when we win and there is a lot of excitement in the air, they get excited too and want to play.

Now throughout this discussion I will allude only to one dog because that is the way we see it. All of the UGAs are connected to form the spirit of one dog. That is the dog who represents the University of Georgia.

In 47 years UGA has had so many great adventures. Over the years I think we've only missed a few regular-season games. I remember that in 1958 we couldn't take him out to Texas when Fran Tarkenton made his debut. I've had to miss a game or two because I was in court, but somebody from my family will always take him. My son Charles has been helping me hold UGA down on the field since he was 15, and he's in his forties now.

I think the only bowl game he missed was our bowl out in Hawaii in 2000. I got a call saying that if we took him he'd have to be quarantined for two weeks once he got out there. Well, we weren't going to do that, so we both missed out on a great trip.

In 1982 UGA went to New York to attend the Heisman Trophy dinner when Herschel [Walker] won the award. He had a great time. The dress was formal, so we had a white collar and black tie made for him. And I'll never forget all the stares from those New Yorkers when I was walking him down to Central Park.

We attended a cocktail party for all the past Heisman winners. Herschel, of course, spent a lot of time with UGA, and we have some great pictures from that night. But what I remember most is when the Heisman winners lined up and were getting ready to walk into the dinner. Only one former winner broke the line and came over to rub UGA's head. That was Steve Spurrier, who played and coached at Florida, our bitter rival. I will never forget that and because of it, I have a tender place in my heart for Spurrier.

UGA had one of his greatest days in New Orleans when we played Notre Dame in the Sugar Bowl for the national championship. They gave us a nice big suite at the old Fairmont Hotel so that UGA would be comfortable. When it came time for the game I never thought we would get him out of the lobby and down to the stadium. People just gravitate toward him. They want to rub his head and get a picture with him.

Because of the love that the Georgia people have for UGA, our annual team picture day in Athens is absolutely incredible. The number of fans who want to have their picture taken with him has grown so large that we need about 15 people to get it organized. It takes place in August, so it is usually a pretty warm day. We give him one break in a two-and-a-half-hour session, and he just stands up there and takes every picture. He is a real trouper.

Another thing you need to know about UGA: he loves a parade, especially when he's in it. He knows that people are paying a lot of attention to him. I remember that one of the proudest days of my life was at the Orange Bowl Parade of 1959. I looked up to see UGA riding on the hood of a 1959 red Cadillac going down Biscayne Boulevard while the band was playing "Glory, Glory, to Old Georgia."

UGA has also had his moments on the silver screen. He had a cameo appearance in the movie *Gator* with Burt Reynolds back in the seventies. But he pretty much played a starring role—at least I thought it was—in *Midnight in the Garden of Good and Evil*, which was shot in Savannah and directed by Clint Eastwood.

Let me tell you this: UGA and Clint Eastwood hit it right off. Clint came down to Savannah before shooting to check on a couple of things, and he asked if he could meet UGA and sort of size him up to make sure he would work in the movie.

Well, as soon as Clint saw UGA he immediately dropped down to his knees and started wrestling on the floor with him. UGA was loving it! Finally Clint looked at UGA and said, "UGA, I'm going to make you a celebrity."

That's when my wife, Cecelia, said, "Oh, Mr. Eastwood! UGA is already a celebrity!"

By the time Clint finished shooting down in Savannah he found out that Cecelia was right.

Now, I'm not trying to tell you that UGA is perfect. I do remember that one year he did commit a flagrant breach of social etiquette on Vanderbilt's brand-new artificial athletic turf. Let's just say that he christened it as only a Bulldog can.

And in 1986 UGA injured the ligaments in one of his hind knees when he jumped off a bed before the game with Vanderbilt. UGA was put on the injured list and his brother, Otto, took over for four games. Georgia went 3–1 in those games, including a win over Georgia Tech.

Because Otto came off the bench and performed so admirably, he has always been a favorite of coach Vince Dooley's.

Coach Dooley said of Otto, "He had his day in the sun and performed like a champion when we needed him."

Of course, UGA was having a grand time in the early eighties when we won three straight SEC championships. He really walked around with his chest stuck out! And it was hard for him to take when we went from 1982 to 2002 without winning another championship. Twenty years is a long time, especially for a dog.

UGA loves our new coach, Mark Richt, because coach Richt loves UGA. Coach Richt has started a new tradition of having every incoming freshman player take a picture with UGA on the first day he arrives at Georgia. Then he sends a copy of the picture to the player's parents and another copy to the player's high school coach. I'll bet a bunch of those are hanging in locker rooms and coaches' offices all over the South.

I could go on, but what UGA would want you to know is this: he is proud to be a Bulldog. He is proud to be chosen to do what he does. And he does it with great dignity. Just watch sometime and you will see that he stands at attention for the "Star Spangled Banner" just like everybody else.

Someone once said that UGA and I have probably seen more games at field level than anyone alive. And that is probably true. But it has been a joy for both of us, and every year, when football season draws near, UGA starts getting excited. I can tell that he is ready to get back in the car and head to Athens. We can't wait until the first game of 2004.

Sonny Seiler, who played the judge in *Midnight in the Garden of Good and Evil,* has teamed with Athens writer Kent Hannon on the book *Damn Good Dogs,* which chronicles the adventures of UGA I–VI. A film about UGA and his life is expected to be released in 2004.